THE
ZABERN AFFAIR,
1913-1914

by
Richard William Mackey

UNIVERSITY
PRESS OF
AMERICA

Lanham • New York • London

Copyright © 1991 by
University Press of America®, Inc.
4720 Boston Way
Lanham, Maryland 20706

3 Henrietta Street
London WC2E 8LU England

Library of Congress Cataloging-in-Publication Data

Mackey, Richard William.
The Zabern affair, 1913-1914 / Richard William Mackey.
p. cm.
Includes bibliographical references and index.
1. Zabern Affair, 1913. I. Title.
DD228.5.M34   1991   943.08' 4—dc20   91-23426 CIP

ISBN 0-8191-8408-X (alk. paper)

 The paper used in this publication meets the minimum requirements of
American National Standard for Information Sciences—Permanence
of Paper for Printed Library Materials, ANSI Z39.48–1984.

CONTENTS

PREFACE

During the nineteenth century the rapid rate of change in industry, commerce, invention and ideological questioning of man's place in the world, brought stuctural change of a social nature. An increasingly mobile, disorderly and confused society sought a new social structure that would reflect the importance of financial position and replace the outworn and increasingly warped institutions of the Ancien Regime. Indeed, new institutional forms evolved to serve the needs of those newly freed from the restrictions of birth, position, and place. Such institutions revolved around the assembly and how it would represent the people and what social and religious groups would be represented in it. Such representation brought the necessity for political parties and other organizations such as corporative structures and trade unions to represent special interests. New discoveries in medicine and health brought greater prominence to doctors, sanitation officials and nurses. The evolution of change brought class and mobility to replace caste or "estate" ideals.

During the nineteenth century the collaboration of institutionalized absolutism and aristocratic privilege managed to dominate the forces of modernity. That is, these remnants of the Ancien Regime that had been reconstituted by the Concert of Europe after the demise of Napoleon at Waterloo had kept in-tow the reform-minded industrial, educational and military forces by controlling political institutions. As the population of Europe became increasingly literate and censorship of publications diminished, and as public opinion within various countries reflected social, economic and political views in opposition to remnants of the eighteenth century Ancien Regime, these same reform-forces became frustrated over their lack of influence. They found that intransigent traditionalism, that maintained medieval institutions such as aristocratic privilege and absolute monarchy, diametrically opposed the increasing tendency for social distinction to be based upon a monied economy producing differentiation of wealth through capitalistic competition, and opposed politically the

v

developing ideal of a nation of people constituting the state.

The subject with his assigned place in society had been replaced by the citizen and thereby represented a change from a social to a political orientation of values. The fixed estates or <u>Stände</u> had given way to the relationship of the individual to the state and while the former corporative structure remained as an ideal, organizational and practical need in a monied society turned to a newly defined institutionalization finding middle-class linguistic inventions for old words such as "bourgeoisie", while ideological extremes found new meaning for the term "bourgeois". Such old institutionalized nomenclature had given way in the late eighteenth century before the need for a new bureaucracy of experts to organize the state's institutions for the benefit of the state. In so doing these bureaucratic practitioners of organizational expertise created a new institution that sought financial remuneration, place, and political recognition, repectively, for their new position of power. Hence these revolutionary experts supported laws that developed and maintained their new responsibilities to the state. Hence old social "estate" and corporative-custom laws became replaced by new class and organic laws that brought increasing state direction and control through an institutionalized state bureaucracy. Thus the wealthy monied interests were harnassed in service to a state whose regulatory and protective nature came increasingly to serve their interests and at the same time for whose interest this emerging middle-class willingly participated. The "withdrawing roar" of disapproval by the Ancien Regime's aristocratic institutions was muted by the necessity of cooperation with the new forces for the preservation of the state when faced with threatening competition for international power in the late nineteenth century. Occasionally the roar of the wounded lion forcefully voiced its displeasure through regression and this retrenchment brought new life to the old body. While much of that roar and bodily spirit was lost during World War One, the period before the war was characterized by its revival.

Especially in the German Empire the celebration of the eighteen-thirteen "war of liberation" at the centenary revived such memories of the law of the state regulating the needs of the army through new constitutions or promises thereof. After all in opposing Napoleon, the opponents had taken on the characteristics of that conqueror; hence state law for German needs came to threaten aristocratic preserve, yet the pride in that army that had won that war brought a revival of aristocratic values a century later and the "modernizing forces" of the modern state found themselves faced with the conflict of pride in the elite officer corps that had led Prussia and the German people to victory in liberation and unification on the one hand, and, on the other, the need for financing technological advancements that would weaken the privileged aristocratic officer corps in the fundamental basis of its ideology, in its ownership of property. Democratic elements welcomed the political change that potentially would limit the votes that property ownership contributed to aristocratic domination of the political system, but that had not been the primary goal of the majority of these modernizing elements. Nevertheless, common goals for democratic and other modernizing elements brought cooperation and then coalition. Particularly in Prussia the opponents to change reacted by maintaining control of their army, their property, and their legislature when faced with this coalition.

This work, The Zabern Affair, 1913-1914, reflects the culmination of these antagonisms within the German Empire. However, in these years of the twentieth century, instead of the institutionalized anachronism of absolutism and aristocratic privilege habituating universal retrenchment within the German Empire, the industrial, educational and military reform groups coalesced in solidarity against this Ancien Regime. This solidarity against the governmental institutions, however, faced disruption and dissention brought about by hostile foreign and internal public opinion against these same anachronisms and consequently the political parties reflecting the solidarity position retrenched and regrouped when faced with foreign and internal threats to the nation-state and to Imperial unity. Yet, despite this nationalistic protective mechanism, this "nation-state" was not the same as that of the nineteenth century German Empire. Although the opposition within the coalition of political parties here in 1913-1914 could reflect that fragmentation that became so characteristic of the century, nevertheless, on one issue the Centre, National Liberal, Radical, and Social Democratic Parties were in agreement. All believed in the necessity of a parliamentary system being the basic form of government for a modern Germany both as an ideal and, as a consequence of the reactions and attitudes formulated during the Zabern Affair, as a reality.

The center of this affair, Zabern, was a town of approximately 9,000 inhabitants in Alsace. Its people spoke a dialect of German, but were deeply rooted in French culture because it had been a part of France from the end of the seventeenth century until it had been conquered by the Prussian army and made one of the German Imperial territories in 1871. In 1911 the Imperial Chancellor, Bethmann-Hollweg, had attempted to integrate Alsace more fully into the German Empire by giving it a new constitution, but this had not salved the wounds produced by forty years of Prusso-German occupation. Some of these wounds were reopened and became running sores as a result of the brutal disregard for civil law and human decency that characterized the actions of Lieutenants von Forstner and Schad and their commanding officer, Colonel von Reuter, against the townspeople of Zabern.

The Zabern Affair began as merely a local incident in which it seemed that the Prusso-German military had been unwilling or unable to discipline an unruly lieutenant. It became an object of national and international concern in which polarized opposition threatened the very existence of an Empire, a nation, and an aristocratic caste-system. In its initial stage the question was whether there was to be the militaristic domination of the army over the people of an Imperial province and the civil laws that governed them. However, this stage was superseded by one of greater magnitude involving whether such domination would or could be applied to all German citizens, and thus this ultimately involved the question of the survival of the German Imperial Constitution in the form in which it existed. Indeed, when faced with the threat of this Prussian army-nationalism, some thoughts of secession had been voiced in Bavaria and Saxony. Yet, of even greater importance was whether the nature of the German Empire, of the political system, or even of the state itself would be changed by a coalition of parties in the Reichstag demanding a new German constitution which would include the separation of the armies of the various states and the participation of a parliamentary system in the governance of an Imperial state.

Historians analyzing the Zabern Affair within its framework of 1913-1914 have viewed it from the vantage point of what the democratic-liberal elements gained in terms of democratic goals dear to the Social Democrats, rather than from the point of view of what conservatives lost in terms of what they needed if they were to maintain the status quo. Thus, although the Left and Middle political parties did not gain what the conservatives lost, the stage was set by the losing for future gain by the mere questioning of the status quo which weakened its power-base. Thus, this Affair shortly before World War One left a hitherto relatively powerful social and political element, the Conservatives, in a position of relative weakness and created a power void in which a coup d'etat would be possible. World War One furnished a catalyst that brought about that coup d'etat, but would not have done so, and, some say, would not even have occurred, if it had not been for the disruptive events of 1913-1914 within Imperial Germany. Among these events the Zabern Affair is the most important and not only sets the stage for but evokes the spirit of opposition of later attitudes toward the government that contributes to the weakening of its major support. That a democratic-liberal government did not appear in Germany as a result cannot be made the fault of the failure of the Zabern Affair to realize the hopes of the Left and the ultra-liberals, as some historians have maintained. Since far too much was expected immediately of this affair both at the time and by historians reviewing its influence, there could be nothing but disappointment over its quick demise and short-term outcome. On the other hand, the small victories that were achieved and the loss of power and prestige of the Right and the army were overlooked in the disappointment over what might have been. The outbreak of World War One for a time halted inroads upon Imperial governmental authority by the Reichstag and made change in the political system appear dependent upon international defeat and/or internal revolution. Yet, in retrospect, that war seemed merely to have postponed what seemed by the beginning of 1914 to be the trend of the future. The post-war revolution seemed to be a mere continuation of the sequence of events that had led to the culmination of the Zabern Affair in which the power-base of the German Empire had been threatened. The Constitutional issues concerning the relative power of the legislature and the executive appear in the debate over the Weimar Republic in 1918, and the President assumed the powers that the dominating party coalition in the Reichstag during the Zabern Affair had envisioned as necessary for an executive to have in a parliamentary state. The mood of the Social Democratic, Centre, National Liberal, Radical Party coalition that had brought about the mistrust vote of the Imperial government on the fourth of December, 1913, reappeared in 1918 as if four years of war had not intervened and the Zabern Affair had just taken place.

This study is based primarily on printed primary sources consisting of selected documents and statements of private as well as public opinion. That I was able to research on this subject and complete this work is due to the patience as well as the aid of my family despite the inattention I was forced to maintain towards them due to my teaching load and long absences for research/writing purposes. Most recently, my sister, Dorothy Mackey, and my wife Phyllis, have given me the benefit of their criticism of my writing style and syntax. In addition I owe a debt of gratitude for the help given to me with this study by Eugene and Pauline Anderson. Any faults within this study are my own.

PART I

DEVELOPING COALITION

CHAPTER I

CENTRIFUGAL FORCES IN IMPERIAL GERMANY 1913

There comes a time in the history of a nation when the pent-up pressures of frustration explode in wrathful denunciation of the regulators of society; when the angered elements burst forth from their restraining social shell and bombard the offenders with accusations of repression; and when, for a short while, almost all elements are polarized into enemy camps, which denigrate not only each other but also the few remaining groups emphasizing moderation or compromise. For the polarized forces, there can be no compromise on issues that have produced such passionate hatred; thus the entire future of the nation becomes the issue at stake. Just such a period in the history of Imperial Germany occurred from November 6, 1913, until January 23, 1914, the days during the Zabern Affair, when the newspapers of all political parties in Germany gave to the events that took place at Zabern the most desirable space and the most complete coverage of any event since the Daily Telegraph Affair of 1908. During this time the Reichstag suspended all other business; even the important request by Winston Churchill for a naval holiday lay in abeyance until January 25, when the decision of the Kaiser concerning questions raised by that Affair was awaited and the Zabern Affair had no longer the central place in the interpellations in the Reichstag. Only then did the Imperial Chancellor Bethmann Hollweg believe it to be safe to turn to this so vital issue concerning the future of the Imperial German Navy.

During these seventy eight days until January twenty-third, the Zabern Affair was the center of attention not only in the German Empire but in France, England, and Italy as well. The newspaper and periodical press featured long articles on the threat which the Affair presented not only to civic freedom in Alsace-Lorraine but also to what little autonomy still remained to the federated states of the German Empire. As events

1

unfolded, the newspapers and periodicals in France kept up a thorough daily report on the Affair, including quotation of long comments from the German Press, given, however, without criticism until after the Trial of Colonel von Reuter on the sixth of January, 1914. The Times of London had its Berlin correspondent carefully record every detail and indicate the momentous importance of the Affair for that time and its significance for the future in terms of internal German politics and German-French relations. J. Ellis Barker, who was in South Sicily at the time of the Zabern Affair, stated that every newspaper he read, both Italian and other, contained long columns on the Affair that prognosticated its bearing upon the future in direful tones.[1]

Fundamental to the Zabern Affair were the actions of the protagonists in this, at times, ludicrous drama-both Lieutenants von Forstner and Schad and their protectors, Colonel von Reuter, the commander of his regiment, and General von Deimling, Commanding Officer of the Provincial District. Yet if the issues in this Affair had concerned merely the disciplining of a young, unruly Lieutenant, the whole incident would have been of considerably less significance than it became.   Such was not the case. Not only were the issues provoked by the Lieutenants' actions complicated, but the timing of the Affair after the animosities of the preceding ten months involving the army made these issues a focal point for all liberal as well as conservative elements that opposed the central-ization of authority within Imperial Germany.   These elements used the Affair as an occasion for demonstrating their displeasure and lack of both faith in and support of the centralized government that had been created by the Imperial Constitution of 1871.   Yet, again, the Affair would have been limited if only these elements had been involved.   In fact, the Affair expanded to include the matter of German unity, the relative power of the army and civil government, the extent to which the army or the government would have the power over the other in time of disorder, the relative power of the Prussian Army and the semi-independent armies of other federated states, the Prussian franchise, whether Alsace-Lorraine should be a province as it had been, a federated state within the Empire, or an independent state in Europe, and to what extent, if any the French had used this Affair to promote anti-German sentiment by emphasizing that the mailed-fist militarism was characteristic of Germany, rather than of Prussia.   Yet, the most important result immediately and in the long-term was the issue of whether the Reichstag should be a legislative and influential force within Imperial Germany, in which case it would cease to be an Empire as established by the 1871 Constitution, or whether it should continue to be merely a parliamentary appendage to a nonparliamentary state; subsidiary to this the question, whether as representative of the public opinion of various socio-economic groups, it could force the Imperial regime to make fundamental changes with respect to the other issues mentioned. Since so many of these sources of dissatisfaction over the Zabern Affair involved the role of the military in the German Empire and the provinces, it is necessary to examine the preliminary Army-related events which built up the pressures that finally exploded in the Zabern Affair.

In 1912 Lieutenant Colonel von Ludendorf criticized the German Army Bill of that year because he considered the two new corps authorized by the bill inadequate for Germany's defense; he insisted on the addition of three new corps in the next Army Bill. His superior, General Wandel, the director of the General War Department of the War Ministry, censured him for uttering remarks like those that could be construed as a threat that might lead to a revolution in Germany. The Prussian War Minister, General von Heeringen, had supported General Wandel's censorship of von Ludendorf and the result was that the latter was removed from his post as head of the Deployment Section and sent to command a post at Dusseldorf.[2]

Within military circles, there must have been a group of considerable authority who had the ear of the Emperor and who had agreed with von Ludendorf, or had come to the same decision independently, for in 1913 the largest army increase in the military budget in the history of Germany was requested. It seemed to many observers that the Emperor was giving this cause his full support through conducting a great advertising campaign which recalled the greatness of the army as it had been a hundred years before, in 1813, and through maintaining that in this great centenary year of the liberation of Germany from the oppression of Napoleon that it was no less great.

Indeed, the year 1913 had been planned as a great festival year. It was not only the centenary of the War of Liberation but, of course, of all the battles fought for this purpose therein; the battle of Nations fought at Leipzig, October 16 through 19 was given special attention. After all, it was here that the German Army had reached great glory in defeating Napoleon decisively and forcing him to cross the Rhine and leave what was in 1913 German territory. It was also the twenty-fifth anniversary of the Emperor's reign and the forty-second anniversary of the German Empire. For everyone, however, the primary celebration was to be that of the freeing of Germany from the military occupation, martial law, and domination of the Napoleonic Imperial power France. No longer after 1813 had the tentacles of France's Napoleonic octopus strangled the nationalistic feelings of good Germans. By 1913 a new empire had come into existence embodying the foresights and hopes of that same nationalistic minded Germany which had thrown off the yoke a hundred years before. Yet, for some Germans one yoke had been substituted for another and for others the French yoke still remained in the provinces and in the south.

Apart from the expulsion of the French, there had been no agreement either as to what goals had been set in 1813 or as to what the people of Prussia, Bavaria, and the other smaller German federated states had hoped for in the future. One hundred years later, therefore, there was no agreement as to what exactly was to be celebrated during the glorious Centenary festivities. For instance, the South Germans of Baden, Wurttemburg, and Bavaria had received soon after 1813 liberal constitutions emphasizing civil liberty,personal freedom, legal equality, security of person and property, and freedom of conscience and of press; certainly, it was said, these were purely institutionalized ideals rather than practical realities because the impotence of the representative bodies rendered them to be nothing more than academic in nature. On the other hand, those constitutions had represented the hopes and desires of liberals then, and in this centenary year, said many, those hopes and desires should be realized. In 1913 the liberals in all parties took up the cudgels of reform through emphasizing the liberal accomplishments and aspirations of Baron vom Stein and von Hardenberg and the glorious successes of the Scharnhorst-developed Landwehr and Landsturm forces. The achievements of the combined German armies in 1813 had foreshadowed the great unification of Germany that Bismarck had brought about in 1871, said those liberals as well as others of opposing views. Thus, they pointed out, this War of Liberation was one fought on an equal basis by all elements of the German population. All classes fought side by side for the overthrow of the oppressor and all sacrificed alike in doing so. These views were generally voiced in the newspapers and speeches in this year of celebration. The best example of this attitude occurred in Berlin on March tenth at the commemoration of the speech An Mein Volk, made at Breslau, Silesia by Frederick William III in order to arouse the patriotism of the Prussians against Napoleon. March tenth was also commemorated as the birthday of Frederick William III's wife, Queen Louise, and it had been selected by Emperor William II as the official anniversary of the founding of the Order of the Iron Cross. In Berlin the Kaiser extolled the virtues of the patriotic self-sacrifices of 1813 for the benefit of King and Fatherland; he commemorated the magnificence of that great army that had won the War of Liberation and assured the assembled people that these virtues still existed in 1913 and that all should support the glorious army which in that year one hundred years ago had been the great protector of Germany.

Praise for these two pillars of Prussia, the King and the army, was met by the efforts of the Liberal Press and public to make it commemorative also of the reforms of the King's ministers, Baron von Stein and von Hardenberg, whose statues had been solemnly decorated by party deputations at a commemorative park.   Nearby, the statue of Scharnhorst had been the focal point of large crowds listening to the speeches about the democratic nature of his army reforms.   Flowers and evergreens had been placed in such profusion upon this statue that it had become a mound of color, now rendered drab and drooping by the incessant rain.   Despite the disparity of victory of King and army as pillars of the state, on the one hand, and that of the democratic reforms in the government and the army on the other, the opposing views found common cause in celebrating the official military program of strengthening the army.[3]

Neither the liberals, the Kaiser, nor the official representatives of the Kaiser in speeches parroting him took an outwardly anti-French attitude on this day commemorating the defeat of the French.   Instead, both in the Kaiser's speech made at Königsberg on February fourth and in the thirty rirst of January "Rescript" acknowledging the loyal congratulations received by him from all quarters on the occasion of his fifty-fourth birthday, the emphasis was put on the great possible achievements of modern-day Germans if they but did as their forefathers had done in 1813, putting their trust in God and giving "their last drop of blood and last possessions for King, country, freedom and honor."   The Kaiser continued in this "Rescript," "May the memory of the past spur our generation to emulate the faith, devotion and union of their fathers."[4]

The Kaiser was certainly going to extremes in his appeal to God for this emphasis on God was not due to William II's basic religious nature. Throughout the War of Liberation celebration during 1913-1914, this Emperor-Monarch emphasized trust in God and Emperor or King in all his speeches.   Yet he was not basically a religious person; rather, as Ursula Countess von Eppinghoven, Dame du Palais to Her Majesty the Empress Queen, said: "In contrast to the Empress, the Emperor is not a religious person, but like her Majesty, firmly believes that godliness does very well for common People."[5]   His use of religion as a tool was further implied by Franz Schoenberner, who, in his Confessions of a European Intellectual, recalled the visit of the Kaiser to the University of Berlin on the centenary of its founding (1910) and his unplanned speech, in which:

His style and his diction were those of a provincial army sergeant addressing his recruits on the drill ground.   He strongly recommended the fear of God, for him more or less identical with loyalty to the Kaiser (underlining mine) invested by God.   And he did his best to make God alone, not the University responsible for what he called 'Prussia's glorious resurrection in 1813 after the total collapse of 1806.' 'Was that the work of man?' he bellowed. 'No, that was the work of God.' He seemed so startled by his discovery that he pounded the pulpit like a beer-hall politician.[6]

The insistence on God's responsibility differed also from the 1813-1914 Imperial insistence that the Prussian Army was solely responsible for victory, although one might have inferred that as the agent of the King in 1813, this army could have been indirectly an agent of God.

Neither the Kaiser's veiled reference to his Divine Right powers in his speech of the fourth of February, nor his earlier "Rescript" of January thirty-first reflected the mood of the elected representatives of the people in their assembly, the Reichstag. Indeed, on that same day the Reichstag voted 227-97 in disagreement with Imperial Chancellor and the Kaiser over their support for the Prussian law passed in January that allowed the Prussian army-Junker aristocracy to expropriate Polish Lands.[7] This was the first legal vote of distrust of the government in history. Of course, the Prussians supported the Kaiser as was shown on the twenty eighth of January when the conservative-led lower house of the Prussian Landtag condemned the debate on the issue as "interference" in Prussian affairs by the Reichstag. The Reichstag was criticized for breaking the Constitution by attempting to rule legislatively a federated state. Yet, the Reichstag had gone further than merely voting a disagreement as was indicated by the Centre Party, when, seemingly, it had voiced the will of majority when it made the point quite clearly that more opposition to the government was forthcoming and that it did not fear a dissolution of the Reichstag.[8]

Although the so-called "liberal voice" was heard in the Reichstag disagreeing with the government on the twenty eighth of January, the "conservative voice" found expression on that very day that the Kaiser had so carefully avoided insulting the French, on the tenth of May, 1913. On this day the Kölnische Zeitung seemed to be in complete disharmony with the government for on this celebration of the Centenary of An Mein Volk, this journal published a leading article entitled "The Disturber of the Peace," in which the French were vilified as a menace to Germany. The London Times summarized this article as stating that the German government "would have little difficulty in explaining the necessity for the new Army Bill if it plainly and without any obscurity, pointed to the quarter whence Germany is menaced, the quarter where the whole world feels the menace, to France." The article continued:

Never has the relationship to our Western neighbor been so strained as today, never had the idea of revenge been exhibited there so nakedly, and never has it become so plain that people in France claim the help of their Russian Ally and the Friendship of England solely for the purpose of reconquering Alsace-Emporia. In whatever corner, therefore, the world may catch fire we--that is quite certain---shall have to cross swords with the French. . . .[9]

The Times correspondent in Berlin believed that this article did not represent the opinion of the Foreign Office of Imperial Germany. He considered the author unfair, because the German Government had labeled the Army Bill a defensive measure made necessary by exigencies of the Balkan conflict and "the consequent alterations in the balance of power and unfair in that the sudden cry that France is the real enemy provokes suspicion that German politicians once more desire to float their patriotic sacrifices on a wave of passion, and thus arouse doubt in European minds that any German Army Bill might be defensive in nature."[10]

The reference to the impending conflagration above and the allusion to the necessity of using the sword were, however, quite in keeping with the attitude of the Crown Prince, who contributed a significant introduction to a book called Germany in Arms, written for the Centenary of the War of Liberation. In this he lauded the readiness of the German army and emphasized that only by the might of the ready sword would Germany emerge victorious from the impending conflagration that would engulf all of Europe and preserve its place in the sun, for," he said, "the sword will remain the decisive factor till the end of the world."[11]

Neither examples of chauvinistic aggression seemed to have been representative of the spirit of the Kaiser's policy. Although he proclaimed the "well built structure of the German Empire, equipped against every attack," his main emphasis in his speech of the fifth of February, 1913 was on the strong moral fiber of the people, which had to be maintained at that time when "instead of warlike deeds we see the fruitful works of peace. Trade flourishes, arts, science, and invention progress, and town and country prosper."[12] Yet at a banquet given here at Königsberg on the same evening he too seemed apprehensive of a future world cataclysm, for he said that:

If an extension of the principle of universal military service should be known to be necessary, he had no doubt that the German people would be cheerfully prepared to make further personal sacrifices, after the glorious examples of their forefathers.[13]

Gerhard Hauptmann, the great author, had quite a different view of the goals of the forefathers in the War of Liberation from that expressed by the Kaiser. In a Festspiel which he wrote for an exhibition in Breslau,

Silesia, in commemoration of the Wars of Liberation of the years 1813 through 1815, he commemorated not so much the armies or the glory of the War of Liberation as the freedom achieved. He did not mention Frederick William III, and he characterized Germany as Pallas Athene in suitable Greek attire and arms. She "sends her children to war with the command first, to free Germany from foreign rule; secondly, to care for her unity, and then themselves to be free."[14] Eleven performances of the Festspiel had taken place when the Crown Prince, who had been the patron of the exhibition, caused the magistracy of Breslau to cancel the remaining four performances; his attention had been called to the character of the work. Herr Hauptmann considered the whole affair the result of a "web of intrigue of a political character originating in Berlin."[15] The conservatives in the controversy that followed, considered Hauptmann's Festspiel not an appropriate expression of German feeling. The Radical Press, on the other hand, treated the whole incident as if a distinguished poet had been insulted.[16] The controversy lasted for almost a month and left the people of Silesia in silent anger at the Imperial Family over this rebuff to their poet-laureate, who had only the year before received the Nobel Prize in Literature.

Whereas in his Festspiel Herr Hauptmann emphasized liberation, unity, and freedom in that order and not the power of rulers over people, quite a different approach was evident at the Assembly of Princes at Kelheim on the twenty-fifth of August, 1913. Here William II stressed the importance of Prussian aid in the unification of Germany and the continuances of unity under its princes. The Prince Regent of Bavaria emphasized Bavaria's aid in the unification and liberation process and the continuance of unity, but he showed some of the inner stresses within Germany when he warned foreigners that they should not count on the divisions in the Empire as weakness in any possible future altercation between the states of Europe. William II replied to that Bavarian Prince Regent by stating, "The enthusiasm with which all classes of our people have taken part in the celebrations of this year bears witness to the depth with which the feeling for the Fatherland has taken root and shows how closely the German nation feels itself bound to its Princes."[17]

The necessity of the allegiance of the people to the ruler was again emphasized at Breslau on the thirty-first of August, 1913, at the commemoration of the Centenary Exhibition where the Kaiser brought out the importance of Frederick William III's role in calling for this crusade to liberate the Fatherland from the chains of the oppressor. Here, too, he proclaimed the willingness with which the people sacrificed their blood and treasure for the honor and freedom of the Fatherland. His concept of freedom was connected with freedom of Germany from foreign rule, but nowhere did he stress freedom of the citizen as a value in itself. Here he glorified the deeds of the <u>Landwehr</u> military force of Silesia and the motto "with God for King and Fatherland," and he asserted that as long as this loyalty and manly temper were cultivated in Silesia, "we need not allow our gaze into the future to be a troubled gaze."[18]

The Kaiser's autocratic views were in sharp contrast with those, also in Silesia, of Gerhard Hauptmann, but they were also at odds with those of Prince Bernhard von Bulow. This former Chancellor lauded the inspiration of Scharnhorst and Stein in linking the interests of the greatest number of individuals to the interests of the state by giving them an interest in the state through representative institutions. This Centenary speech commemorative of the great victory of the Battle of Dennewitz seemed to voice liberal views found among the radical and socialist supporters of Hauptmann's views.[19]

Perhaps the culmination and high point of the long series of celebrations took place at the Centenary of the "Battle of the Nations" at Leipzig on the nineteenth of October, 1913. The monument, which had been under construction for fifteen years, was unveiled, and representatives from all the Princes of Germany, as well as one from the Tsar, came to commemorate the great event. C. Wickham-Steed, the Berlin correspondent of <u>The Times</u> at that time,reported that on that day there seemed to be rejoicing over the Centenary in all parts of Germany, but that the extent was somewhat difficult to ascertain because of the great sorrow widespread over the catastrophe to the naval airship L. II. He also reported that patriotic fervor was "to some extent counterbalanced by the cynical abstention of the Socialists who are even stronger in Saxony than elsewhere. In their press they have rewritten from their own point of view the history of the 'War of Liberation' and have attempted to organize counter-demonstrations."[20]

Not only was there opposition during the whole year to the official view of the War of Liberation and ideals and celebrations thereof, but there were even suggestions that there was really no enthusiasm at all for the concept of a centenary of the War of Liberation. This was indicated as early as the twenty-sixth of October, 1912, when there appeared in Maximilian Harden's <u>Die Zukunft</u>, a poem entitled "Festal Song" written ostensibly by one Herwart Raventhal, which was a pseudonym for Walter Rathenau. The poem, of biblical nature, emphasized that "pride goeth before a fall" and quoting a text from Ezekiel, prophesied through an apocalyptic vision, "An end, the end is come upon the four corners of the land." In general, the poem was a protest against the organized enthusiasm falsely worked up for the Centenary. Barbara W. Tuchman in <u>The Proud Tower</u>, said that "Voices like that of Rathenau, who did not have quite the courage to sign his own important name but used a pseudonym, were not heard."[21] This was not true. Among the many examples occurring within that Centenary year itself that reflected the general mood of opposition was that of the Bavarian Clerical Representative in the Reichstag, Deputy Speck, who in criticizing the taxation proposals for financing the Army Budget Bill of 1913, protested:

> against the whole attempt to carry the scheme upon a wave of false enthusiasm about the centenary of 1813. When people talk about public enthusiasm they misunderstood altogether the real opinion of the people. About that there was no doubt whatever. The people were groaning under an enormous burden of taxation, and it was not the worst part of the people which looked with anxiety to the future and regretted the orgies of sham patriotism. If the people accepted the proposed burdens it was only in order to preserve peace.[22]

This view was not generally shared by the Reichstag. The National Liberal Deputy, Herr Paasche, opposed it by expressing regret over Herr Speck's pessimism and argued that the "Memory of 1813 was the real moral basis of the present discussion, and that it was necessary to give foreign countries an exhibition of Germany's strength, wealth, and unity."[23] But, in arguing thus he gave credence to Herr Speck's charge that the enthusiasm over the centenary was unnatural, false, and mere "sham patriotism" by that National Liberal's intimation that the real reason for working up this enthusiasm was to impress foreign countries with Germany's strength.

A foreign comment supporting Herr Speck's contention that there was a direct link between the celebration of the War of Liberation and the Army Budget Bill was made by the financiers and economists in Paris concerning the means by which the milliard of Marks necessary for financing the Army Bill would be obtained. Their suggestion, as reported by the Paris Times (London) correspondent in a dispatch dated the sixth of March, was that the levy of a "contribution" of one milliard was an expedient of an irresponsible statesman and that a responsible and experienced individual would have taken for that amount a loan that would not have prejudiced the highly complex German economy as this contribution would have. It was further suggested that this expedient was a primitive one which would have appealed only to the mind of an average lieutenant of the hussars and would have, at the same time, recalled to the minds of the people of Germany the spirit of giving found in those who gave diamonds, pearls, wedding rings, and money to the Army in order that the War of Liberation could be fought and that the people of modern Germany, as the Kaiser has emphasized in his speeches, would be no less than their forebears willing to give their all to make Germany free from foreign domination.

This correspondent also made a suggestion that the principle of taxing those who were most able to pay by applying a Federal State-applied-land tax would pacify the Social Democrats and "controvert the Socialist assertion that the well-to-do classes, particularly the Prussian landowners, always manage to shove the burden of military expenditure onto the shoulders of the working classes by means of indirect taxation." However, he suggested, that there might be difficulty applying such a tax due to the statement of the Secretary of State for the Imperial Treasury, Herr Kuhn, that the inheritance tax, a direct tax was illegal and, he said, could not be applied.[24]

The linking of the centenary of the War of Liberation and the Army Budget Bill was noticed by many and, indeed, it would have taken a persuasive advertisement and consequent motivation to have considered this Bill in other than extraordinary terms. This Army Budget Bill for 1913 contained requests for increases and changes that made it more extraordinary than any previous ones submitted by Prussian War Minister von Heeringen. The very enormity of the increase in requirements argued that an entirely different policy had been taking hold in the German Army from that of a relatively small professional army philosophy, that of the Prussian Junkers and their representative, the War Minister von Heeringen. This army philosophy would have maintained control in the hands of the Prussian aristocrats. But, the Army Bill reflected, instead, what Lieutenant Colonel von Ludendorff had demanded in 1912 which had brought about his transfer to more tranquil surroundings. In fact, von Ludendorff in 1912 had advocated exactly what was often implied and sometimes openly expressed in the Kaiser's War of Liberation speeches in 1913:   that Germany must become a "nation in arms," as she had been in 1813.[25]

The vast increases that gave the impression of "a nation in arms" were supported vigorously by the policy of the newspaper, the Lokalanzeiger, when, on the twentieth of April, 1913, it criticized von Heeringen's promotion of the inadequate Army Bill of the preceding year that had been passed. The Times reporter on the twenty-first of April said that it was impossible to say whether the Lokalanzeiger was trying to push War Minister von Heeringen out of office or if it had heard of his being forced to leave.[26] Others, however, were not in doubt. The Centre Party organ, Germania, printed the following interesting item:

> We are face to face with the fact--hitherto regarded as almost an impossibility in the Prussian Army with its much lauded discipline - that Army circles are working for the fall of a Minister of War.[27]

Certainly it would seem that there was some basis for this belief. The Kreuz Zeitung, an ardent supporter of the army, after some formal reservations, hinted that it had been very inconvenient that the disclosures concerning Krupp's bribing of army officers in order to obtain secret information on future weapons contracts had taken place at the moment that the Reichstag had been about to vote "the largest Army Bill that has ever occupied its attention," and when: "Germany (it stated) needs more than ever the confidence of the German people in the military organization and administration, and in view of the international situation, can less than ever put up with a public degradation of German military institutions."[28] The Kreuz Zeitung implied that von Heeringen, who had been consulted by the recipient of information condemning the Krupp officials, Karl Liebknecht, should have chosen another time for the disclosures or that they should not have been made at all. The conservative journal, Lokalanzeiger, went even further in stating that von Heeringen had concluded a bargain with the deputy Liebknecht.[29] This attempt to oust the Prussian Minister of War coincided with the scandalous disclosures at the Krupp trial, the legal proceedings of which had been announced by von Heeringen.[30]

The Army Bill was sufficiently shocking to the people of Germany without the scandal of army corruption to reinforce the shock. The Kaiser had tried to prepare the people for the surprises in store for them by emphasizing in speeches as early as February, the concept of a "nation in arms," which was the primary concept contained in the Army Bill. Yet, until the second of March, 1913, no one had the slightest hint of what the Army Bill was to contain, nor how large the forces required for the coming years would be, nor the size of the expenditure of the funds necessary in order to bring about the needed growth in the Army. According to The Times, of the third of March, 1913, the Imperial government was at last beginning to take the public into its confidence regarding the proposed increases of the German Army and the provision of money for these increases. The correspondent for The Times in Berlin at this time mentioned that he had heard through "well informed" channels that the proposed expenditure was to reach figures which almost everybody in the nation would regard as incredible. The increases were "to be at least fifty million pounds as an initial and nonrecurring expenditure," and the annual recurring expenditure was to be about one-fifth of this amount.[31]

Certainly the public mind was unprepared for this tremendous figure. The government had attempted to keep the intentions secret until its plans were made; but the sensational paragraph about the plans in the Nord Deutsche Allgemeine Zeitung on Saturday, the fourth of March, according to the Berlin correspondent of the Frankfurter Zeitung, was provoked by the appearance that morning of an accurate forecast in an unofficial publication.[32] It seemed that the only people who knew about the plans in the first week of March were the officials of the South German governments whom the Secretary of State for Imperial Trade had consulted that week. It was definitely not the aim of the government to disclose the terms of the Army Bill at that time, for Treasury Bonds and Consols were being sold and the result of the disclosures would have been to reduce the number of applications for them because the announcement of a levy on property would have had a depressing effect upon government loans and upon the money market in general.[33]

Charges had been made of delay in announcing the enormous sums, and the Nord Deutsche Allgemeine Zeitung had sought to justify this by publishing a note of explanation. This government spokesman claimed that the decision to strengthen national defenses had been reached by the Kaiser immediately after the revolution of conditions in the southeast of Europe and that the most careful consideration was taken in order not to alarm the other nations of Europe, but that the intention had been to build up the defenses of Germany by employing the concept of a "nation in arms" and to muster all the reserve population able to bear arms. According to this journal, the Emperor had arrived at this decision as early as the month of January. On the other hand, although the government took its time in arriving at its decision, the Nord Deutsche Allgemeine Zeitung maintained that the bill had to become a law by at least Whitsuntide or the necessary preparations for the increases in the army could not take effect on the first of October of this year, when it would be absolutely necessary that this occur. Public impatience over the long-expected announcement of the army budget bill was evident everywhere, the Nord Deutsche Allgemeine Zeitung stated that the "public enthusiasm will not cool down by being kept waiting for such a long time"; and furthermore, it stated, no army bill for a long time past had been so surely based upon a "deep-rooted conviction of the necessity to strengthen further the German armaments if Germany is to continue to make her way in the world."[34]

Apparently, the army authorities and the Imperial Cabal had decided to take enough time before announcing the requests and their costs in order to prepare the population for the surprises of so large an expenditure and the enormity of the change. By doing so they had hoped to develop the receptivity of the population by stressing the great contributions of all people in the War of Liberation and by emphasizing that the German people had not changed and that therefore their generosity would be expected. Thus the enormous sums expected by the army bill would be given in a generous spirit without that opposition that a shocked populace might have been expected to display. At the same time the immediate necessity of the bill's being passed in order that Germany might be protected in the immediate future made very long discussion and opposition a threat to the safety of Germany, and therefore, would have been an unpatriotic act in this year commemorative of the great human and material sacrifices of one hundred years ago. Any hesitance on the part of the Federal Council of the Empire or of the Reichstag might be a fatal blow to Germany's chances in the European-wide armament race that was, at that time, foremost in the minds of the German General Staff, Admiral von Tirpitz, the Kaiser, and Germany's European allies.

Nevertheless, despite the immediacy of the occasion, the Nord Deutsche Allgemeine Zeitung spokesman of the government, was willing to state only one definite fact that might in any way weaken the chances of immediate acceptance of the requests and that was that the German princes would no longer be free from taxation, that they had waived their rights of nontaxation for the purposes of this patriotic special levy. It was presumed then that all or most of the federal states, perhaps notwithstanding their antagonism to the idea of an Imperial property tax, had, at least in principle, consented to the new scheme.

Initial press comment in Germany on the announcement by the above journal was perhaps too hurried and too shocked to be of interest or of note. Nevertheless, the first reaction came from the Frankfurter Zeitung and might well be considered a fair indication of the first impressions that would be coming from other such liberal journals, and, indeed, from perhaps a majority of all. Most seemed to regard this as a huge increase, and many of the more liberal ones including the Frankfurter Zeitung, accepted this army bill as an initial effort to solve the problems of Germany in that it imposed the burden of paying for armaments upon the classes that could bear it. They agreed that it was in terms of ability to pay for these armaments that the burden for doing so should be apportioned. The Frankfurter Zeitung did sound a note of warning when it cautioned that the withdrawal of an investment potential of one-hundred milliards of Marks was a rather risky proposal and a very serious matter.[35] Yet, not all liberal journals gave even limited support. The correspondent for the London Times reported that one South German liberal journal was in complete opposition. This journal had regarded such a desperate measure as this army bill as applicable only to the problems that might arise in a state of total war, and Germany was not at war. It asked why such an imposition upon the people would have to be made in peacetime and why it was necessary to make fantastic demands of the type found only when nations were at war.[36] In truth, the Frankfurter Zeitung although supporting the principle of the increase in the army bill, was not altogether in support of it, and to some extent even echoed the view of this South German liberal journal when it pointed out that the public did not demand such tremendous armaments on a tremendous scale; it declared that the demands for these armaments had to have come from the army people and their pan-German following.[37]

The more conservative journals were also not at all happy about the prospect of paying for the increases by taxing "loose" capital, which could easily be hidden at home or invested abroad. Examples of this viewpoint were found on the second of March in an article in the agrarian-conservative Kreuz-Zeitung[38] and in a similar article in the Vossische Zeitung. The latter was usually considered a good index to the feelings of the financiers who, in this issue, wrote in condemnation of the South German activities of the Secretary of State for Imperial Trade, Herr Kuhn, who, they said, had brought back this heinous idea of Imperial taxation of estates from his tour of the South German states. They maintained that "the proposal will make a bad impression abroad and suggests that Germany is again at the end of her national resources."[39]   On the other hand, the Bavarian government organ, the Bayrische Staatszeitung, foresaw just the opposite effect. It suggested that few people will be able to pay the tax out of their current incomes, and therefore they would have to draw upon capital and thus "make a sacrifice for the national idea, which would effectively strengthen the power of the Empire, wring respect from foreign countries and remove the ground from under the feet of Socialist agitators."[40]

Further evidence for pressure having been put upon the populace for the swift passing of the army bill was found in the National Liberal Kölnische Zeitung of the eleventh of March in which it was pointed out that the immediate danger for Germany from attack was from France and that Germany had to be ready to withstand such an attack from the revanche (revenge) minded antagonistic French.[41]   This anti-French viewpoint might not have represented the opinion of the German Foreign Office, as was suggested by the Times (London) correspondent, but it did seem to have aided the propaganda in support of the army bill. That this viewpoint might have followed some suggestions from the Kaiser and the German General Staff seemed to have been indicated by the Kreuz-Zeitung, which had even gone so far as to say that the simultaneous appearance of several such condemnatory articles reflected the thinking of official backing from Berlin and that the reason for the semi-official repudiation of the anti-French article from the Wilhelmstrasse was that the ". . . form (my underlining) of the article then accorded so little with the requirements of the Foreign Office that it was held wise to put on the brake by means of yesterday's publication in the Nord Deutsche Allgemeine Zeitung."[42] This explanation seemed to agree with the emphasis during the centenary celebration which the Kaiser had put upon readiness to meet any foreign attack by expanding military training, a policy that was a part of the new army bill and which was inserted just the day before (thirteenth) in the Nord Deutsche Allgemeine Zeitung.

All the efforts of the Kaiser, the Imperial Chancellor, the Prussian War Minister, and the German General Staff bore fruit on the twenty-seventh of June when the Reichstag passed the army bill in almost its original form. The government, therefore, could congratulate itself on having achieved more than it had in any army bill before and with the least amount of compromise of any army bill in the history of Imperial Germany. It had won a great victory, but a victory that might well be in the future a Pyrrhic one. The final vote on the bill had revealed a new coalition in the making in German party politics, one of the Centre Party, the National Liberals, and the Radicals. The Conservatives and the Free Conservatives had now formed the opposition to the new coalition. Even the Socialists had given their support to the new coalition in response to the government negotiation with the various parties. The entire situation was new; it constituted a radical departure from former coalitions. Before 1907 the Imperial Government had had a Conservative-Centre majority. From 1907 until 1909 Prince von Bulow had depended upon a Liberal-Conservative Bloc. In 1909 the Centre Party had broken the Bloc over the question of inheritance taxes, undermining the position of Prince Bulow and then forming an alliance with the Conservatives. This alliance lasted until the general election of 1912, which produced no trustworthy combination of any kind.[43] Since that time there had been no real test of the Parliamentary situation. Certain questions arose out of this unique situation in which for the first time in Imperial German history the Conservatives were left out of the ruling group. Were the Socialists abandoning their traditional opposition to the government? Was the government really becoming more liberal? Could it be said that the Centre Party was moving toward the Left? The most important question, however, was, were the Conservatives being isolated or were they isolating themselves?

There was no doubt that in this instance the Conservatives were isolated. The final vote on the finance bill had found them to be the major portion of the minority of 63 against the bill, while the 280 who had supported the bill included individuals from all parties except the Conservative Party. The latter opposed the finance bill because it introduced a new form of taxation, that would be unconstitutional in the sense that it would be a direct tax on increment of property value, on income, and above all, on inheritance. The Imperial government had left imposition of direct taxes to the various states in the past. Now the Conservatives feared that the new tax revenues would supersede the financial support of the Empire by the individual Federal states. They saw in this action by the Reichstag an attempt to increase the power of this assembly at the expense of the power of both the individual federal states as well as of the Imperial government. They foresaw that in three years, when this finance bill would have fulfilled its purpose and expired, there would be no reason to question and, considering the international situation at that time, little reason to doubt that the same remedy would be applied again with a further reduction of the authority of state as well as federal authority. The Conservatives feared the effect of this finance bill on their own power, for the incidence of this tax would fall heavily on them as property owners and upon the inheritance of their sons. They might very well need to sell property to pay taxes, and the loss of such resulting in the lowering of their taxes would give them less representation in the Prussian Landtag under the three-class system of voting, and would inevitably threaten the Conservative domination of this body by making possible a successful attack on this body by making possible a successful attack on that three-class voting system, the reform of which had already been threatened by Chancellor Bethmann-Hollweg over the last few years. The speech of Count von Westarp in the Reichstag sitting of the thirteenth of June, 1913, sums up the attitude of the Conservatives:

> This Bill opposes the Imperial Constitution, opposes the independence of the Federal States, and, as the Social Democrats have claimed, it is in the spirit of Social Democracy and stands as the first step towards the democratic ruled unitary state; therefore, the Conservatives could not support such a law at any time.[44]

In his view this law, instead of aiding the government in building up the army, would destroy the government and replace it with a democracy.

Indeed, it would seem that the army bill had been passed with great rapidity in order to get it out of the way so that the really important business could be addressed, that of the finance bill. The Reichstag even gave in to the Imperial desire for six new cavalry divisions, after at first holding out for a reduction to three such divisions; it did so without hearing any persuasive arguments on the part of the government in support of the demand. The very fact that the army bill seemed, in its nature, to be the creature of the militaristic, extremely nationalistic Defense League (Wehrverein) and the General Staff did not deter the Reichstag from passing it with only token opposition. It was true that in his Reichstag speech of the ninth of April, 1913, the Reichs-Chancellor had denied that he and the government had surrendered to the Defense League and the General Staff, but his argument for this denial was the very weak one that he and the General Staff had come to the same conclusion coincidentally and that that conviction was shared by the Minister of War.[45] This did not seem to have satisfied the Reichstag, as was shown by the jeers from the Left and also by the Centre Party's notice of opposition by having allowed the well known views of Major General Haeusler, a Bavarian member of the party, to have been voiced in opposition to the army bill.[46] After these critical expressions it would have seemed very odd if there had not been great opposition to the bill; but the fact that there had not been, and that the great compromise effort to pass the anti-Prussian government finance bill had taken place seemed to substantiate the theory that the army bill had been passed as a stepping stone to a finance bill that could give the Reichstag future control of the government and the army.

In truth, then, the passing of the army bill was not a victory for the Imperial government, but for the Reichstag and perhaps for the new coalition, for it was still necessary to implement expansion by passing the finance bill. This fact was made very obvious by the admission of Bethmann-Hollweg before the lower house of the Prussian assembly that the Reichstag had refused to accept the financial proposals of the government. It had, indeed, acted in direct opposition to these desires, and had incorporated terms of its own.[47] He said that if the government had not accepted the financial proposals of the Reichstag, it would have been October before the Reichstag met again and it might not have passed an army bill then.[48] His admission of weakness showed the power of the Reichstag and the new coalition of 1913. The four pillars of Prussia, and hence of Imperial Germany as King William II was also the Emperor, were the Monarch, the Junker landowners, the army, and the bureaucracy of Prussia. The Monarch-Emperor and the Junker landowning army officers and hence the army had been weakened by the new coalition of liberal elements that had broken up the old Conservative controlled coalition that had ruled Prussia ever since that coalition had been formed under Frederick the Great. In so doing these liberal elements wanted to weaken the dominating power of Prussia over the German Empire and thus to pave the way for the institution of a representative form of government in which the Reichstag would have a major role as an initiator of legislation. This, then, was one of the steps taken toward that goal which was accomplished, finally, in 1918, but it was also a necessary step preparing the way for the next step which began in 1913 but culminated in 1914 shortly before World War I. Step two was that of the condemnation of the Imperial government and the Prussian Army and the consequent division of two of the pillars during the Zabern Affair by this same coalition.

An element or link not yet evident in the action taken by the coalition in the finance bill, as well as one contributing to the Zabern Affair, was the development of animosity toward the army officer-corps. There is little doubt that this hostility lay dormant, at that time; it was aroused by the revelations of the Krupp trial concerning the corruption of army officers in helping Krupp to gain a monopoly of government contracts for armaments.

The wrath of the Conservatives was not directed toward the army, for they could control it through the Junker domination of its officer corps; it was directed at the coalition of Social Democrats, the National Liberals, the Radicals, and the Centre Party members who had achieved this setback for the aristocracy. Indeed, the virtues of this army, of patriotism and extreme devotion to its King, which the King-Emperor had extolled so often in celebration of the War of Liberation Centenary in the months prior to the passing of the army bill, were virtues that the Conservatives vehemently insisted were dominant despite the lack of the virtue of honesty which had been so palpably evident in the Krupp affair. The Conservatives emphasized that the reputation of the army must not be tarnished by the Krupp disclosures through having its officers convicted of bribery. The army must be saved at all costs, they said, and even justice and the integrity of the German Imperial court system could be sacrificed before the altar of the army.[49]

The Social Democrats took quite the opposite point of view, as was expected. The informer, Brandt, who had given the Socialist Liebknecht the proof of the revelation of army secrets to a Krupp official, had uncovered a mare's nest which the Socialists exploited as much as possible before and during the trials of the officers involved and those of the Krupp officials, especially Brandt. Perhaps a feeling of guilt possessed the Socialists because of their recent mild opposition to the Army Bill. On the other hand, this was a natural issue for them; it provided a good chance to attack capitalism and the army and the militaristic, servile spirit that could produce such corruption. These issues were normally exploited by the Socialists, and this golden opportunity could not be ignored or played down.

The first disclosure of the Krupp affair took place on the eighteenth of April, when the Reichstag seemed to be dragging its feet when faced with the great costs attendant to passing the army bill and when it gave every indication that it would give it its most careful and detailed study. Representative Liebknecht's accusations disrupted this studied concentration when he announced that bribery and other types of corruption had been committed in the agreements of various armament firms with the government and that primary among these was the firm of Krupp, which had kept an official in Berlin with the sole purpose of perpetrating this felony by obtaining military secrets of proposed types and numbers of arms. His revelations included the statement that the War Minister, General von Heeringen, had dutifully opened proceedings against some six or seven of the culprits.[50] The link between these revelations and the horror evident among the representatives as a consequence, on the one hand, and the Army Bill, on the other, was brought out very openly in the Reichstag debate of the twenty-second of April, 1913.

On this day the evidence of this corruption was published in every major newspaper, as were most of the debates in the various state and national assemblies, and the reaction of the public and its elected Reichstag representatives was antipathetic to both the Army and the Bill that bore its name. At the same time, evidence of the growing solidarity of that aforementioned coalition and further reason for such solidarity came with these revelations of corruption in the supply of armaments to the government by contract. This event caused that coalition to bring about a demand by the Budget Committee of the Reichstag that there be set up a commission of inquiry in order to deal with armaments supply. The spokesmen for the Centre and National Liberal Parties showed approval and voiced a deep distrust which also reflected public opinion at that time of the army administration. The Free Conservative, Dr. Delbruck, suggested that this would be unconstitutional. He maintained that the constitution did not allow the Reichstag to have the powers of an executive nature which it would assume by the establishment of a committee of inquiry. He further suggested that the Chancellor would be quite willing to set up such a committee of his own appointees. Several members countered that appointment of a Reichstag committee was constitutional because the Reichstag's right to control expenditures would include such power.[51]

Representative Erzberger echoed this view and even went further when he suggested that whatever Dr. Liebknecht might have revealed of a questionable nature, he had stated one fact admitted by the War Minister, that in 1907 the Deutsche-Waffen und Munitionsfabrik,[52] in order to increase its production and profits, used an advertisement in a French newspaper to show that France was extending its production of machine guns and had used this as proof that Germany should do the same. Furthermore, said this influential Centre Party member, because of the obvious nefarious machinations of the German armament industry the Reichstag should employ its right of controlling expenditure in order to investigate army supply contracts with private companies; it also ought to examine the feasibility of establishing factories owned by the state to perform the function of producing armaments without the possibility of corruption and without the possible betrayal of military secrets to any foreign country.[53]   His statements were supported by his party colleague Herr Spahn, who said succinctly that the government underestimated the extent of mistrust that the public maintained toward the army administration.   This was also the view of the distinguished National Liberal Party leader, Dr. Paasche, in these debates.   Indeed, he had earlier criticized Representative Speck's views that the army bill was to be passed on the crest of a mounting wave of enthusiasm engendered by the sham patriotism of the centenary by remarking, defensively, that the army must be protected in order to show German's strength, wealth, and unity. However, at this juncture, when faced with the evidence, he admitted that not only was there public mistrust of the army administration but that this mistrust was well justified.[54]

When the motion by the Budget Committee for setting up a commission of inquiry was brought to a vote in the Reichstag, as in the case of the Army Bill and the Finance Bill, the only party in opposition was the Conservative Party.   It was obvious that at the end of April the army's reputation was at a low ebb and that it would take almost a miracle to bring about the passage of the Army Bill.   It had seemed that the War of Liberation propaganda had failed.   Nevertheless, the miracle that appeared was that of the government's proposal of a finance bill that provided that until the tax levy would come into operation, the Imperial states would voluntarily apply a direct tax which the various Princes would apportion in their areas based on property, income, and inheritance. The coalition in the Reichstag quickly grasped this proposal and turned it into a Federal direct increment tax.   There was not any evidence that great patriotism had been a deciding factor in passing the Army Bill; nor do the records of the Reichstag show any change toward a pro-army view, nor any great fear of any enemy's outdistancing Germany in armaments, nor any deep concern about military strength as major reasons for passing the Bill.

The animosity toward the army and the War Office in July and August, 1913, did not take the form of a cry for vengeance against the soldiers who had sold military secrets to the Krupp representative in Berlin.   Indeed, it seemed that the convicted men were the unwitting dupes of a master manipulator of men, Herr Brandt.   Therefore, when the sentences meted out in punishment for the crime were mild compared to what the public prosecutor had demanded at this Berlin military trial, the public breathed a sigh of relief.   There was, of course, no doubt that crimes had been committed; but whether one believed the claim of the

Socialists represented by Herr Liebknecht's accusations of gross crimes against the state and humanity, or that of the Conservatives represented by the Kreuz-Zeitung claim of the sixth of August, that "It's only a petty theft,"[52] one had to admit that the army and the War Office were put in a bad light and had seemed, because of the assumptions by the soldiers that Krupp and the state were one and the same thing, to be even more at fault than the soldiers who had committed the crimes. Both the Centre and Conservative parties were greatly shocked at the whole affair. When the guilty verdicts were announced, however, the Conservatives mounted a considerable campaign against the Left in general and Liebknecht in particular. Even the Left-leaning Berliner Tageblatt, under Theodor Wolff's editorial expertise, had played down the guilt of the soldiers and had dwelt on the evil effect all of the publicity would have on Germany's reputation and the resulting deleterious effect on her international relations.[55]

The "dirty linen" had been washed in public, and the complicity of the army and the Krupp officials had been proved, although at the trial of Brandt in October and November the defendant was to hint at even further revelations. This seemed to be a veiled threat, but no disclosures were made. The relatively light sentence received by Brandt of four months' imprisonment, which was counted as already served because of the equivalent period spent incarcerated while awaiting trial, could perhaps be linked to the threat of further disclosures, but evidence is lacking upon this point. Certainly, there were many who suggested that Brandt had served Germany just as Bismarck had in forging the Ems Dispatch and Yorck von Wartenburg had in violating the order of his sovereign in 1812 and aligning his forces with Russia against Napoleon; yet they had not been condemned, and indeed, they were even praised for their duplicity; therefore, why should Brandt be condemned for serving Germany through serving Krupp for, as had been pointed out by the soldiers in the previous trial, was not Krupp identical with the government? This had been the defense of Brandt's lawyer and had been intimated in various conservative journals, such as the Kreuz-Zeitung,[56] the Nord-Deutsche Allgemeine Zeitung,[57] and in those representing Herr Keim's Wehrverein.[58] Indeed, of all the newspapers in Germany, the Vossische Zeitung was the only one to suggest that the whole system of army contracts had to be overhauled.[59] The Conservatives had hinted that justice should be a consideration secondary to the primary responsibility of all Germans, including the members of the court system of the Empire, to preserve the prestige of the army and the War Ministry. Yet the conviction of Brandt had proved beyond a doubt that the Social Democrats had been right.

The trial of Brandt had not even disappeared from the front pages of the newspapers when the revelations of yet another and even greater scandal had shaken the foundation of public trust in the whole military establishment of Germany. This shock, the Zabern Affair, exacerbated the many quarrels that had produced the new coalition against the Conservatives and again isolated them as the coalition was now renewed. The Zabern Affair was to produce the second anti-government vote in the Reichstag within one year.

NOTES

[1]J. Ellis Barker, "Autocratic and Democratic Germany: The Lesson of Zabern," The Nineteenth Century, February, 1934.

[2]Walter Goerlitz, History of the German General staff, 1657-1945 (New York: Praeger, 1960), p. 149. According to this author, von Ludendorf helped retired General Keim set up the Wehrverein with the aid of von Moltke in 1912. It is possible that this group together with the Pan-Germanists were responsible for the Kaiser's new emphases in 1913.

[3]The Times (London), March 1, 1913. All references in this work are to the London Times.

[4]Ibid., February 1, 1913.

[5]Private Lives of William II and His consort: Secret History of the Court of Berlin. From the papers and diaries of Ursula Countess von Eppinghoven, dame du Palais to Her Majesty the Empress Queen, Vol. I (New York: World Publishing Co., 1909), p. 128.

[6]Franz Schoenberner, Confessions of a European Intellectual. (New York: Macmillan Co., 1946), pp. 57-58.

[7]Nord Deutsche Allgemeine Zeitung, January 28, 1913. A vote of disagreement by the Reichstag was allowed by a law of 1911.

[8]Ibid.

[9]The Times, March 11, 1913.

[10]Ibid.

[11]Ibid., May 1, 1913. In his Memoirs he states that his only intention was not warlike as it had been labeled, but merely to awaken the German soldier to patriotic support for the Fatherland to protect it from potential enemies. The terms and language he used, however, are quite inflammatory and regardless of his intention brought fear to the hearts of both foreigners and countrymen. Crown Prince of Germany, Memoirs, (New York: Charles Scribner's sons, 1922), p. 108.

[12]The Times, February 6, 1913.

[13]Ibid.

[14]Gerhard Johann Robert Hauptmann, Festspiel Am Deutsche Reiman, Sämtliche Werke Herausgeben von Hans-EgonHass, Band II Dramen, Propylaen Verlag (Frankfurt M.: Verlag Ullstein GmbH. Berlin, 1965),

pp. 1003-1006.

[15]The Times, June 18, 1913.

[16]Ibid.

[17]Ibid. August 25, 1913. See pp. 11-12, for Herrs Rathenau and Speck's denial of enthusiasm.

[18]Ibid., August 31, 1913.

[19]Prince Bernhard von Bulow, Memoirs, 1900-1919, trans. Geoffrey Dunlop (London: Charles Whittingham and Griggs Ltd., Chiswick Press, 1920), IV, p. 99.

[20]The Times, October 19, 1913.

[21]Barbara W. Tuchman, The Proud Tower: A Portrait of the World Before the War, 1980-1914 (New York: Macmillan co., 1966), p. 345.

[22]Stenographische Berichte des Verhandlungen des Reichstag (hereafter cited as Verhandlungen des Reichstag), Sitting 170, 1913, pp. 4629-4639.

[23]Ibid., 4638-4639.

[24]The Times, April 11, 1913.

[25]Hans Herzfeld, die Deutsche Rüstungspolitik vor dem Weltkrieg, as stated in Alfred Vagts, A History of Militarism: Civilian and Military (rev. ed.: New York: Meridian Books, Inc., 1959), p. 377.

[26]The Times, April 21, 1913.

[27]Ibid.

[28]Ibid., April 21; Kreuz-Zeitung, April 20, 1913.

[29]Ibid., April 21, 1913.

[30]Verhandlungen des Reichstags, Sitting 170, p. 5961.

[31]The Times, March 3, 1913.

[32]Frankfurter Zeitung, March 6, 1913.

[33]The Times, March 6, 1913.

[34]Nord Deutsche Allgemeine Zeitung, March 1, 1913.

[35]Frankfurter Zeitung, March 2, 1913.

[36]The Times, March 3, 1913.

[37]Frankfurter Zeitung, March 3, 1913.

[38]Kreuz-Zeitung, March 2, 1913.

[39]Vossische Zeitung, March 2, 1913.

[40]Bayrische Staatszeitung, March 3, 1913.

[41]See above, pp. 10-11.

[42]The Times, March 14, 1913.

[43]This is in opposition to Arthur Rosenberg (Imperial Germany) who said it lasted to 1914. The new coalition against the Conservatives and against the government in the Army Bill, Finance bill, and the Zabern Affair also questions his views.

[44]Verhandlungen des Reichstag, sitting 173, 1913 (see also for further

support of anti-government attitude on military bill p. 5895 c, June 28, Sitting 172--Scheidemann's speech--"two majorities").

[45]Ibid., Sitting 170, pp. 4609-4610.

[46]Ibid.

[47]The Crown Prince in his Memoirs condemns the Imperial Chancellor for not having accepted the Defense Bill of 1913 immediately. Indeed, he said that this bill which gave the much needed augmentation of Germany's military resources had to be forced down the throat of Bethmann-Hollweg. Crown Prince of Germany, Memoirs, p. 96.

[48]Stenographische Berichte uber die Verhandlungen des Preussischen Hauses der Abgeordneten (22 Legislatur-Periode, 2 Session, 1914-1915), Vol. I, p. 140. Hereafter cited as Verhandlungen des Preussischen Hauses der Abgeordneten.

[49]Nord deutsche Allgemeine Zeitung, August 6, 1913; Kreuz-Zeitung, August 6, 1913.

[50]Verhandlungen des Reichstag, Sitting 143, 1914, p. 4913.

[51]Ibid., Sitting 146, pp. 5047-5056.

[52]Trans. German Weapons and Munitions Industry. A promotional organization for armament sales.

[53]Verhandlungen des Reichstag, Sitting 143, 1914, p. 5048.

[54]Ibid., pp. 5059-5060. This is a turnabout from his earlier view of the end of April (see above, pp. 10-11).

[55]Theodor Wolff, The Eve of 1914, trans. E.W. Dickes (London: Victor Gollantz Ltd., 1935), pp. 330-334.

[56]August 6, 1913.

[57]August 5, 1913.

[58]The Times, August 6, 1913.

[59]Vossische Zeitung, August 6, 1913.

CHAPTER II

ALSACE-LORRAINE AND THE EVENTS IN ZABERN

In the years 1871-1914 Alsace and Lorraine became united as never before in one common thought: the dislike of German occupation and influence. Never in these years did Alsace-Lorraine cease reminding the German Empire and especially Prussia that German soldiers were unwelcome in Alsace-Lorraine. Even after the Dreyfus Affair terminated in France in 1906 and anti-clericalism was the foremost expression of what was typically French in Europe, although the pro-French ardor was cooler, the anti-German feeling did not diminish.

Alsace was united with France by 1697 when Louis XIV had completed his conquests and satisfied himself with this legacy of the Treaty of Westphalia. Lorraine became a province of France in 1766 when the King of Poland, Stanislaus I, died and willed this Duchy to France in fulfillment of his agreement with Louis XV. In 1871 as a result of the Franco-Prussian War, Alsace and Lorraine were given to Imperial Germany and became the united Imperial Province (Reichsland) called Elsass-Lothringen. In the intervening years Alsace with its predominately German speaking population and the predominantly French speaking Lorraine had become French in culture and affinity. Thus Imperial Germany in 1871 found itself possessed of an Imperial province which resisted all efforts to Germanize it. Despite the attempted repression of French culture through legal forbiddance to speak, write, or read the language of France and despite, since the law of 1904, the settling of retired army noncommissioned officers and soldiers, "Old Germany," as they were called, in the area, the people of Alsace-Lorraine remained primarily French in culture and sympathy. The Decree of March, 1904, which gave the "Old Germans" 50 percent of all small official posts, was a source of irritation that was not helpful in "Germanizing" the natives.

29

Many attempts to placate the Reichsland people were made. As the Crown Prince in his Memoirs points out, it seemed that after every period of a repressive Stadthalder's administration that a mildly liberal one was initiated by the appointment of a less repressive Stadthalder by the Emperor.[1] One of the most important attempts to placate them occurred in 1911 when the Imperial Chancellor Bethmann-Hollweg was able to issue a new constitution for Alsace-Lorraine. This act was considered by Imperial Germany to be a great sacrifice, for it gave to Alsace-Lorraine a bicameral legislature with a lower house elected by universal male suffrage and an upper house consisting of one-half Imperial appointees and one-half locally elected representatives. It allowed Alsace-Lorraine representatives in the German Imperial Reichstag, but their functions were limited to matters not directly pertaining to Alsace-Lorraine. For on matters that directly affected their homeland they were allowed only to listen and comment; they could not vote on these matters.

Yet the constitution, which was a step toward political self-government independence for Alsace-Lorraine. was not enthusiastically accepted; it did not fulfill the hopes of the democratic elements in the population. The Emperor-King as sole possessor of executive power, could not only nominate one-half of the members of the upper chamber, but had the right denied him by the Imperial Constitution to veto the Landtag's decisions.

The lower house of the Landtag was refractory from the beginning and, composed of twenty-six clericals, ten members of the Lorraine bloc, twelve Liberal-Democrats and eleven Social-Democrats, opposed the upper house often. As a result of such show of opposition, the Emperor, at Strasburg, in May, 1912, threatened that unless there was more cooperation between the houses of the Landtag, he might have to take away their constitution and annex them to Prussia. (The Social Democrats laughed at the implication that becoming part of Prussia was a punishment.) No less ludicrous was the fact that the Emperor was powerless to do what he had suggested for the spirit of conciliation in Germany was fighting for ascendancy with this northern exponent of autocracy.[2]

According to Theodor Wolff, the Constitution of Alsace-Lorraine was arbitrary and welded two very different cultures into a single unit. The French speaking Lorrainers and the German dialect speaking Alsatians were not naturally bound together by linguistic or ethnic ties. The nationalism of the Lorrainers was never really fractured, but the German speaking Alsatians were less under the influence of Paris and it seemed from time to time that some headway might be made in this area, of which Zabern was a part. Yet, the Alsatian capitalist stratum completely cut itself off from Germany after 1870 as far as social contact was concerned and it seemed that under the influence of this class many others had no intention of becoming Prussian and were quite determined to remain Alsatian. Indeed, most of the Alsatians wanted separation from Germany although that did not necessarily mean union with France. They knew that this would not come about without a war and they did not want war.[3] Many would much rather have had Alsace-Lorraine an autonomous state within the German Empire than be the center of a war.

A great many of the people of Alsace-Lorraine considered this constitution to be little more than a sop thrown to dissidents as a bone was thrown to a barking dog. To them it seemed that this was an attempt to restrain the radical influence through their pacification of the liberal elements with the goal in mind that they would restrain their compatriots.

The altercations arising in 1913, therefore, fanned the flames of an already smoldering fire and for many seemed to come at a very inopportune time for the welfare of the German Empire. The first altercation involved the attempt by Von Wedel, the Stadthalter, in conjunction with Pan-Germanists again to attempt to repress the influence of France by asking the Reichstag and the government to apply a heavily enforced censorship on all means of communication in Alsace-Lorraine. This would have been a breach of the Imperial law passed in 1908 guaranteeing the right of free association (Vereinsrechts) and the speeches in the Reichstag were sufficiently inflammatory to prevent such radical curtailment of human rights, even though there were already in existence laws forbidding advertising and publication in the French language in Alsace-Lorraine which prevented equality of product-competition in Germany and Alsace-Lorraine and was bitterly resented by the inhabitants of the latter.[4] The reaction to this censorship was not only against Von Wedel but equally against the army which had agitated for such censorship for years.[5]

A further altercation concerned the Army Bill of 1913, which Alsace-Lorraine opposed. It showed this opposition by a 47-5 vote of the lower house of the Diet condemning the instructions of the Stadthalter to the Alsace-Lorraine pleni-potentiaries in the Imperial Federal Council to vote for the bill. There was no doubt in the minds of the framers of this resolution that the course of events would not be changed by their resolution, but they knew that it expressed public opinion and could be disregarded neither in Imperial Germany nor in France. But all of these altercations seemed to be merely minor compared with the Zabern Affair.

In 1913 the population of Zabern was about 9,000 persons and consisted mainly of Catholics. It was a tourist town in the summer with the visitors being predominantly French. The French influence of Catholicism contrasted with the presence of the predominately Prussian-

Lutheran ninety-ninth German Infantry Regiment, which had been stationed there since 1890. Through the city ran the Rhine-Marne Canal and the workers on the canal boats going between France and Zabern often found that the German soldiers opposed such constant French influences, and fights often resulted from confrontation between such workers and these soldiers stationed there. Officers and soldiers spent their money in the city and thus benefited industry and business.

One of these soldiers, a Sergeant Höflich, wrote much later that there was no way that Alsace-Lorraine, this two hundred year old possession of France, could become Germanized by the mere drawing of new boundaries and that the predominantly French culture and anti-German population both prevented this assimilation. He maintained that the people equated German with Prussian and the spirit of Potsdam with the spirit of the German fatherland. They saw Germany as the land of the Reformation; the land of Luther, and referred to that Bismarckian Kulturkampf satirically as an example of German toleration of religion. According to Hoflich the Alsatian priests were very influential in this protracted cultural war. As far as his own case was concerned, he said he had not known whether the people had been anti-German or just anti-military when he had been an active protagonist in the infamous Zabern Affair.[6]

The major protagonist in the drama that unfolded in the town of Zabern in Alsace was a Freiherr Lieutenant von Forstner. This twenty-year old representative of Prussian militarism belonged to a family of soldiers and had been educated at the famous Cadet School at Gross Lichterfelde. After graduation from this military academy he had received eighteen months' experience as an ensign and then in 1912 had been promoted to the officers' ranks. His time in Alsace had not been without incident and already by the twenty-eighth of October, 1913, when the notable events of the famous Zabern Affair had taken place he had committed actions which were pending inquiry as breaches of military duty.[7]

The Affair began with the zealous practice by this representative of East Elbian Junkerdom of the traditional virtues of this aristocracy; the foremost of which was that of confidence in the superiority of the officers within the Prussian Army and the inherent inferiority of all other human beings. Outstanding among those inherently inferior he deemed the French and the inhabitants of Alsace-Lorraine, of whom the townspeople of Zabern, who had so often taunted and mocked him, became the lowest. The outcome of this young man's contemptuous manner was growth of animosity within him over slights to his honor, both real and fancied, and this animosity had exploded in epithet-laden remarks concerning not only the local citizenry but also the recruits under his command of Alsace or

Lorraine origin. He also voiced his animosity toward the French Foreign Legion.

There are several accounts of the actual words spoken by Lieutenant von Forstner on the twenty-eighth of October, 1913. The earliest account that had been read in Germany, given by the Strasburger Post, was that this Lieutenant during the instructions hour for new recruits had spoken of some recent assaults on soldiers. He had said that it was the duty of recruits to refrain from exciting or initiating disturbance, but that if they were attacked by any of the Wackes it was their duty "to lay about them and to consider this proper behavior." If the recruit in the process should stick these Wackes with his bayonet, then he would give him not the three months in prison that others had recently received, but ten Marks instead, as a personal reward from himself. Sergeant Höflich, a native Alsatian, second in command, added to this that he would contribute a Thaler to the same cause.[8] This is, however, not the view published in the Alsatian newspapers. The predominant view in these was that the occasion for the remarks was the sentencing of a soldier to two months' imprisonment for stabbing someone, and that Lieutenant von Forstner had used the word "Wackes" with reference to the man stabbed and had said that the assailant would not have been sentenced if it had been "an Alsatian Wackes" that he had stabbed.[9] The official Telegraph Report had been the same, but without explanation of the word Wackes as meaning a rowdy. The Strasburger Post had sought to excuse the lieutenant's usage of the word on the grounds that he had not known the real meaning of the word to the local citizens and had considered it just to be a generic term for rowdy.

On the sixth of November, the remarks of this young lieutenant had appeared in the local newspapers with particular emphasis given by a Sergeant Baillet and his nine fellow informers that the lieutenant had insulted the people of Alsace as a whole by the application of the word Wackes to all Alsatians. That evening noisy demonstrations of public displeasure took place in front of von Forstner's quarters. The next day he was pestered on his way home by a mob of men whose noisy, insulting cries brought threats from the merchants that if these demonstrations did not stop they would close their shops. Lieutenant von Forstner was forced to enter a restaurant, Zum Karpfen, and telephone for help. He then was escorted home by two soldiers with loaded rifles. In the evening a crowd of over a thousand people made a demonstration and many cries were heard demanding that he be lynched. The commanding officer of the Ninety-ninth Infantry Regiment, Colonel von Reuter, appeared on the scene and tried to calm the crowd but to no avail. The Burgomaster also failed in his efforts and finally finding that both the police and gendarmerie were helpless he called upon the fire brigade to drive off the crowd with their power hoses.

The firemen were loath to use their hoses against the crowd and, at first, refused to do so. It was only when the Burgomaster insisted that they acquiesced, but instead of using the power of their hoses to push the crowd apart, they pointed the nozzles skyward and merely rained down upon the crowd a shower of water. This was no deterrent at all; the crowd promptly put up umbrellas and continued their demonstration and, in any event, the shower soon stopped, as someone had cut the hose. Indeed the crowd did not disperse until a company of soldiers was brought to the scene with ready-rifles and arrested those who refused to leave.

The "semi-official report" noted that several soldiers had been assaulted, that violent threats and balled fists had greeted the minions of law and order, and that the cries of "We are Alsatians but not Wackes" had drowned out the pacific efforts of the commanding officer, Colonel von Reuter, to explain away the insult to the townspeople. The noncommissioned officer, Sergeant Hoflich, who had offered a Thaler in support of Lieutenant von Forstner's higher offer for sticking a Wackes, had been forced down a dark alley and had been assaulted. This "semi-official report" went on to say that in consequence of the extreme excitement, military persons had been exposed to ridicule throughout the town and as a result of these insults and the consequent reactions of the military, soldiers had been forbidden to visit the cafes and public houses.[10]

What this "report" had omitted was that the excitement had not been over and that Lieutenant von Forstner, who was the round-officer, had led an armed patrol through the street to enforce a curfew that had been called; this and other such patrols, following regimental commands, had cleared the streets and had even gone so far as to clear the inns of patrons. Then four young officers had been left alone on the streets with loosened sabers and a great dane.[11]

Yet, these efforts had not quelled the excitement. According to the Frankfurter Zeitung, on the tenth of November, school children had jeered at Colonel von Reuter and he had disciplined them. A large crowd had assembled on the street where von Forstner lived. This time there had been no violence and little disturbance, except for whistling and singing and the explosion of a few firecrackers. Nevertheless, they had been very roughly handled by the mounted police and this left an aura of extreme annoyance in its wake. According to this report, the local press had been quick to take advantage of the already mounting animosity toward Prussian martial law and had not missed this opportunity to emphasize an anti-Prussian sentiment. Yet, the people of Zabern had been able to breathe a sigh of relief when, on this day, they had discovered that Colonel von

Reuter had left for Berlin. Whether von Reuter had resigned, had been asked to resign, or whether he was merely taking a leave of absence had not been known at that time.

On the eleventh of November the <u>Official Statement on the Zabern Case</u> was issued and according to the Schulthess <u>Deutschegeschichtskalendar</u> the investigation by the commanding general, von Deimling, had drawn different conclusions. The investigation had brought out that Lieutenant Freiherr von Forstner during the exercises on the twenty eighth of October, 1913 had in front of his Corporal admonished his recently punished recruits in regard to illegal weapon carrying and other grave offenses and to avoid strife with Civil persons and brawls. At the time, he said the following: "Take care when you go alone into the city now. They appear to be inclined to fight and it is easily able to come to such in Zabern. Restrain yourself also in your thirst for action." At this he had adjoined an instruction, how the recruit had to restrain himself unless he were to be attacked and then he said to them: "If you however are attacked, then make use of your weapon: if you thereby stick one down then you will receive from me 10 Marks." The Squad Leader-Corporal added to this, "And from me you will receive in addition 3 Marks." The statement then concluded that it would have been impossible for the Lieutenant in this (with reference to the sticking) situation to have meant by the expression "so einem Wackes" (thereby any Wackes) the whole Alsatian people, and that with the expression he had only meant the fight-seeking individuals and rowdies.[12]

Lieutenant von Forstner did not go unpunished for his escapades. It was reported by the <u>Berliner Tageblatt</u> newspaper on the twenty-first of November, that he had been sentenced to a period of detention and transferred to a different company of his regiment for having used the insulting word "<u>Wackes</u>" with reference to all Alsatian recruits. This contradicted the official view given above, and it was apparent that either additional facts had come to light with regard to the young lieutenant's conduct or that this was an attempt to placate the civil authorities of Alsace-Lorraine. On the other hand, it seemed that the army in such a situation had to maintain its prestige. As a result, on that same day, the so-called "informers" who had informed the local press of Lieutenant von Forstner's remarks, a Sergeant Baillet and nine other Alsatian soldiers, were arrested and the other Alsatian recruits in the Ninety-ninth regiment, fifth Company, were transferred to neighboring garrisons. Furthermore, according to this journal, Colonel von Reuter, who had submitted his resignation on the tenth of November and had had it refused by Kaiser William II, returned from his leave of absence. It was also suggested that his return was brought about by the Kaiser in order to silence reports that he had been removed and to remind the Alsatian people that the army was still in command in Zabern.

The punishment of Lieutenant von Forstner and of the Alsatian recruits was given complete sanction by the commanding general of the Fifteenth Army Corps, Meldung von Deimling and also by the commander of the Thirtieth Division, General Lieutenant von Eben. In Zabern, the evening of the twenty-fifth of November they reviewed the case against Lieutenant von Forstner and delivered a sharp reprimand. The use of the term "Wackes" was strongly forbidden--a confirmation of a measure already taken by Regimental Command--and the most stringent punishment was promised to any soldier not maintaining the secrecy of all affairs dealing with his military service.[13]

Yet, despite this reinforcement of punishment it was again Lieutenant von Forstner who was in trouble on the very next day, November the twenty-sixth. Almost a week before, the local press had provoked trouble by reporting language which Lieutenant von Forstner was said to have used on previous occasions. One of these alleged remarks consisted of an insult to the flag of France. This had been promptly denied by von Forstner at the time, but the newspaper published a confirmation signed by a large number of the recruits whom Forstner had been addressing. The occasion of the trouble on the twenty-sixth was the celebration of a going-away dinner for one of the young lieutenants and the over-indulgence of Freiherr von Forstner and others in strong drink. On the way back from the Train where the going away celebration had taken place, Lieutenant von Forstner and others had heard some boys calling after the former some remarks which reminded all of them of expressions connected with the history of the incident regarding von Forstner's alleged remarks concerning the flag of France. Nearby, some citizens conversing together laughed and a Lieutenant Chad (Schad) hastened to the guard, who with fixed bayonets rushed to the scene and quickly occupied themselves with arresting those pointed out by this young Lieutenant.

By this time the actions of von Forstner had become news, and the journals all over Germany and others in Europe had brought out stories of the latest offense in Zabern. The military journals, of course, denied any offenses of any consequence and retaliated that these events would never have happened if there had been discipline among the recruits and the words of a commanding officer had not been divulged to a newspaper.[14] Simplicissimus, a Munich newspaper renowned for its cartoons vividly descriptive of ludicrous situations they satirized, published a cartoon representing a German officer riding down the crops on the German side of the Franco-German frontier, while on the French side a spectator cries: "Bravo, You are riding under our colonies."[15]

Yet, this small turbulence of the twenty-sixth was but an anticlimactic prelude to the great upheaval of the following day. The news of this did not reach Berlin until the twenty-eighth, after the Prussian Minister of War, von Falkenhayn had answered representative Delsor's question concerning the insults to the Alsatian people by Lieutenant von Forstner. The Minister of War had tended to treat the events in Zabern as merely part of a "tempest in a teapot" and had answered representative Delsor's question by citing the above mentioned semi-official report which the expression "Wackes" had been said not to have pertained to the population of Alsace in general, that Forstner had not known his words would be published, that their disclosure had been a gross breach of duty by informers, and that, anyway, von Forstner like himself, when he had spent four years in the provinces, had not known the local meaning of the word "Wackes" and therefore had not been cognizant of how great an insult the usage of this word would be to the Alsatians. Furthermore, he said, a very young officer was concerned here and, although young officers could not be excused just because of their youth, what an uproar there would be if public attention were called to every case in which a young man went "overboard" in the conscientious discharge of his duty.

War Minister von Falkenhayn considered that a far greater danger to the nation lay in the public excitement drummed up by irresponsible newspapers which had exploited the affair in the most extravagant and provocative way, without regard to the immediate official publication of the actual facts, and had done so even after it was generally recognized that the law must take its course.[16] This ministerial effort to excuse the actions of an individual on the basis of inexperience, to show that it was not the organization, nor the law of the army, nor the system of militarism pertaining thereto that was at fault, was really saying that army affairs were not the business of the civil authorities and certainly not of the Reichstag. Indeed, what he had implied was born out by events in Zabern on that same day. Martial law was imposed upon the people of Zabern without proclamation and despite the fact that the civil authorities had not called upon the military authorities for aid, nor given up their own powers.

Just a week prior to this day, Colonel von Reuter had been encouraged to action by the refusal of the Kaiser to accept his resignation, and by the support of his past actions by von Deimling who had written a letter on the twelfth of November to William II calling the proceedings of von Reuter in all particulars good and condemning the newspapers and the local population for agitation in Zabern.[17] Thus, when Colonel von Reuter was questioned later concerning his actions, he maintained that the actions of these two days had been brought about not only by encouragement, but by command from "higher authority" and that therefore his actions had been justified.

According to the Frankfurter Zeitung's carefully written report of Saturday, the twenty-ninth of November, on Friday afternoon, just at the time that the Minister of War was making his statement in the Reichstag, Lieutenant von Forstner had gone shopping for chocolates accompanied by four soldiers with fixed bayonets and by so doing provoked laughter from the citizens of Zabern. The mood of the people was one of contemptuous amusement and was heightened by the remarks of a number of continuation school pupils which seemed offensive to some young lieutenants just returning from fencing school. One of these, that same Lieutenant Chad who had two days earlier called on troops to arrest laughing civilians, now acted again with precipitation and soldiers immediately arrested the nearest civilians. Yet, this was only the beginning for in a few minutes sixty men were drawn up in two lines in the Schlossplatz and Colonel von Reuter stood behind them and gave the order to load rifles. Drums were beaten and the command was given to use force against all civilians who did not retire at once.

Just at that time, rather late in the afternoon, the civil judge and counsel were emerging from the district court. They were arrested, and except for the judge who proclaimed his office, incarcerated in the coal cellar of the barracks along with several people of importance within the community such as a public prosecutor, the publisher and owner of the largest newspaper in Zabern, the Wochenblatt, who just happened to be out taking a walk for his health. Also arrested were a young man formerly belonging to the volunteer fire department who had heard drums and assumed that a fire was in the courtyard and had come rushing out of the house only to be chased back by the soldiers all the way to the third floor where he had hidden under the bed and the soldiers with fixed bayonets forced his seventy-eight year old mother back from the door and forcefully extricated him from his cover, and a young man who had been on his way to the pharmacy to buy a toothache remedy. These and many others, eighteen in all, were forced to spend the night in a very cold damp cellar where there was just enough room to stand up, no room to sit down and in a space where the frigid November wind came freely. There were no places to perform the natural functions. A corner was used but the odor nauseated some of the unfortunate group and had made matters worse. At ten in the evening the blankets had been provided but these were not enough to keep them very warm. They were forced to stay there all night and were not brought before the civil magistrate until noon the next day, at which time all of them were immediately freed by the judge and their cases dismissed.[18]

That afternoon the Zabern Rural District Council in a special meeting gave voice to its indignation in telegraphed resolutions to the Imperial Chancellor, the Statthalter, the Prussian Minister of War, and the president of the Reichstag. It recited the facts stated above and declared that there was no reason for the arrests, protested strongly against the continued actions of Colonel von Reuter, which were in open contempt of the law and obviously provocatory, and demanded the necessary protection for the people of Zabern. The Prussian Minister replied that he had given the necessary instructions to the responsible military authorities at Strasburg. The Imperial Chancellor replied, "I have received your telegram and informed the Imperial Statthalter. In case the introduction of strong investigation shows illegalities, redress will be given."[19]

In the succeeding three weeks after the violent demonstrations against von Forstner for his notoriously abusive language against Alsace had first come to public notice, a series of petty incidents had taken place in this small garrison town which had produced a scandal because they had been handled by the military too slowly and with too much regard for military discipline. The Frankfurter Zeitung had characterized the Affair as of the twenty-ninth of November when it further represented it as:

> ...scandal which has shocked and distressed public opinion more than any 'incident' of recent times and one which is evidence of the most damaging illustration of conditions in the Reichsland that has been shown since the annexation and for which the responsibility lies between the military and civil authorities whose animosity toward each other has helped to produce the Zabern Affair.[20]

Yet, even at this time there is still one more act in this farcical drama called the Zabern Affair. This involves the actions of that Affair's principal protagonist, Lieutenant von Forstner, and although it takes place in a nearby town called Dettweiler, nevertheless it fits well within the boundaries of the Zabern Affair in terms of attitude on the part of the protagonist, in terms of violence, and in terms of locale. According to a German semi-official telegraph agency (Wolff's) report on the second of December, 1913, Lieutenant von Forstner and his company passed through Dettweiler at seven o'clock that morning. This already notorious young man was recognized by some nearby workmen and was "insulted by contemptuous cries." He called a halt, tried to capture the culprits but to no avail. His ensign, Wies, captured a lame cobbler who "with all his strength resisted arrest." In the ensuing battle, Lieutenant von Forstner "drew his sword and cut the cobbler over the head," opening a wound approximately six inches long on his forehead. He then marched the cobbler (Herr Blanc) to the Burgomaster of the town who questioned him. Even though the Burgomaster considered the wound dangerous, Lieutenant von Forstner stood with his sword ready, waiting impatiently while the questioning went on. Wolff's Telegram Agency published an account later that evening which was described as semi-official, but did not give the source of its information. According to this statement, the cobbler threatened a corporal who was pursuing him, and "put his hand in a pocket in which there was later found a pocket knife." When the corporal who was pursuing him attempted to arrest the cobbler, the cobbler punched him in the face and then turned against von Forstner who drew his sword and struck him over the head.[21]

In a Statement to a correspondent of the National Zeitung, the Burgomaster of Dettweiler claimed that those who were baiting Lieutenant von Forstner were only children. The poor wounded cobbler was dragged bleeding to his office and forced to undergo cross-examination for two hours under the supervision of guards with their bayonets drawn. The Mayor told the correspondent that the public in the town of Dettweiler was greatly excited due to the continuous insults by von Forstner's troops. They had been provoking civilians every morning when they passed through the village.[22]

The events included with the Affair at Zabern were concluded with Lieutenant von Forstner's wounding of the lame cobbler; yet the Affair was to go on long after the events for the reaction to these events seemed to rise to new heights with each succeeding event and this reaction demanded an explanation at its climax on the third of December. Both the press and the general public were disgusted with the militaristic excesses, which could have been prevented by the swift punishment of a young officer who called the Alsatians a name for which a workman had been sent to prison recently. Adequate, swift punishment of von Forstner would have prevented the display before the entire world of the cleavages within Germany, the feeling of Alsace and southern Germany which was adamantly opposed to the militarism, and, above all, the seeming disenchantment of people of all classes with the military. This disenchantment was not assuaged by the official view of the military as put forth in the Kreuz-Zeitung that the military in Alsace had no choice but to defend itself against attacks from civilians not properly policed by local constabulary, that the civil authorities failed to stop the violent and insulting actions of the populace, and that the re-establishment of order had to be accomplished in what was primarily a matter of military jurisdiction.

Those who were disenchanted did not know at that time what the

Emperor thought of the situation as he was seemingly in seclusion at the estate of Prince Furstenburg at Danaueschingen and the only knowledge of any Imperial action at this time was rumor.   These who questioned also found no answer to the troubles coming from the Reichstag as the Reichs-Chancellor Bethmann-Hollweg had postponed the consideration of the Zabern Affair Interpellation until after the first reading of the "estimates" for the military budget of the coming year and this reading had not yet occurred.   The newspapers thus had free rein in developing agitation without refutation of a forceful or convincing nature from the government.   However, on the first of December, the Reichs-Chancellor reiterated that he would deal with the Zabern Affair as soon as debates on estimates were begun, probably Wednesday, the third of December.[23]

NOTES

[1]Wilhelm, Crown Prince of the German Empire and Prussia, Memoirs, p. 95.
[2]W.H. Dawson, The German Empire 1867-1914 and the Unity Movement (New York: MacMillan co., 1919), II, 364-365.
[3]Wolff, The Eve of 1914, p. 339.
[4]Abbé E. Wetterlé, Behind the Scenes in the Reichstag, trans. from the French by George Frederic Lees (N.Y.: George H. Doran Co., 1918), pp. 202-206.
[5]Some said that Zabern events and trial and outcome were a military plot to destroy the Constitution of 1911 in Alsace and the rights it guaranteed and that censorship was round 1, and Zabern round 2. That failure of 1 had caused 2. The Times, June 17, 1914.
[6]Sergeant Höflich, Affäre Zabern: Mitgeteilt von einem der beiden Missetator (Berlin: Verlag fur Kulturpolitik, 1951), pp. 9-12.
[7]The Times, December 1, 1913.
[8]Strasburger Post, November 6, 1913.
[9]The Times, November 10, 1913.
[10]Ibid.
[11]Ibid.
[12]S. Schulthess, Europaischen Geschichtskalendar, Vol. LIV, p. 351.
[13]Ibid., p. 366.
[14]The Times, November 22, 1913.
[15]Simplicissimus, November 20, 1913.
[16]Verhandlungen des Reichstags, Sitting 177, vol. 291, pp. 6040ff.
[17]Hans Gunter Zmärzlich, Bethmann-Hollweg Als Reichskanzler: Beitrage zur Geschichte des Parlamentarismus und der politischen Parteien-Band II (Dusseldorf: Droste Verlag, 1965), pp. 114-115.
[18]Frankfurter Zeitung, November 29, 1913.
[19]Schulthess, LIV (1913), p. 371.
[20]Frankfurter Zeitung, November 29, 1913.
[21]Ibid., December 3, 1913.
[22]Ibid., December 4, 1913.
[23]Verhandlungen des Reichstags, Sitting 177, Vol. 291, pp. 6040ff.

CHAPTER III

THE PRELUDE TO THE VOTE OF MISTRUST

The Reichstag meeting of the first of December, 1913, was crowded in anticipation of the forthcoming debate over the events of the preceding month in Alsace-Lorraine. The views of the Prussian Minister of War, von Falkenhayn had already been put forth on the twenty-eighth of November, when he had refused to consider the events of great significance and had dismissed the Affair as nothing more earthshaking than the pranks of an impetuous young lad of twenty years of age who had "gone off the rails" in devotion to the principles of his profession. He had refused to comment on whether the punishment was a satisfactory atonement for the crime because this was an issue to be decided upon by Lieutenant von Forstner's superior officers at his forthcoming trial. The greatest damage done, however, was not caused by the young lieutenant, but by those who had broken army discipline by reporting the affair to newspapers, that immediately expanded it out of proportion.

Three days earlier than Falkenhayn's remarks, the Imperial Reichs-Chancellor, Bethmann-Hollweg; had refused to comment on the events of the Zabern Affair and indicated that he would wait until the debate on the estimates of the 1914 Army Bill had begun. This statement had been a coercive attempt to have the army bill at least begun to be considered. It had been a form of blackmail for he had known that such a controversial issue as the Zabern Affair would draw the attention of the Reichstag and that this, as well as the already existing disinclination to deal with this painful subject, might have postponed the consideration of the army bill until a dangerously late date. On the first of December, he could not but remember the great difficulty with which army bills of the past had been adopted.

His anxiety over the reading and passing of the estimates was shown subsequently to have been well founded when on the fifteenth of January,

1914, he would stand before the Prussian Abgeordneten Haus (House of Representatives), as Minister-President, and would be forced to answer the criticism of his handling of the Zabern Affair. He would be forced to justify the delay on the basis that the proposed Army Bill of the first of October, 1913, had to be passed by the first of June of the next year or Imperial Germany would lose at least one-half, if not a whole year, in its arms race with other powers and, that considering the international situation, this loss of time could be disastrous. Certainly, he had not anticipated such interpellation, but he was aware that the financial provision of the Army Bill of June, 1913, to expand the military forces had been made in such a manner that part of the payment had to be included in the 1914 Army Bill and thus any delay would have crippled the provisions already made in 1913 as well as hold up expansion for the current year.[1]

The parties in the Reichstag, outside of the Conservatives, had demonstrated throughout the year that they intended to expand their authority and had been aware that a continuing control of the government and an enhancement of the power of the Reichstag could be obtained by insuring continued supervision of the Army Budget in this manner. Bethmann-Hollweg was equally aware of the possible limitations that could be imposed upon the government until the complete Army Budget Bill went into effect and was begun to be paid for in 1917. It was therefore mandatory first, that he get the estimates considered, and, second, fearing the antigovernment majority of the preceding year's army budget debate, break up this most complete anti-government majority in the history of the German Empire.[2] Yet, first the bill had to be introduced and the Zabern Affair furnished an opportunistic lever for the accomplishment of that purpose.

However, the public furor had grown to such huge proportions by the first of December, because of the latest provocations of Colonel von Reuter and Lieutenant von Forstner that Bethmann-Hollweg was forced to appear before the Reichstag and calm the roiling waters by promising to deal with the members' interpellation by the third of December when "he would interrupt the estimate-readings already begun if the results of the official inquiry had been obtained." The quid pro quo was obvious. He continued:

> Events of so regrettable a nature (had taken place) that I myself regard it as most important to make a statement with all possible speed to the Reichstag and the country in order to remove any doubt that the authority of the laws (underlining mine) would be protected as well as public order and the authority of the executive.[3]

The Prussian Minister of War, von Falkenhayn, had not made the attainment of Bethmann-Hollweg's goals any easier because he had suggested on the twenty-eighth of November, that military discipline had to be maintained and that the insults from the civilian population could not be accepted by officers in the army. He further pointed out that in opposition to the reports published in almost all the newspapers in Germany, Lieutenant von Forstner had not known what the word "Wackes" had meant just he, the War Minister, had not known it when he had been stationed in Alsace-Lorraine some years ago.[4]

On the second of December, four days after von Falkenhayn's seeming justification of von Forstner's actions on the basis of youth and ignorance, this ignorant youth attacked the lame shoemaker, Herr Blank, at Dettweiler.[5] Nothing of note concerning Zabern took place in the Reichstag on this day as everyone had expected a declaration of the Government's position from Bethmann-Hollweg and he had not appeared in the Reichstag. However, the Estimates-reading was begun and disapproval was immediately shown of these army financial estimates given by the Secretary of State for the Imperial Treasury. The Reichstag then suspended its ordinary business, and, not hearing the expected traditional speech on foreign affairs by the Reichs-Chancellor following the Estimates, adjourned early. Also, on this date, the Prussian Minister of War returned from Prince von Furstenburg's estates of Donaueschingen, where he had consulted the Emperor and the Imperial Military Cabinet.

Both the officer in command of the Fifteenth Army Corps at Strasburg, Lieutenant General von Deimling, and the Under-secretary in the Strasburg Ministry, Herr Mandel, were on hand in Berlin to hear the Reichstag debate on what the military insisted had become essentially a dispute between the military and the civil authorities over jurisdiction in Alsace-Lorraine. According to the reporter of The Times, the military took this jurisdictional question as a way to weaken the possible actions of the government.[6] Yet, the dispute seemed much broader in nature than just a dispute over jurisdictional authority in Alsace-Lorraine. This had been evident when the Kölnische Zeitung on the first of December explained that Alsace was so completely stirred up by the "military dictatorship" in Alsace-Lorraine that in some areas, notable Mulhausen, people had suggested the calling of a general strike until the issues were settled.[7] Yet, the excitement and interest were not limited just to Alsace-Lorraine; they were found everywhere and the reporter for The Times questioned whether the decision-making authorities would be allowed to show any signs of giving in to public opinion by making an important decision. He further pointed out that the only "indication of a decision was an unconfirmed statement that the Ninety-Ninth Infantry Regiment would be transferred from Zabern to Hagenau."[8]

The debate in the Reichstag on the third of December was primarily concerned with the central issue of Alsace-Lorraine and the Zabern Affair. However, this Affair was broadened in scope to include subjects which had been problems ever since the Empire and been established. Indeed, some of the issues and examples brought up included controversies which had existed ever since Frederick the Great in the eighteenth century, but which had become outstanding problems only recently in the late nineteenth and early twentieth centuries.

Militarism was the first problem raised by the Alsatian Progressive Party representative, Herr Röser, in his remonstration against the attitude of the military in Zabern. His remonstration was that the whole Zabern Affair had been created through wrong military conceptions of honor which did not allow punishment for injustice in due time. The honor of one young lieutenant was held to be more important than the good will of not only the 8,000 people of the town of Zabern, but of the entire population of the Imperial province of Alsace-Lorraine. Von Forstner had brought about the animosity of all by the application of the term "Wackes" to the soldiers of Alsace.[9] Representative Röser provided another example of the values of militarism when he described the events of Sunday, the ninth of November. It was on this day that Lieutenant von Forstner, who had been the subject of ridicule for the previous three days due to the publication of the Wackes incident in the Zabern newspapers, was officer of the day and, according to Representative Röser, had patrolled the streets with soldiers in an unnecessary and unusual fashion and in a provocatory manner brought on further criticism. It was obvious that the honor of the military had been trodden upon, for soon after this a regimental order had been issued clearing the streets of all troops and ordering all officers back to their barracks except for the four lieutenants. They had been subject to ridicule the preceding day and seemed to be seeking retribution for having been forced to seek refuge from the mob in a restaurant for now they had walked the streets leading a Great Dane and with sabres drawn had sought their oppressors. Representative Röser continued his attack by saying that all this took place on the same day that Colonel von Reuter had prepared to declare a state of siege if necessary:

> the day he had ordered to get the machine guns and cartridges ready for use --gives cause to the suspicion--and there is almost no other way of thinking about this--that they were searching for a motive to be able to make use of all the war preparations that had been made in the barracks.[10]

The honor of the military demanded that civilians not be allowed to stand up against the military and the walk of these four lieutenants among the irritated people was a demonstration of the domination of the military and of militarism over the populace and civil authorities of Zabern.

Yet, this was just the beginning of this display of militarism, Deputy Röser continued.   In the succeeding days the recruits from Alsace-Lorraine had been arrested, because they had been under suspicion.   The only one who had remained free was the Lieutenant himself, the perpetrator of the whole affair:

> the gentleman--who had been subject to laughter because of some misfortune during the maneuver--had to stay, probably as a decoration and also to maintain the prestige of the uncompromising super-militarism; and so he gave further reason for all the sad incidents that happened later.[11]

The comments of the Socialist representative, Peirotes, were also in a low key but no less vitriolic than those of his Progressive Party colleague.   In referring to the incidents in Zabern he had heard that these incidents had been part of a nationalist plot and he reacted to this:

> No other statement could be more wrong than this one.   It is true, that the people of Alsace-Lorraine are not especially in favor of the existent militarism.   A system which produces people like the Captain from Koepenik and the Postman from Strasburg cannot suppress these people.[12] The whole institution of militarism does not impress them. An institution which has no similarities whatsoever with the Napoleonic army, in which every soldier carried the Marshal's baton in his knapsack, but one in which one could rather find a sack full of sand in every knapsack, an institution like that just does not appeal to the people of Alsace-Lorraine.[13]

Representative Peirotes then ridiculed the culture which this "Militarism" represented.   He stated that the people of Zabern had been unusually friendly with the soldiers and had been quite harmless, and yet they had still been mistreated.   He said, "In this hour militarism has exposed its highest potential of cultural standards."   His comments on Colonel von Reuter further brings out his contempt for "militarism" when he said:

> They have had 50 soldiers on the Schlossplatz confronting fifteen or twenty civilians.   Now, isn't that a peculiar form of playing a war-

game? To do things like that, to have the first row (of soldiers) kneel and the second one level the guns and it was not a lieutenant giving orders, no, it was a Colonel, fifty or fifty-five years of age, giving orders, not in front of the soldiers, but standing behind them, of course. . . . When things like that can happen, it shows us how far militarism has progressed in this country, it has reached a limit which you will realize when knowing that a lame shoemaker has been made unfit for service by Mr. von Forstner.[14]

The Social Democrats, as Herr Peirotes had suggested, wished the destruction of the institution of militarism without destroying the military. Peirote's object was to free the German citizen from that institution that maintained artificial differences and destroyed the unity of the Empire with its provinces and created animosity between the military and the civil government and at the same time maintained an anti-liberal attitude.[15]

The only rebuttal that Bethmann-Hollweg gave against these charges was that the army was obligated in all circumstances to protect itself against the insults of the populace and must defend not only its honor but also its physical being "even if the consequences of the measures that were taken, did not remain within the limits of the law."[16] His emphasis was on the inviolable nature of the King's uniform and that aggressions had been committed against it and if there were no punishment for these acts there would not be armies in the world.

War Minister von Falkenhayn sounded very much like an echo when he said:

it is one of the vital necessities of the army, that authority, discipline and the sense of honor be protected and respected. . . . Anybody who had fought in the front lines of a war, knows what the "sense of honor" of an army means. I ask the soldiers in the Reichstag to be my witnesses. In those solemn hours, when the fate of the home country is being decided on the battlefields of honor, the soldier would not be able to derive any help from words and speeches, but only from discipline and the sense of honor. . . . I am talking about the sense of honor which keeps the soldier from doubting one single moment at the point where he has to decide between death and disgrace. It is no easy task, gentlemen. to inject such a sense of honor into any man, be he an officer or just a plain soldier.[17]

The War Minister was much more articulate and convincing than the Reichs-Chancellor and his remarks brought forth increasing cries of agreement from the Right while, at the same time, the cries from the Left, which had been so loud and continuous at first that von Falkenhayn had found it impossible to speak, were reduced in intensity and feeling with the continuance of the forceful and sincere remarks of the General. He continued:

> I am quite sure, gentlemen, that even the most efficient theory of a respectable old man cannot replace ONE outstanding example of a youthful officer or noncommissioned officer in the battle. . . . The army needs the young leaders so badly that it gladly accepts the accompanying phenomenons which are inseparable from the sometimes clumsy way of showing youthful courage. . . . But the golden rule of our regiment even applies in this case: omission and failure are still much worse than erring in selecting the right means.[18]

The War Minister was adamantly opposed to the definition of militarism assumed by Deputy Ledebour of the Social Democratic Party when the latter asked whether the army should meddle in politics when von Falkenhayn had suggested that the army was not created to take police measures. The War Minister said:

> Certainly not! It is indeed lamentable and even detestable as has been proven to me in this case by the repeated warnings the military authorities have pronounced to the civilians, if the army has to intervene in such a case. Once it has intervened, however, a certain amount of severity cannot be prevented.[19]

The National Liberal representative, Dr. von Calker from Strasburg, was quite condemnatory of both Bethmann-Hollweg and General von Falkenhayn's treatment of the Zabern Affair because they had maintained a false prestige of the military, which, he said, was exactly what the latter had just condemned. This remark brought acclamations from all parties in the Reichstag, except the Conservatives. He continued:

> And now, gentlemen, let us turn to the facts of the case of Zabern . . If right after the affair became publicly known--the administration had said: "In case the lieutenant actually used the expressions--we don't know that yet, the matter will be investigated immediately-- there will be appropriate punishment--I am sure that things would not have developed the way they did. . . . Why did the military administration do no such thing? This is really something that has to be brought out clearly at this point! Nothing has been said about

the punishment--because of a policy of prestige which is completely improper in my opinion-a policy of prestige that makes believe that the authority is in danger even when something that has been done wrongly, is being admitted. Gentlemen, I think it is just the other way around, I think that the authority is in danger when one tries to extenuate a mistake! . . . If that had happened, everybody would have been satisfied and the hard work of the Reichs-Chancellor would have been made easier.[20]

The opinion of Dr. von Calker was of great importance in that it represented both the opinion of the National Liberals as a party, as was shown by the great acclaim that he had received from the National Liberals, and from the "Old Germans" in Alsace-Lorraine.[21] Thus, this was doubly condemnatory of the militaristic practices condoned by the way in which the government of Reichs-Chancellor Bethmann-Hollweg, representing Kaiser William II, handled the Zabern Affair.

The militaristic spirit was not only associated with maintaining the honor and the prestige of the army but was also found associated with the destruction, or condemnation for that purpose, of liberalism in the form of the liberal press and the Reichstag's questioning of the army. This liberal attitude which emphasized that civil authority should not be controlled by the military and that a representative assembly should be a primary part of any government, was a direct threat to the independence of the military officer corps, the Junkers, and therefore threatened the continuance of the caste system of the Prussian Junkers that had dominated the officer corps of the German Army.

A prime representative of this liberal attitude was Socialist representative Peirotes. He insisted that the Reichstag had the right to ask the Reichs-Chancellor what he would do to prevent future occurrences such as Zabern from happening and why Lieutenant von Forstner had been punished so lightly. He suggested that the Reichs-Chancellor would be powerless to interfere in military affairs directly but that he could "appear before his Imperial Master and tell him that he can no longer bear the responsibility for incidents like that" and that the Kaiser should "cooperate with us in the transformation of the German Reich into a modern, liberal nation."[22]

Concerning the Minister of War, von Falkenhayn, Representative Peirotes said:

that he is responsible to the Reichstag for all the things that happen in this army; and if such a mild sentence is being given for things like that, we have the right to call him to account in this house.[23]

The rebuttals of both Reichs-Chancellor, Bethmann-Hollweg and War Minister von Falkenhayn were critical of the obstinate, persistent examination of the Zabern incident. Both implied that the Reichstag was stepping outside the bounds of its authority in demanding that the Reichs-Chancellor judge the von Forstner case, and that he comment on the punishment, and that he assure that body that no such occurrence would happen again, and that the Reichstag could call to account the War Minister.

Bethmann-Hollweg refused to consider Peirotes' pleas and implied that the Reichstag was interfering in a matter which was brought about by special circumstances that would not happen again and that there was not any long lasting controversy between the military and civil authorities.[24] According to him the dispute had been brought about by the activities of Lieutenant von Forstner which included an impertinent remark which insulted the Alsatians and an insult to the French Foreign Legion and that these having being reported in the newspapers brought on riots which ended in the incarceration of thirty people. The actions of von Forstner and his commanding officer had not been legal, according to Bethmann-Hollweg, but the army had the right to protect itself against aggression, if the civil authorities could not do so and, although the civil authorities had denied it, the army had stated that there had been no law and order. He believed the controversy could not be settled and therefore nothing could be done. He said:

So, as you see, the local authorities have completely divergent opinions on this actual question, not the legal part of it, the actual question. I am not able to decide who is really right on the basis of the result of the investigation. Whether or not this can be decided in the future, I do not know and leave the question undecided, gentlemen.[25]

The comment from the floor at that time was ". . . this is your declaration of bankruptcy,"[26] and indeed so it seemed at the time. His only suggestion was that the authorities work out their own problems by cooperating with each other and that the people of Alsace-Lorraine help to bring about a peaceful solution. In effect he was saying that the incident was out of his hands. He could do nothing about it. It was a fait accompli by the military and, although it was illegal that the military arrested innocent spectators, it was necessary in order that worse things should not follow from the insulting of officers. He was saying that the military had made the decision and it could not be reversed. At no point did he suggest that there was any reason for the Reichstag to be concerned nor that it had any right to make queries about the law. Indeed, his suggestion was that "the judge will have to determine whether there has been violation of the penal law and whether there will be any claims of indemnization according to the civil law."[27]

War Minister von Falkenhayn was even more directly condemnatory of the liberal spirit than was Reichs-Chancellor, Bethmann-Hollweg. He conceived of the whole affair as a "plot." He said:

> This is a regular attempt to achieve some illegal influence upon the decisions of the competent authorities by riots, inflammatory newspapers, systematic insults of military personnel and by hindering them in the normal fulfillment of their duty.[28]

He further suggested that an organized plan of action existed when he stated, "To avoid excuses--and I am sure that those who originated the present scandal, would have been perfectly able to fix up something for that purpose. . . " [29] This was in direct contradiction to representative Peirotes former statements that there had been no German nationalistic plot upon which the Zabern incidents had been based as had been suggested in the semi-military, pro-Prussian, conservative newspapers, Deutsche Tageszeitung, Die Post, and the Kreuz-Zeitung.[30]

The War Minister alluded to the spirit behind these actions in the following short speech:

> We will keep discipline in the army, you can be sure of that. I ask you to see to it that the spirit that now stirs up portions of the population be . . . eliminated--the spirit that has led to the lamentable incidents.[31]

Quite in opposition to these views was the liberal opinion of Deputy Peirotes. He believed that the spirit behind the incidents was much more conservative and that it had been first brought out by then Colonel von Deimling on the twenty-sixth of May, 1906. This uncompromising military despotism that was so contemptuous of the Reichstag was still in command in Alsace and was the spirit behind the whole series of provocatory actions in Alsace-Lorraine for he was the commander at the time of the Zabern Affair in this year, 1913.[32]

When this conservative-militaristic anti-Reichstag spirit associated with Colonel von Deimling was condemned by a heckler during von Falkenhayn's rebuttal, the Minister of War for Prussia said to the heckler that von Deimling's actions took place seven years ago and should be forgotten. When the heckler parried with "but he has not changed," von Falkenhayn countered with "that is his best quality."[33] Obviously, not only was the War Minister referring to von Deimling's attitude in general, but in particular his attitude toward the Reichstag; this was an effective summary of the combined attitude of the military in this incident. Indeed, this view had been suggested by Deputy Röser in the opening speech on this day when he said it "is the result of the attitude that has once before become apparent in this House of the desire of enabling one single lieutenant and ten of his men to clear out this House."[34]

According to Deputy Röser, this spirit that he had seen demonstrated went all the way back to the eighteenth century when King Frederick the Great ruled as an absolute despot.[35] Deputy Peirotes even traced this spirit back to the early sixteenth century when the farmers of Alsace were fighting in Zabern with the young squires and when the latter cut down the former in the same courtyard where Colonel von Reuter had set up his machine guns seemingly to follow this precedent three hundred and eighty seven years later.[36] Deputy Fehrenbach, representing the Centre party, commented on this spirit as being the same that he had seen demonstrated thirty years before and he criticized the army for not having learned anything in the intervening years.[37] This spirit was that of a dominating caste system allowing no question of its power, prestige, and authority even by the duly appointed and constituted authorities of the civil government. Deputy Fehrenbach criticized this power as one that operated outside the law and he finished his remarks very emphatically by saying that if this was to happen in Germany it would mean finis Germania.[38]

For forty-three years since the 1870 conquest by Germany, the natives of Alsace-Lorraine had wanted in ascending order of desire the following: a voice in their destiny, representation in the Reichstag, representation in the Imperial Council, a constitution, recognition as a province, and finally autonomy. All of these would have given to Alsace-Lorraine at each step increasing degrees of self-determination. Alsatians had gradually acquired all but the last two, ending with the 1911 Constitution that had been given to them through Bethmann-Hollweg's influence on the Kaiser. Yet, the constitution meant little because there were no means to enforce it, and furthermore it was considered too weak and allowed too little self-determination. Therefore, it was not unnatural that the Zabern Affair was used as a tool in order to pressure the government into giving one or both of the last two desires.

Alsatian Deputy Röser began the explanation of the factors behind the development of the Zabern Affair by referring to the lack of both self-determination and the power to enforce the constitution when he said of the Zabern Affair:

The Affair developed because of the weaknesses of our civil authorities, who were not capable of protecting the country from shocks like this one because of the incomplete constitution in Alsace-Lorraine and because of their dependence on Berlin.[39]

Alsatian Deputy Peirotes was equally vehement in his denunciation of the weaknesses of Alsace-Lorraine's constitution when he echoed Deputy Röser: "The incidents at Zabern have also demonstrated the powerlessness of our constitutional system in Alsace-Lorraine."[40] He explained this by saying:

At the meeting of the local government authorities we had to pass resolutions in which we asked the central government to present a petition to the Imperial Government asking it to intervene so that the people of Alsace-Lorraine were no longer subject to insults and abuses. The mere fact that we have to file these petitions in such a way shows how powerless our government really is.[41]

After taking this negative view toward the present constitution he proceeded to suggest what should benefit Germany and Alsace-Lorraine mutually in the future:

I think that, if you really want to work in the manner Mr. Röser indicated, if you wish to guarantee world peace to a certain extent, you will above all have to strive towards a reconciliation with the people of Alsace-Lorraine and you will have to grant them self-reliance and autonomy.[42]

In this instance Deputy Peirotes paraphrased what the well-known French Socialist Jaures had said concerning world peace. This pleased neither the center nor the right in the Reichstag because it seemed to indicate that the Alsatian Peirotes had accepted both French and French-socialist views and neither were popular in a Germany that was well aware of France's Revanche (revenge) minded population.

The issue of Alsace-Lorraine being a weak province of Germany with little self-determination was, perhaps, less important than the issue that pervaded the Zabern Affair of fear of the domination of Prussia to the point at which there would be no self-determination at all and at which Alsace-Lorraine would exist merely as a slave-state to Prussian Junkerdom. The Prussian officers could drill and develop the discipline to perfection and thus could revert to Medieval aristocratic values. This fear stemmed from the practice by the Kaiser and other military officers of placing

Prussian officers in positions of authority in Alsace-Lorraine as propagandist-examples of good German citizens who were expected to stay there and "educate" the natives. Often, this worked to the opposite effect resulting in antagonizing many of the so-called "Old Germans" who had been placed there and who were not Prussian. They became more often good citizens of Alsace or Lorraine than the natives became good German or Prussian citizens. This fear of Prussianization was always present, but seemed to become much more apparent in times of crisis. Yet, for the most part, even in times of crisis, the town of Zabern remained the most calm and the least anti-German or anti-Prussian of the towns in Alsace-Lorraine.   It was thus most extraordinary that the people of Zabern became riotous and this indicated the great provocation that produced such action.

Animosities among the "Old Germans" appeared not only in Zabern but elsewhere in Alsace-Lorraine. The provocations at Zabern produced opposition to the Prussian system in Strasburg where Dr. von Calker, an "Old German," mirrored the objectives and opinions of many others:

> Gentlemen, the Emperor sent me to the University of Strasburg not only for the purpose of teaching subjects "Penal Code" and Criminal Procedure," but also for me to work for the German development and the German rights. I have--and I can honestly say this--tried to see my job under these principles--sixteen years so far--and I have tried to work for a policy of reconciliation of differences which still have not been overcome; for a policy, which fully recognizes the rights of the Alsatians--of the native population--but which on the other hand naturally also tries to bring the influence of the "Old-German" rights, the rights of the entire German country to hear. This is why it is so very hard for me today to discuss this problem. I can assure you that not only the Alsatians are deeply grieved over what is happening today . . . after sixteen years of work . . . everything is lost again.[43]

Another example, as quoted by Deputy Röser, of an "Old German" comment was less diplomatic than Dr. Calker's and called the "Old Germans" by the name befitting what he considered their spirit to be, "Old Prussian." Deputy Röser said:

> The reason for these incidents is typical of the treatment given to the people of Alsace-Lorraine by the so-called "Old Prussians," e.g., the "Old Germans"-- who want to transplant the spirit of the absolutistic era of Frederick the Great into our times. The expression "Wackes,"

which now is officially presented as if only used in connection with vagabonds--according to its origin--is actually an expression generally used in this part of the country by the so-called "Old Prussians": this word is being used in a derogatory sense when referring to the natives.[44]

He condemned this treatment further by stating that many of these men who had occupied important positions had returned home without ever having known the Alsatians; without ever having gained any insight into the feelings or character of those over whom they had ruled for so many years. He justified this by quoting again from the letter of that "Old German":

> In cases where the so-called Old Prussians are superior in number in any public office, they actually form an obstacle for the objective of Germanizing the natives. They are a "nursing home" of the Old-Prussian reactionary spirit in the borderlands--a nursing home that is separated from the native population by our insulating layer made of heartlessness and lack of understanding for anything different. . . . Unfortunately the traditional pride of place is often considered superior to the high duty of Germanization and unfortunately one seems to consider the power of the conqueror to be the only means of subordinating a people.[45]

The views of Centre Party Deputy Hauss were not dissimilar to those of Deputy Röser. However, in order to show that the opposition to the Prussian influence and coercion was not just based on one party he cited the National Liberal newspaper, the Hannoversche Kurier, of the twenty-sixth of November, the editor of which wrote:

> In case it is our desire to make the Germanization of the Alsatians impossible there is no better way of achieving it than with cases like the one in Zabern. Men like General von Deimling, who deliver war speeches; men like the colonel who immediately sets up machine guns, as well as the Lieutenant who uses very little judgment when choosing his words, should not be stationed in the Imperial provinces.[46]

The antagonism between the people of Alsace and the so-called "Old Prussians" was based primarily upon an attitude of authoritarian domination on the part of the latter and was found at the same time in both civil as well as military affairs. An attendant, yet at the same time far more important matter for the whole of the Empire, was the entirely separate question asked during the Zabern Affair of whether the authority of the military or that of the civil government was to dominate in the provinces and, in its extension, whether the military would dominate over the civil government in all of the Imperial German confederated states. Of course, a crisis would have to exist in which civil authority ceased to be responsible, but in that case would the Prussian military dominate over, for example, a Saxon area?

These questions seemed not to have been applied to the Zabern case at hand, but will be applied to the Affair that develops. Indeed, Deputy Röser cited the authority of a retired German officer in Zabern and that of others of the "Old German" population showing that the population of Zabern was not pugnacious by nature. This officer, Colonel Barth, said that there had never been any conflict between the civilian population and the military and this led Deputy Röser to state that there was none now, but only a conflict with several military individuals.[47]

The outstanding issue here in the Affair was one of the very basic reasons for any civil law to exist, the protection of oneself, family, and possessions from uncontrollable actions on the part of individuals or groups acting violently as mobs. On the other hand the justification for military protection was to maintain law and order when no civil government existed. In a province such as Alsace-Lorraine, could the military determine when civil government had ceased to exist and, if so, could it in the form of an organized group making laws for itself and for the community, be responsible without the consent of the community for maintaining law and order for the good of the community?

In the Zabern Affair the people protested emphatically in the newspapers, in the town council, through representatives to the provincial diet at Strasburg and finally to the Reichstag that the army had not the welfare of the province in mind when its actions were taken into consideration. This, they said, could be seen very clearly in the army's assumptions of military honor and prestige which later led to incidents in protection of these falsely valued attributes. It could be seen in the attempt to subordinate the Zabern population to a despotic, Prussian set of values emphasizing obedience to military authority wielded by officers who had to be shown proper respect. Yet, the ramification that illustrated this attitude most clearly, they said, was the demand that civilians show obedience to Prussian military authority and to its concepts of honor and prestige, and that this was forced upon them with complete disregard for the Imperial Civil law and authority that were still operating at the time.

The military view, of course, stressed that the military could not be subjected to the ridicule of the populace whether it deserved this ridicule or not. This ridicule would destroy the faith in the army and the army's self esteem as well. The army, according to its supporters, was the protector of the Empire and its provinces and it had to discipline its members so that they believed themselves to be of value to the army itself, and to the country which it served. Therefore the values of this fighting force of self-protection and honorable, prestigious conduct must be maintained both in times of peace and of war and these must not be in any way questioned or ridiculed by the populace or that public law that served it. The army had to be a law unto itself and its authority should not be questioned or its protective shield would be questioned and by so doing weakened, and the Empire it served and protected would be liable to destruction.

Thus a very modern conflict had arisen here between the military and civil authorities. It had as its source a fundamental disagreement over whether the individual was to be benefited by the laws of his country, thus becoming a valuable, productive potential asset to his country, or whether that person must survive under a law benefiting the country by maintaining its striking force, its military, yet be in such a servile position that this force determined what that law was. This latter view was based upon a value system alien to the civilian, but one which was rationalized by the necessary for military protection and ultimate victory in war. Yet, a law that served only war conditions in time of peace, as Röser said served only those who prepared for war and was detrimental to those who served peace.[48]

The encroachment of military power on civil law was not new when it appeared in the Zabern Affair. Both Deputies Röser and Peirotes gave examples of the domination of the sabre over the civil authorities and the denial of civil rights and equal opportunity to the people of Alsace-Lorraine. Deputy Peirotes emphasized that the Zabern Affair was just the last straw in a long line of military encroachments that finally broke the camel's back. He was eloquent in his condemnation of the actions of the military which at one time had led to the overthrow of a local governor and at another to the illegal persecution of the newspapers, Souvenir Francais and the Souvenir Alsace-Lorraine by Generals Prittwitz and Gaffron, respectively. At another time the head of the police at Muhlhauson had been transferred as a result of conflicts with a Major-General. The actions of the military affected the population as a whole by the military influence bringing about a denial of rights of foreigners in Alsace-Lorraine, and thereby depriving the populace of a source income. Another example of this population control he found in the denial to provincial soldiers of the right to hold confidential positions in the army. Peirotes pointed out that the most recent act of discrimination had occurred only a few days before when a captain had become enraged because eight of his First Jägers were of Alsace-Lorraine descent.[49]

Deputies Röser and Peirotes were joined by Deputy Hauss, a member of the Centre Party from Alsace-Lorraine, in fixing the blame for these denials of civil rights on Berthold von Deimling, the commanding officer in Alsace-Lorraine. Deputy Hauss, in particular condemned the General's anti-civil-authority-attitude by citing how General von Deimling had acted in the Reichstag on the twenty-sixth of May, 1906.[50] Deputy Peirotes added to this that there was more than an anti-Alsace-Lorraine approach in the threat of military law replacing civil law in time of peace. He compare von Forstner's "breaking up" of the Wackes with other such similar slogans, all of which climaxed in the idea expressed some years before of "we the strikebreakers can do anything, we can even kill somebody."[51]

As stated before in this monograph,[52] the War Minister had defended General von Deimling by taking the attitude that such acts committed seven years before should be forgotten. Outside of this reference neither Reichs-Chancellor Bethmann-Hollweg, nor War Minister von Falkenhayn commented on the past actions of the military nor on the past illegal denial of civil rights to the people of Alsace-Lorraine. The War Minister seemed to have denied the rights of civil authority when he emphasized that the army would have to take the law into its own hands if the spirit that had directed the actions of the people in Zabern recurred.[53]

That military actions conflicting with civil law in Zabern actually took place, was undeniable said all of the speakers in the Reichstag on this day but there was quite a difference of opinion over whether there existed a chronic state of opposition between military and civil authorities. Both Alsatian Deputy Röser and a group led by Deputy Delsor agreed with the Reichs-Chancellor that there was no such chronic state of dissension in Alsace-Lorraine nor in Zabern. All saw the Affair arising out of isolated incidents perpetrated by certain individuals. Deputy Röser even went so far as to say that, ". . . out of thirty-five military officers of this military regiment, only the Colonel and four of the younger lieutenants organized everything."[54] He cited evidence to show that retired officers in Zabern had viewed the people as not being opposed to the military and stated that there had been no tension between the military and the civilian authorities before the affair and that the affair had been brought about by belligerent individuals of the military establishment. Colonel von Reuter had ignored the pleas of civilians, closed the post office, and ignored the protests of the civil authorities that no military law could dominate in peacetime and had countered objections by stating that he was following the commands of his superior officer. Despite the fact that the District Court Judge had volunteered to hear the case against the twenty-eight incarcerated prisoners this plea had been ignored until noon of the following day. Even after the surrender of the prisoners the armed patrols had continued to roam the streets despite the fact that the civil authorities had informed the colonel--in accordance with the ministry's instructions in Strasburg--that they alone wished to take the responsibility of maintaining order in Zabern. Again on the twenty-ninth of November it had been an individual who had been at fault, said Deputy Röser. Lieutenant Chad (Schadt) had entered a house illegally when following a boy who had laughed.[55] Röser cited the evidence of the Town Council of Zabern, the Association of Middle Sized Towns of Alsace-Lorraine, and the Alsace-Lorraine Association [56] as representative of the broad outcry that had been against these infringements of the police-authority of the mayor of Zabern. Throughout, however, he stressed that the actions of individuals: von Forstner, von Chad, von Reuter, von Deimling had been responsible for causing the problems and not the animosity between the military and the civil authorities in general.

On the other hand, Deputies Peirotes, Hauss, Haass, Fehrenbach, and von Calker took a broader view which was quite emphatically in opposition to that of Deputies Röser, Delsor, and to the Reichs-Chancellor. War Minister von Falkenhayn concurred with the former view that this was a question of conflict between the two authorities, civil and military. Peirotes suggested that Lieutenant Forstner had invited violation of the law by setting up a reward for knocking down a Wackes and had taken the law into his own hands when he had chased people who had insulted him instead of appealing to the civil tribunal. Peirotes even suggested that such provocations had been planned and cited the memoirs of Prince Hohenlohe-Schillingsfurst of 1873, the former Reichs-Chancellor, as evidence that "the military want to reduce the people to despair so that they will rebel and then the military can repress the rebellion bloodily."[57]

Deputy Peirotes asserted that the military had no right to intervene in the affairs of the civil authorities. He said, "It can only intervene in the case of a siege and the siege has to be proclaimed by the Emperor . . . the military can also intervene upon the request of the civil authorities and there was no such request."[58] Although, his statements had been taken from the military law of 1837, which was still in operation, nevertheless, Deputy Peirotes was not content to follow this law; he suggested that while the Reichs-Chancellor had assured the Reichstag on Monday that this law would be maintained, he "would have preferred for the Reichs-Chancellor to have mentioned the kind of rights that we were born with."[59] This statement referred to an inherent, inalienable right above the government-made law that had to be maintained, and Peirotes even went so far as to call those who transgressed that right, traitors and insisted that they were unfit to be stationed in Zabern. He cited the French example of a General Boullard whom the French government immediately transferred in 1907 for having given a "sabre rattling" speech in front of the garrison at Nancy, and Peirotes suggested that the same transfer be given to the whole ninety-ninth regiment at Zabern.[60]

Hauss of the Centre Party from Alsace-Lorraine was in agreement with Peirotes that a military dictatorship in Alsace-Lorraine had been instituted after von Forstner's punishment and after von Falkenhayn's speech on Friday. He insisted that both the punishment and the speech had been inadequate and indeed seemed to provoke rather than prevent further illegal actions involving the arrest and imprisonment of peaceful citizens. Not only did these illegal actions include the arrests, but also the Colonel had violated the law when had he ordered a lieutenant and four soldiers to break into the office of the editor of the Zaberner Anzeiger and search for a manuscript.[61]

An important difference between the approach of the Reichs-Chancellor, and the War Minister, was found in the basic assumptions of the two men. Both assumed that there would be a trial for the protagonists of the drama at Zabern, but Bethmann-Hollweg clearly assumed that the trial would be civil. The judge would have to determine whether there had been a violation of the penal law and whether there would be any claims of indemnification according to the civil law.[62]

He insisted that the measures taken by the army officers, although illegal, had been necessary for self-protection against the mob "in order to prevent worse incidents" and because "the military felt that the civil authorities failed completely to function and could not have offered them sufficient protection at all."[63]

Von Falkenhayn also stressed that harsh measures had to be taken if the populace could not be restrained by civil authorities,[64] but he assumed that a military courts martial would decide the case and not a civil tribunal. Von Falkenhayn said, "Even the most stupid person in the country knows that this matter will be solved according to law and order by their superiors."[65]

The difference, of course, lay in their orientation. Although Bethmann-Hollweg used the military reports as factual information in relating the events of the time and although von Falkenhayn used the comments of an Alsatian resident who had moved there from France, to prove the lack of authority in Zabern, nevertheless, the reference to civil law on the part of Bethmann-Hollweg and to military law on the part of von Falkenhayn indicated the differences between the two with respect not only to Zabern, but to the German Empire as well. Bethmann-Hollweg assumed the army to be subject to civil law and civil discipline administered by a civil court system, while von Falkenhayn could envisage only a military trial to enforce or determine military discipline and this meant no civil interference in army matters.

Neither Bethmann-Hollweg nor von Falkenhayn had any conception of the principle of law that protected the public, according to the South German Center Party Deputy Fehrenbach. To him, justice and laws could not be destroyed without destroying the very essence of Germany. If the military could decide when and where and whether it will follow the law, Fehrenbach asserted, then there was no law and if none there could be no Germany. He was in complete opposition to von Falkenhayn's views that only the military could judge the military. He said:

> if the rights and laws have been violated by somebody, even by the public powers (such as the army), it is up to this House (Reichstag) to take care of the remedies. It is also up to them to intervene in favor of the weakened laws and rights.[66]

Fehrenbach declared that the officer was subject to civil law and must act within its scope just as would any other citizen. The process which both must follow was: identify the individual; keep him in custody; turn him over to the police; but under no circumstances must the officer take the law into his own hands as had occurred at Zabern. In such a situation the civil authority must govern the actions of the military and the authority of the military must obey.

In a situation which demanded a decision from the Reichs-Chancellor on a series of actions the nature of which was disputed by the military and civil authorities, Deputy Fehrenbach condemned the use by Bethmann-Hollweg of the military reports of the disputed actions to the exclusion of the civil reports. He affirmed that the bias of the military was thus put forth as fact by the Reichs-Chancellor and resulted in an unjustified acceptance of this by the populace.[67]

The dispute over whether military or civil authority should rule, according to Fehrenbach, was an extension of simple, earlier issues which had gone beyond their initial stage when adequate punishment or a leave of absence might have settled them Now, he said, it was in a state of hopeless confusion and the statement of the Reichs-Chancellor that nothing could be done and that of the War Minister, that nothing had happened, could not even find support in the far right side of the Reichstag. "We cannot allow something like that to open up a chasm between the military and civil administration, of our German Empire." The civil authorities had been willing to do their duty but were not allowed to do so. These incidents "have been used here again to set up a dictatorship in Alsace and to discredit the constitution that has been built up with such great efforts and with a chance of success."[68]

Fehrenbach's approach was in opposition to von Falkenhayn's. The War Minister insisted that the affair had been insignificant and that it would have ended if it had not been for the inflammatory press and riotous actions; the offender had been punished by the military and that was all that could be desired and he was not allowed to reveal the nature of the punishment.[69]   The War Minister at no time referred to a constitution and did not take the opportunity offered by Fehrenbach to deny either the dictatorship by the military or the discrediting of the constitution. He ignored them and instead merely emphasized that worse happenings had been prevented.

Deputy von Calker was much more familiar with the situation in Alsace-Lorraine than Deputy Fehrenbach.   The former had lived in Strasburg for sixteen years and was a personal friend of the governor of the province, Governor Wedel. He said he had been shocked by the actions in Zabern, but had been even more shocked by the military accusations that there had been no civil protection for the military, who therefore had to protect themselves. He said that if conditions had been so bad, the civil authorities ought to be eliminated, but he was convinced that Governor von Wedel was being wronged if such accusations were made.

That officers of the Prussian Army were ignoring civil law and civil rights and were not being punished, was known and condemned throughout Germany. Equally exasperating, however, was the fact that in this affair the officers were also ignoring military law with impunity. This was brought out by Deputy Röser when he stated that Lieutenant von Forstner knew that the use of the word "Wackes" was illegal; he had signed as having read a military order to that effect.[70] This ignoring of military law was also shown by Roser in the Panduren Cellar episode in which the twenty-eight citizens had been incarcerated in violation of the instructions Nos. 118-130, and No. 134 regulating garrison duty. These listed among other regulations that civilians had to be handed over to a Civil-Judge for interrogation when arrested, and it was shown by Röser that judges of the civil court had volunteered their services at the time but that they had been rejected by Colonel von Reuter.[71]

Concerning the actions of Lieutenant von Forstner and his calling his recruits Wackes, Deputy Peirotes showed the illegality of this action by citing Article 121 of the military criminal code which indicated that any superior who insulted one of his inferiors might receive up to two years imprisonment.[72]

The reply of the War Minister to these questions regarding what he should do about these violations was that the punishment of Lieutenant von Forstner was up to his superiors and that he had no responsibility for this matter. This was tantamount to telling the Reichstag that this was army business and that the Reichstag had no right to interfere.

Deputy Peirotes replied that anything that concerned the army was within the province of the Reichstag's authority and von Falkenhayn as War Minister was responsible to that assembly for all these occurrences and therefore that body had the right to call him to account before it.[73]

This approach of expanding the constitutional rights of the Reichstag was also what Deputy Fehrenbach of the Centre Party was insisting upon; indeed he used almost the same words as did Deputy Peirotes.[74] Furthermore, this revolutionary view was implied in the questioning of all of the speakers of this day. These speakers represented four different parties: the Alsatians, the Social Democrats, the Centre Party, and the National Liberals. When Deputy Peirotes asked the Reichs-Chancellor to cooperate with his party in bringing about a modern liberal state, the Reichstag records show that the only opposition or displeasure came from the hisses and shouting from the Conservatives. The helplessness of the Reichs-Chancellor, the ignoring of the major issues by the War Minister, and the persuasive speeches by both Fehrenbach and von Calker had put the Reichstag in a very liberal mood and one which was very definitely anti-authoritarian. According to von Falkenhayn, it had been this liberal spirit which had caused the incidents by compelling the army to enforce discipline upon the civilian population and it was this spirit which had to be eliminated.[75] The answer the Reichstag had to this demand was found in a motion signed by the Deputies Dr. Ablass, Fischbach and colleagues that:

> The Reichstag resolve to state that the way the Reichs-Chancellor handled the question with which the interpellation of Röser and colleagues dealt, is not in accordance with the opinion of the Reichstag.

This motion was carried and a further discussion of the interpellation of Röser, Albrecht, Delsor and colleagues was scheduled for December fourth, the next day.[76]

NOTES

[1]Stenographische Berichte uber die Verhandlungen des Preussischen Hauses der Abgeordneten, January 15, 1915, 22 Legislatureperiode, 2 Session, vol. I, pp. 246-319.

[2]The majority coalition cited above is that substantiated supra. pp. 15 and 32, and deals only with the major issues there stated.

[3]Verhandlungen des Reichstags, 291 (1913), p. 6096.

[4]Ibid., (1913), pp. 6041 ff.

[5]See above, pp.39-40.

[6]The Times, December 2, 1913.

[7]Kölnische Zeitung, December 1, 1913.

[8]The Times, December 3, 1913.

[9]Verhandlungen des Reichstags, 291 (1913), pp. 6340-6341.

[10]Ibid., 291 (1913), p. 6242.

[11]Ibid.

[12]The "Captain from Koepenik" by donning the uniform of a Prussian army officer and masquerading as an officer was able to command a squad of troops, arrest the mayor of a town who was an officer in the Reserve, and abscond with the town treasury equally powerful in a uniform as the postman in Strasburg who marched 1500 troops around in a polygon.

[13]Verhandlungen des Reichstags, 291 (1913), p. 6143.

[14]Ibid., p. 6147.

[15]Ibid.

[16]Verhandlungen des Reichstags, 291 (1913), p. 6157.

[17]Ibid., p. 6159.

[18]Ibid., p. 6160.

[19]Ibid.

[20]Ibid., p. 6169.

[21]The "Old Germans" were those sent to Alsace-Lorraine to Germanize the population in the years 1870-1913. Mostly they consisted of retired army officers and soldiers along with bureaucrats and educators.

[22]Verhandlungen des Reichstags, 291 (1913), p. 6151.

[23]Ibid., p. 6149.
[24]Ibid., p. 6157.
[25]Ibid.
[26]Ibid.
[27]Ibid.
[28]Ibid., p. 6158.
[29]Ibid., p. 6159.
[30]Ibid., p. 6145.
[31]Ibid., p. 6167.
[32]Ibid., p. 6150.
[33]Verhandlungen des Reichstags, 291, (1913), p. 6167.
[34]Ibid., p. 6140. This is a reference to the remarks of Oldenburg-Januschau and leaves out a part which stated that the Kaiser ought to be able to tell a lieutenant to take ten men and close down the Reichstag--Oldenburg-Januschau, Erinnerungen (Leipzig: Verlegt bei Koehler and Amelang, 1936), pp. 109-110.
[35]Verhandlungen des Reichstags 291, (1913), p. 6141.
[36]Ibid., p. 6145.
[37]Ibid., p. 6161.
[38]Ibid., p. 6162.
[39]Ibid., p. 6140.
[40]Ibid., p. 6154.
[41]Ibid., p. 6151.
[42]Ibid.
[43]Ibid., p. 6168.
[44]Ibid., p. 6140.
[45]Ibid., p. 6141.
[46]Ibid., p. 6154.
[47]Ibid., p. 6141.
[48]Ibid., p. 6142.
[49]Ibid., p. 6150.
[50]Verhandlungen des Reichstags, 291, (1913), p. 6154. See p. 69, this monograph.
[51]Ibid., p. 6158.
[52]See above, p. 55.
[53]Verhandlungen des Reichstags, 291, (1913), p. 6167.
[54]Ibid., p. 6141.
[55]Ibid., p. 6143.
[56]Ibid., p. 6144.
[57]Ibid., p. 6147.
[58]Ibid.
[59]Ibid.

[60]Ibid., p. 6151.
[61]Ibid., p. 6154. Herr Wetterlé, the editor of the <u>Zaberner Anzeiger</u> was warned and removed the manuscript in time.
[62]<u>Verhandlungen des Reichstags</u>, 291, (1913), p. 6157.
[63]Ibid.
[64]Ibid., pp. 6259, 6170.
[65]Ibid., p. 6159.
[66]Ibid., p. 6162.
[67]Ibid., p. 6167.
[68]<u>Verhandlungen des Reichstag</u>, 291, (1913), p. 6167.
[69]Ibid.
[70]Ibid.
[71]Ibid., p. 6144.
[72]Ibid., p. 6148.
[73]Ibid.
[74]Ibid., p. 6162.
[75]Ibid., p. 6170.
[76]Ibid., p. 6171.

CHAPTER IV

THE VOTE OF MISTRUST

According to the Agenda at the end of the Reichstag meeting of the third of December, 1913, the discussion of the fourth of December would include three items: one, the third deliberation of the proposed bill concerning commercial relations with Great Britain; two, a continuation of the discussion of the interpellation of Ablass, Röser, Albrecht, and Delsor concerning the events in Zabern; three, a continuation of the discussion of a proposed bill dealing with the Imperial Budget and the budget for the protectorates during the year 1914. Actually, only the second of the three was considered. The reason for this was that great public indignation had been aroused over the "army dictatorship" and the infuriating insults to the Reichstag by both the Reichs-Chancellor and the War Minister on the preceding day.

The question for all of Germany seemed to have become: Will the Postman of Strasburg and the Captain from Koepenik rule over the civilian population as well as the military without regard for either civil or military law, or will this spirit of Prussian militarism that seemed to have emanated from the actions of the military in Zabern be subject to German Imperial law and justice that applied to all persons within the Empire, whether Prussians, Saxons, Bavarians, or members of any other group, whether members of the army or not? As Deputy von Calker had said the previous day, "a serious political question is now being presented to the nation and the nation is aware of the issues at stake."[1] The newspapers of the fourth of December showed very clearly this understanding by their almost unanimous condemnation of the speeches of the Reichs-Chancellor and War Minister of the preceding day. Comments taken from the newspapers of this day printed in the Frankfurter Zeitung defined the problem and stated the attitude toward it. An example of this from the Social Democrat newspaper, Vorwärts, stated that the Zabern

71

Affair constituted a conflict between the constitution and militarism with the latter being represented by the War Minister and the Reichs-Chancellor and no one supporting the constitution. On the other hand, it did say that there was a contrast between the views of the Constitution of the War Minister and the Reichs-Chancellor with the latter being aware of the guilt of the military for acting in opposition to the constitution but being unable to do anything about it. Vorwärts declared that the Reichstag had begun a war against military anarchy.[2]

To the liberal Berliner Tageblatt this regime was "saber-rule" and one which disheartened the best ministers and brought down upon itself the distrust of the people.[3] According to the Vossische Zeitung, which represented the moderate liberal elements, the regime echoed the "high command" so closely that Bethmann-Hollweg should have donned a uniform. It said that the War Minister in his speech of the day before had been as energetic as the Reichs-Chancellor had been listless and that the latter did not seem to have had his heart in the sentences he had spoken. The paper implied that these sentences had been dictated to him rather than having been an expression of his own opinion. On the other hand, it noted that the War Minister seemed to be the epitome of "Krautjunkertum." The Frankfurter Zeitung quoted the Vossische Zeitung as not viewing the future with optimism within the present governmental system. It emphasized that even though a new Reichs-Chancellor might be appointed if a vote of mistrust in the Reichstag should go against Bethmann-Hollweg, this would not change the army dominated state system and Bismarck's dictum that the bayonet should govern would still apply. It further explained that a lesson learned from the debate over Zabern in the Reichstag of the previous day was that Bethmann-Hollweg representing the civil-authorities could not win in competition with von Falkenhayn's representation of the Imperial military authority. The fact that von Falkenhayn had been invited to an audience Monday, the first of December, with the Kaiser and his military cabinet at Donaueschingen while Bethmann-Hollweg was kept in Berlin in ignorance of the issues and the decisions was proof that the War Minister had won the game.

According to the Frankfurter Zeitung, the Kreuz-Zeitung of the fourth of December, 1913, recognized in the stormy activities of the preceding day in the Reichstag only the stirring up of artificial excitement. The Kreuz-Zeitung considered that the War Minister represented the army point of view commendably in the Reichstag. Concerning the Reichs-Chancellor, it considered that he had said everything that could be said in justification of the military authorities in the Zabern case. However, according to the Kreuz-Zeitung, he should have said more, namely that the civil authorities had been to blame for the events of the preceding few days because they had not opposed the November outbreaks of the populace and because the Strasburg directed administration of Zabern had not understood the conditions of life in the army.

Generally, however, the Kreuz-Zeitung regarded the speech of the Reichs-Chancellor as satisfactory and of course this showed the distance between the opinions of this newspaper that represented the army and those of the general population which reflected the opinion of the vote in the Reichstag of the fifth of December which condemned the Reichs-Chancellor, Bethmann-Hollweg, 293-54 or 6 to 1 against him, the army, and Prussian militarism, according to the Berlin reporter of The Times who wrote on that date.

The Deutsche Tageszeitung had mild praise for the Reichs-Chancellor but the Frankfurter Zeitung pointed out that the paper was no lover of parliamentarism. On the other hand, the Berliner Neuesten Nachrichten considered the third of December to be a black day for the Reichs-Chancellor. This was quite a different view from that taken by the conservative Post which remarked that the nation owed a debt of gratitude to both the Reichs-Chancellor and the War Minister for saving the army from injustice. An opposing view was found in that of the Tägliche Rundschau. The author pointed out that the storm aroused in the December debates in the Reichstag was greater than any since that against the Kaiser in November[4] and that it not only was against the government but was also against the army. Indeed the dissatisfaction was so deep that the middle-class parties not only did not dampen nor repress the hostility, but actually stimulated it. This author insisted that the events at Zabern and their justification portended ill for the future of Germany.

The Germania believed that no politician could have gone into the Reichstag the day before with any hopes for a friendly reception, but that not even the greatest pessimist foresaw that the outcome of the meeting would be the drafting of a motion of distrust. It agreed with Dr. von Calker that all that had been built up in Alsace-Lorraine had been destroyed. It concluded that the people would be justified in expressing its displeasure by a vote of distrust.

The National Zeitung stated that the Reichs-Chancellor had ignored the central point that had stirred up such trouble in Germany as a whole and had made Germany the butt of foreign ridicule. This point was that the honor of a citizen should be just as important as the honor of an officer in the army. The authority of the civilian official "carries the cloak of the Kaiser just as much as the authority of the army officer" and Bethmann-Hollweg had ignored it and indeed had spoken the preceding day as representative of the ultra-conservative right. He should have said that, as long as he was the supreme representative of civil authority, civil power and civil law would be upheld in Germany. He did not. He capitulated before the military which War Minister von Falkenhayn represented.

The capitulation caused great depression in Alsace and particularly in Strasburg where the newspapers echoed the words of Dr. von Calker in the Reichstag, "Alles kaput, alles kaput."

The press in Vienna reported fully the debate concerning the Zabern Affair and, of the newspapers there, only the Deutsche Volksblatt gave one-sided support to the military. The Frankfurter Zeitung of the fourth of December commented on the thorough coverage of the Zabern affair by the Parisian newspapers and stated that French politicians were astounded there at the resoluteness with which both the Reichs-Chancellor and the War Minister supported the military against the civil authorities. Comparisons were made in Paris of the Zabern Affair with the French Dreyfus Affair in which a war minister also consistently had given unflinching support to the General Staff and the General Staff members had been in the wrong. The French press expressed sincere doubt as to whether the Reichstag could muster a majority vote of mistrust?

The whole of Europe, including Germany, on this day of reckoning awaited eagerly the outcome of the initiated vote of mistrust. Was the Reichs-Chancellor in the wrong? Even the traditional, conservative newspapers in Germany were not altogether sure that he was not culpable. The Kölnische Zeitung condemned Bethmann-Hollweg for supporting militarism and not advising the Kaiser against it and foresaw the development of anti-militarism in Germany for the first time in history.[5] Considering these opinions, it seemed apparent that the Reichs Chancellor had no other choice but to try to calm the storm of opposition which had arisen in all parties with the limited exception of the Far Right. He had to make some concessions or try to explain away his remarks of the day before.

The debate in the Reichstag on the fourth of December was no less vitriolic than that on the preceding day. Indeed, passions had been aroused on both sides to a point that bordered on violence. The debate on the "Estimates" was again adjourned. The Imperial Chancellor was the first speaker and began by saying that Dr. von Calker had asked him at the end of the session on the preceding day what the future course of German policy in Alsace-Lorraine would be. He therefore set out to answer this and at the same time to counter some of the attacks against him. He had been accused of maintaining silence about the civil authorities in Alsace, of having in fact disavowed them. He answered this by stating that it had never occurred to him that by silence he could have been criticizing the attitude of the civil authorities. The subject of debate had been the attacks against the attitude of the military authorities and that had been the subject of his speech. He went on to say that he had been accused of using only the reports of the military authorities and of having ignored those of the civil authorities. This was not so; he had used them! The admission that he had used them provoked so much disturbance in the Reichstag that the President had difficulty in restoring order. Bethmann-Hollweg continued with the statement that the civil and military authorities disputed whether or not the civil police failed in their duty and stated that he had expressly declared that the lack of cooperation between the military and civil authorities was largely to blame for what had happened at Zabern and that nothing but permanent contact between the military and civil authorities could lead to the restoration of normal conditions. He then asked how he could have said all that without having considered the reports of the civil authorities? If in describing the events which led to the intervention of the military he had relied upon the military version, how could he have done otherwise? The Social Democrats protested loudly at this and Bethmann-Hollweg answered their protests with his insistence that he had said that the clearing of the Schlossplatz, the arrests and the treatment of those arrested had been illegal and that these facts had come from the civil reports. He then asked how anyone could have discussed such things more impartially. This only provoked laughter from the Left.

Concerning Professor von Calker's question about future policy, the Reichs-Chancellor replied that he had many times in the face of many attacks expressed his views, and that despite the lamentable events in Zabern he continued to hold them. He had not adopted the passionate tone of other speakers and as he was speaking of matters which were still in great part the subject of judicial and disciplinary proceedings he was bound to impose upon himself reserve. The members of the Reichstag had, however, demanded that he declare his attitude and he had complied. He declared that he had been consistent although he knew he would be criticized for not being so. He had insisted upon the introduction of the Alsace-Lorraine Constitution of 1911 in full agreement with the Statthalter. He maintained that his motives were not democratic in nature but were brought about by the necessity of the situation in which he believed no progress could be made unless the fruitless attempt to turn the South Germans of the Reichsland into North-German Prussians was abandoned. What must be considered, according to the Reichs-Chancellor, was the peculiar characteristics of the people which were due to their history and their traditions. Because he had held these views he had appealed to the Reichsländers to cooperate with him in the unification of greater Germany and not to listen to those who sought to divert them by emphasizing their exaggerated sensitivity.

He went on to deny what so many of late had said, "that the cause of all of the trouble was this new constitution," by emphasizing that anyone who had read history would have realized that there had been troubles before and that it was clear that a new constitution would not work miracles. The course must be steadily and quietly pursued and there must not be total chaos whenever a slight relapse occurred. He refused to share Dr. von Calker's pessimism or to believe that the work of several decades had been destroyed. The Reichs-Chancellor said:

> In this grave hour we must direct our gaze to the future. I call
> the hour grave, not as though my position were in any way
> imperilled or because the House has proposed and is about to
> carry a bill of censure against me. It is not for that reason that
> I call the hour grave (much outcry in the Reichstag), but
> because out of the profound excitement has arisen the peril of
> a cleavage between Army and people. That is the gravity of
> the hour, and because I recognized this I said to you yesterday
> that the first business was to produce harmony between the
> military and the civil authorities. (Interruptions and a cry of
> "tell that to the Minister of War.") I am in full agreement with
> the Minister of War.[6]

Here the Socialists' and other interruptions caused the Reichs-Chancellor to pause. After this he went on to conclude his statements with another reference to the preceding day's debate:

> Somebody spoke yesterday of the existence of a second government
> (Nebenregierung). There is no second government. There is a
> government for which I am responsible to the Emperor, and when
> I think that I am no longer able to bear this responsibility you will
> see me no more in this place. But in this case I repeat there is no
> second government. All the authorities concerned are agreed that
> without loyal cooperation between the military and civil authorities,
> such as was unfortunately lacking in Zabern, there can be no
> improvement. From the highest quarter this point of view has been
> repeatedly and emphatically brought to the attention of the authorities
> and the officials concerned in connection with the events at Zabern.
> The General in Command has been ordered to see that there is no
> transgression whatever of the law. It is also the will of the highest
> quarter that the military and civil authorities shall go hand in hand
> with complete respect for the law. As I said yesterday, what has

been proved wanting will be made good.   Only upon the basis of law and right can we for the future restore what has been imperilled. (Cheers on Right, hisses on Left.)[7]

Conservative Rogalla von Bieberstein condemned Lieutenant von Forstner's "instructions hour" just as Reichs-Chancellor Bethmann-Hollweg and War Minister von Falkenhayn and other gentlemen in the Reichstag had done on the previous day, and he insisted as they did also that von Forstner did not mean to insult the whole population of Alsace-Lorraine.   He added that this was behavior quite in contrast to that of Deputy Peirotes who had generalized in the Reichstag on the previous day that all Prussian army officers were traitors.   Furthermore, he stated that Peirotes' questions concerning punishments given in the army to officers and men need not be answered by the War Minister because the Reichstag had not the constitutional power to hold the War Minister responsible nor did it have any authority whatsoever over him.   He suggested that the Reichstag and all of Germany trust the military administration to discipline the army judiciously.   In other words, he was telling the Reichstag to mind its own business and not to attempt to change the constitution.

He indicated that a major source of responsibility for the whole affair lay with the foreign newspapers <u>Le Matin</u> and the <u>Zaberner Anzeiger,</u> which on the same day, the sixth of November, 1913, nine days after the "instructions hour" had taken place, had come out with heated articles concerning the affair.   He suggested that the civil authorities had been at fault on that very same day for not taking the <u>Zaberner Anzeiger</u> off the street before the affair had been printed in newspapers all over Germany and the world.[8]   He thus indicated that press-censorship should have been applied as a matter of course and that the civil authorities by not doing so were inciting riotous activities.   His assumption, of course, was that press censorship was right.

Indeed, Rogalla von Bieberstein supported the actions of the Reichs-Chancellor, the War Minister, and General von Deimling.   He quoted Bismarck in echoing von Falkenhayn's view that a young officer with spirit was worth far more than an old officer who had only experience to guide him. This representative showed his patriotism by referring to the deeds of young officers in the Franco-Prussian War that were heroic.   He commended the Commanding General, von Deimling, for having ordered after the stoning of officers on the nineteenth of November that the military protect themselves if the civil authorities could not do so.   He concluded that the honor and discipline of the army had to be maintained. In sum, he represented the conservative view as was suggested by <u>Die Post</u>, on the third of December, of complete support for the views of the

War Minister and which, to a large extent, had been echoed by the Reichs-Chancellor.[9]

A different view entirely was presented by Deputy Trampczynski, a Pole who supported the Alsatian side with its provincial view. To him, as for the views of provincials in general, the events of Zabern had not been isolated incidents but were the outcome of a system in which the members, such as Lieutenant von Forstner, thinking of themselves as demi-Gods and as good representatives of their class, regard their actions as being beyond reproach. If there should be any difficulty over their actions, the civil authorities and the newspapers could always be blamed, as they had been in the preceding ten years whenever there had been any conflict between the military and civil authorities. The outcome would be the same as it had been for the last ten years; the civil authorities would receive the blame for any altercations or disagreements.

According to him a system existed of hushing up the mistakes and illegal or inhuman actions that the army commited. He cited the evidence of the nine recruits and the sergeant who had been arrested and held without reason and thus medievally tortured in the Zabern Affair. Another example of this hushing-up system, he said, had occurred not long before when the Deputy Liebknecht touched upon the Krupp affair with the War Minister. Thus had been initiated by the military authority an investigation of the involved persons, but at the same time had been initiated in conjunction with the public prosecutor an investigation of the unknown person who had allowed the information concerning the complicity of the military in illegal activities with the agents of Krupp to "leak out." He said that against this system of "hushing-up" army affairs the common soldier had no recourse. He maintained that the investigation of those who had "leaked" the information had been more important to the military authorities than the investigation of the possibility of illegal activities.[10]

The Polish Deputy Trampczynski proceeded to refute the statement of the previous day by the War Minister that " any soldier who has a grievance against his officers need only complain" by the his own examples taken from the experiences in his province. He cited the famous Knittelschen trial in Gleiwitz. Here an officer, Captain Kammler, had upset the market baskets of the women in the market place without apparent reason. The military trial had awarded the accolade to Captain Kammler of being an honorable, exemplary officer and found him not guilty of any conduct unbecoming an officer. Examples of such "exemplary" behavior by officers, the deputy said, deepened the rift between the civil and military population.[11]

His concluding remarks linked the cause of the Alsatians with that of the Poles and he condemned the militarism that forced the soldiers to turn to the civil authorities for redress of their grievances; he condemned the enforced Germanization that would not allow the Polish language to be spoken, nor Polish books read, nor even freedom of religion observed because of the anti-Catholic attitude of the officers and non-commissioned officers. He condemned the system that made the military service of the individual three years of subjection to a military machine, the consequence of which being that the individual himself became a thoughtless machine. He found this army of 1913 to be similar to that of the eighteenth century, when the soldier feared the commissioned and non-commissioned officers more than the enemy, and compared with the great people's army of 1806, he insisted that the former came out second best. He concluded with the suggestion that the attitude of subservience to the Prussian military machine was not one born in the instruction hour, but one which was cultivated in the unconscious daily lives of the people and that the people had to awaken to the increasing loss of freedom that was taking place everywhere.[12]

A view that was somewhat of a compromise in some respects between that of Representative Trampczynski and Representative Rogalla von Bieberstein was that of the Imperial Party (Reichspartei) member Freiherr von Gamp-Massaunen. As a Pole, Deputy Trampczynski usually was associated with the Centre Party in voting, while Deputy Rogalla von Bieberstein represented Prussian conservative opinion. The views of Freiherr von Gamp-Massaunen reflected those of the moderate-liberal branch of the Conservatives. He was quite in agreement with Rogalla von Bieberstein that self-protection was the right and duty of the military and that the civil administration could not protect the military against insults at all times. On the other hand, he agreed with Deputy Trampczynski that the military administration had not made a clear and exhaustive presentation of the events. However, unlike both Rogalla von Bieberstein and Deputy Trampczynski, he laid the blame for the Zabern Affair at the feet of the joint administration of the Reichslande by both the military and civil authorities. To him, both had been at fault, neither one more guilty than the other.

Freiherr von Gamp-Massaunen placed the responsibility for this Affair in the gradual growth of real opposition between the military and civil authorities. He cited as reflections of this opposition in the case of the Zabern Affair the refusal of the civil-administered fire-brigade to respond to the demands of the military that it disperse the crowds with its hoses. He stated, however, that the examples that could be adduced are far fewer in number than those which could be brought to light if it were not for the secrecy surrounding the whole affair. An example of this secrecy was shown concerning the clearing of the Schlossplatz by the army. In this case neither the military nor the civil authorities had revealed whether the police had been present at the time or not. This would have had quite a bearing on the case, he stated, because if the police had been there and had not protected the officers as they should have, then the military would have been justified in clearing the Schlossplatz. If the police had not been present, then proper measures should have been taken to inform them and patience should have been used by the military and thus the actions with the consequent arresting and incarceration of the twenty people would never have taken place. Yet, he insisted, even if the police had been there and the arrests had been justified, this would not have justified the treatment of the arrested persons. On the other hand, he viewed the arrest and treatment as perhaps not entirely the fault of the military, because the civil authorities had failed to act. He had the impression that the civil authorities had not interfered in the affair of the incarceration of the twenty civilians intentionally in order that the military authorities would receive the full blame for a greater crime against humanity than would have been the case if those incarcerated had been freed after a short arrest by the actions of the civil authorities. In other words, the civil administration could have done something had they wished to do so.[13]

This view brought immediate objection from Dr. Muller-Meiningen and others who countered that a judge had offered his services but that these had been refused by the military.[14] To this Freiherr von Gamp-Massaunen replied that the only one who could have tried the case would have been the Amtsrichter (judge in a civil court) and that it had been the Landrichter (judge of a provincial court) who had offered his services. The opposition maintained that the latter should have had jurisdiction, but the Freiherr dropped the subject.

He, however, further developed his view that the civil administration did not want to interfere in the Affair by suggesting that it had not been until the second of December that the Kreisdirektor issued a proclamation warning the people of Zabern to keep the peace and that this should have been issued three weeks before when this warning had been urgently needed. He queried, hadn't the Statthalter or the Staatssekretär the slightest idea of what had been going on? Why had this occurred only after General Major von Kihne had suggested it? To him this further justified his previous impression of the disinclination of the civil authorities to act and substantiated what the Reichs-Chancellor had said that day about the lack of cooperation between military and civil administration. He condemned both for not putting aside their animosities and for not doing their duty.

Freiherr Gamp-Massaunen formally supported this condemnation by the presentation of a resolution embodying the views of the Reichspartei in which he condemned the Zabern incident and the inefficient investigation of it by the nationalistic, clerical, and progressive press that resulted in attacks against the army. Nevertheless, he also stated that his party disapproved of the military action in Zabern that showed the influence of a local remedy-action, rather than that of the military central authority, which invaded the sphere of civil authority and tread upon the rights of the citizen.

His concluding statement supported the Reichs-Chancellor in his quest for cooperation in the future between civil and military administration. However, he was pessimistic and did not believe that harmony could be achieved in Alsace-Lorraine where the attacks of the Alsatian nationalistic press and the party it represented would prevent future statehood for Alsace-Lorraine in Germany. He suggested that this party even went so far as to manufacture propaganda for its ideas in France. Only after the press and the party were repressed could the Reichsland be bound with Germany.[15]

The assumption by the Reichs-Chancellor on the fourth of December that the long term dispute between the civil and military administrations was the cause of the Zabern Affair did not go unquestioned by Deputy Weill. This Social Democrat from Strasburg stated that the Reichs--Chancellor's view of the fourth of December was quite different from that individual's view earlier in the week. Deputy Weill insisted that the Reichs-Chancellor had stated earlier in the week that the Affair was the result of a temporary difference of opinion between individuals within the civil and military administrations and there had been no long-term, general dispute. His reference to the suggestions for cooperation between the two authorities on the fourth seemed to suggest that some word from the Kaiser had forced Bethmann-Hollweg to change his mind. The animated outcries and support from many parties when he made this suggestion reflected the recognition that indeed, the Reichs-Chancellor's attitude had changed radically during the week. These reactions reflected a great awakening of interest as Herr Weill attacked the government with great forcefulness and frankness.

He criticized the Reichs-Chancellor's request for harmony between the military and the people because the type of harmony that Bethmann-Hollweg suggested would be no less than the abdication of the Reichs-Chancellor's and the Civil authority and the substitution for them of a military dictatorship. This seemed to indicate that he was being controlled by the influences of the Kaiser and his military cabinet emanating from Donaueschingen. According to Deputy Weill, this was not the only indication of the weakness of the Reichs-Chancellor's authority. Social Democrat Weill criticized the fact that their only responsible representative of the Imperial Government in the Reichstag, Bethmann-Hollweg, had been called to Donaueschingen to consult with the War Minister, the Chief of the Military Cabinet and the Emperor and the result had been the domination of the Prussian military view over the civil government's view. It was evident, Weill emphasized, that General von Deimling and the Military Cabinet had won and War Minister von Falkenhayn's remark that the best thing about von Deimling was that his militarism had not changed since 1906 when he had addressed this Reichstag was indicative of the rule of the Empire by a military dictatorship-spirit.

On the other hand, according to Herr Weill, this spirit was quite in contrast to the assurances of the Reichs-Chancellor that he wanted to be above parties, to be neutral and objective in his viewpoint; yet any neutrality and objectivity concerning the events in Alsace-Lorraine would be diametrically opposed to his statements that reflected the spirit maintained by General von Deimling and the Pan-Germanists.   The Reichs-Chancellor had said that he had used the Civil Reports and not exclusively the army reports as had been charged against him yesterday; yet he had shown by his statements that he had not read them the day before.

Herr Weill's condemnation of the Reichs-Chancellor was no more scathing than that which he presented of War Minister von Falkenhayn. He charged that the latter sought to escape responsibility for the actions of the military and, indeed, to shift the responsibility for these actions away from the military themselves by blaming the tumultuous circumstances created by the instigating newspapers of Alsace-Lorraine. Deputy Weill, as a representative from Strasburg and a supporter of Count von Wedel's civil administration of the province, regreted deeply that the Imperial Government had flatly abandoned the Provincial Government (Landesregierung) of Alsace-Lorraine and the civil authorities as well. The once commendatory understanding between the Reichs-Chancellor and Count von Wedel had been lost despite the great amount of cooperation between the two in the changing of the Alsace-Lorraine constitution two years before.

Both the Reichs-Chancellor and the War Minister had tried to gloss over and explain away all the illegalities and insults. This had led the people to ask that if what they had said was true, then what had the whole Affair been about in the first place?   Why had there been any questioning of von Forstner's words if there had not been insults meant? The point of view expressed here that "nothing happened of importance and what had happened was over and let us forget it," was not consonant with the earlier view of the Reichs-Chancellor who had admitted before the Reichstag earlier in the week that the actions of the military had gone beyond the legal boundaries and that he would personally see to it that these boundaries would be maintained and that punishments would be applied against the culprits.[16]

This deputy from Strasburg, Herr Weill, stressed that the whole attitude of the military including the terminology used to justify it in the Reichstag was that of Praetorianism and was expressive of the spirit of military dictatorship. The military used phrases like protecting the cloak of the Emperor, protecting the right and honor of the army, but not one word was said of the rights and honor of the citizen nor the protection of the cloak of the citizen. This Praetorian officership acted as if it was the leader and master of the nation (as the old Praetorian guard of Rome had been under Tiberius). Weill's condemnation was not merely negative. He emphasized that "it is time, high time, that the citizen consider the cloak of the citizen and his citizen honor to be higher in value than the uniform."[17]

According to Dr. Weill the relations between Germany and Alsace-Lorraine had been as Deputy von Calker had said the day before, destroyed. The Imperial troops in Alsace-Lorraine were being considered enemy-conquerors. Yet, he stressed that it was not just the constitution of Alsace-Lorraine that had been ignored, but the constitutional position of the Empire had become questioned. The lesson of a democratic nature had been given to the people by the hunters at Donaueschingen, whose words had to be awaited before the question of the day could be considered. Always, the answer given was that the independence of the Generals and officers from the civil law and their honor from that of the citizenry had to be renewed and strengthened.

He enjoined the Reichstag to carry out the clear and simple duty of passing that vote of mistrust so overwhelmingly demanded by the majority of the citizens of Imperial Germany. He recognized that the Reichstag had no power by a mistrust vote to overthrow the Reichs-Chancellor, but he insisted that his power would be shaken. He understood the position of weakness of the Reichs-Chancellor and he met the objections of those who might use this as an excuse for his not acting in the Zabern Affair by stressing that the influence of the Reichs-Chancellor extended far enough so that he could advise the Emperor and bring about needed changes or even a questioning of possible action as in the case at Zabern, but that the Reichs-Chancellor did neither. He had treated the prospect of a vote of no-confidence with contempt, but perhaps compulsion could be used during debate on the estimates in order to save the people's republic. His concluding statement was to the effect that the Reichstag had a responsibility to protect the delegated authority of the people and, especially, the authority of the principle of parliamentary representation against military dictatorship.[18]

Dr. Haass, a Radical (Freisinnige Volkspartei) from Baden, also stressed that the great majority of the German people, with the exception of a small number of conservatives, did not believe that the Reichs-Chancellor would protect the law and justice of the German people. According to Dr. Haass the rift that heretofore existed between the Centre and Liberals and the Progressives and the Social Democrats no longer existed. It had to be shown to the whole world that the people of the German Empire lived not in a military state but in a state of justice where illegal actions by officers responding nervously to mere words would not be tolerated.

The slogan of the army, Dr. Haass continued, was that the cloak of the Kaiser must in all circumstances be respected. To Dr. Haass this was only a half truth and half knowledge. Representing the Radicals, he believed that the Kaiser's cloak would command respect when he who wore it deserved respect. In reply to War Minister von Falkenhayn, he agreed with the preceding speaker, Dr. Weill, that the cloak of the citizen also deserved respect, but, much more, the laws and justice of the German people demanded respect. The carrying of the colors of the Kaiser did not make the army the personal possession of the Kaiser. The army belonged to the German people.

To Dr. Haass, as also to Deputy Dr. von Ricklin the so-called "instigating press" contained representative newspapers from all parties except the conservatives and therefore could well be said to represent the German people; therefore, the attribution by the War Minister of the cause of the affair to a few of the press organs was wrong. The Affair had been taken up by newspapers all over Germany and was no longer merely dealing with insults in a small town in Alsace-Lorraine. It now involved the principle for all of Germany of civil freedom destroyed by revolting officers. The aristocratic officers (Herren) have revolted against civil law. Not only are the rights of the people guaranteed by civil law but the right of trial, the most important, was guaranteed by the constitution as a fundamental right. What the military in Zabern have done is to commit the most shameful deprivation of freedom in the history of German rights since the creation of the penal code and perhaps even before. If the military could be justified in attacking people who laughed at them, then the military had to be justified in attacking all of Germany, France, America, Austria, Italy, and the whole world, for the whole world had been laughing at the exploits of Colonel von Reuter and his cohorts.

Dr. Haass said that there was now in Germany an unpleasant feeling that a system of "class-justice" existed in Germany. This type of class justice existed whereby the military were not subject to the same laws as the citizens. If a citizen insulted an officer the citizen was incarcerated, but if the officer insulted the citizen, the officer was free to do as he pleased because he had the power of the usage of weapons and the citizen could do nothing about this issue.

His concluding remarks included two opinions in the form of suggestions. He suggested that although General von Deimling might be a good soldier, as he was held to be in Baden, yet he mixed politics with military affairs and this was disastrous for the military. Dr. Haass alluded here to the earlier linking of Deimling's name with the Pan-Germanists in the Reichstag and the suppression of civil authority in Alsace-Lorraine. His second suggestion was with regard to the view of the conservatives that the whole series of events and the Affair itself was due to the constitution given to Alsace-Lorraine in 1911 which allowed it representation and a vote in the Reichstag. He insisted that this was in keeping with the general conservative view that any form of representative government was by definition wrong, an attitude taken by the conservatives in 1911 when they opposed Reichs-Chancellor Bethmann-Hollweg's introduction of the new constitution. Representative Haass denied this emphatically, stating that if a province were to wait until the conservatives were ready to give it a constitution, it would be like Mecklenberg, still waiting. As a summary, he reiterated what he considered to be his most important point, that the army did not possess of itself independent power, but served the German people and was subject to the will of the people and the German people's justice and law.[19]

Dr. Ricklin, from Alsace-Lorraine, representing the Centre Party advocated that this province become a Bundestaat, a federated state of the German Empire with full rights. He said that there had been a time when it would have been dangerous for a politician or a political party to have represented such a point of view, but that this time had passed. Today the people of Alsace-Lorraine were ready to be included into the Empire, but were being alienated by the German military. A source of alienation for many might have been the speech in the Reichstag the day before by the Reichs-Chancellor. But for him, the speech did not truly represent the views of Bethmann-Hollweg, and the Reichs-Chancellor in his speech seemed not truly convinced of the validity of the views that he had been expressing. On the other hand, there had been a definite controversy between the civil and military authorities in Alsace-Lorraine, and although it was clear that justice was on the side of the civil administration, nevertheless, "the Reichs-Chancellor did not have the courage to support this standpoint."[20]

Dr. Ricklin concluded his remarks with skepticism about the words of Reichs-Chancellor Bethmann-Hollweg. The latter had suggested that he had no doubts in his mind that Alsace-Lorraine could win the respect of the German people in the future even after the events of the recent past. Dr. Ricklin suggested that the people of Alsace-Lorraine question whether the Reichs-Chancellor has the power of prognostication? Would there be a battle against the great majority of the people as the Rheinisch-Westfälische Zeitung had recently suggested? Dr. Ricklin's answer to these questions reflected the opinion of a great number of journals throughout Germany, an opinion which to him promised that the people of Alsace-Lorraine would win their battle with the aid and sympathy of the whole of the German people and of the whole world.[21]

The resolutions of Albrecht and associates, and Dr. Ablass and associates were set before the Reichstag. They asked the Reichstag to vote "yes" or "no" as to whether the Reichs-Chancellor had handled Interpellation Numbers 1185, 1190, and 1206 concerning the Zabern Affair in accordance with the views of the Reichstag? The result of the vote of the 351 votes counted was that 293 voted that he did not satisfy the Reichstag, 54 voted that he did, and 4 abstained.[22] There had never been in the history of Imperial Germany such a majority opposed to the government.

No doubt existed that the cause of the vote of mistrust had a great deal to do with the entirely ineffective and badly delivered speech of the Reichs-Chancellor on the third of December. James W. Gerard, the American Ambassador to Germany, reported in his book, My Four Years in Germany, that the Chancellor had received that morning:

> family news of a most unpleasant character, which added to his nervousness. He spoke with a low voice and looked like a downhearted and sick man. It was whispered afterwards in the lobbies that he had forgotten the most important part of his speech. The unfavourable impression which he made was increased by von Falkenhayn's appearing for the first time before the Reichstag.[23]

After this, according to Ambassador Gerard, when Bethmann-Hollweg had been accused of having different ideas than the Minister of War, he had said that he had entirely agreed with the Minister of War. This admission, says Ambassador Gerard, was one that clearly contrasted with his remarks not only earlier in the week but even on the same day. It had been as if the War Minister had him given orders after the Reichs-

Chancellor's opening speech to agree with what he said.

This obedient Bethmann-Hollweg, said Theodor Wolff, the editor of the Berliner Tageblatt, and the author of The Eve of 1914 had been following orders and "Once more the mercenary Friesshart was obeying orders of the tyrant Gessler and guarding the ducal hat."[25] The difference in views had been over whether there had been a long-term controversy between military and civil authorities in Alsace-Lorraine, with Bethmann-Hollweg originally taking the negative while von Falkenhayn took the positive view. His earlier suggestion that he would personally see to it that the culprits of the Zabern Affair were punished and that he would support law and order were at variance with his later "following orders" speeches. This attitude was reinforced on the next day the fourth of December, and seemed to be a very important factor in causing the vote of lack-of-confidence by the Reichstag.[26] Theodor Wolff continued by comparing the Reichs-Chancellor with the French Ministers during the Dreyfus Affair who helplessly took refuge in the honor of the army since the army took precedence over the state.[27] Wolff said that in this case the state was that of Imperial Germany and the army was that of Prussia.

To many within the Reichstag it meant that a Bundesstaat was dominating the Empire, and this was unconstitutional. To others it was a matter of militarism or military dominating the Empire, which was also unconstitutional. To some it was a grave error committed by an overzealous lieutenant and his commander who should have been punished but were not; for this omission the government should be censored, but this did not mean that the basic form of government was wrong.

The issues, then, could be seen to have resolved themselves into two types. One was the issue of what was to be done about Zabern and whether this would include the punishment of the officers and men. The other issue was the question of whether constitutional and parliamentary authority should govern in the German Empire. This latter issue became divided into two separate issues. One issue would be whether the Imperial Constitution of 1871 should rule, allowing a certain amount of freedom and exercise of civil rights; two, whether parliamentary authority could be exercised within a non-parliamentary state without destroying the constitution.

NOTES
[1]See above, pp. 57-58.
[2]Frankfurter Zeitung, December 4, 1913.
[3]Ibid.
[4]Probably this refers to the public reaction to the actual actions in Zabern coming immediately after the Krupp Trial outcome condemning the army and Krupp munitions malfeasance.
[5]The Times, December 4, 1913.
[6]Verhandlungen des Reichstags, 291, p. 6175.
[7]Ibid., p. 6176.
[8]Ibid., p. 6178.
[9]Ibid., p. 6176-6179.
[10]Ibid., p. 6180.
[11]Ibid., p. 6180-1.
[12]Ibid.
[13]Ibid., p. 6183.
[14]Ibid.
[15]Ibid., p. 6184.
[16]This is a paraphrase of the stenographic report that was read by Herr Weill before the Reichstag. Ibid., p. 6187.
[17]Verhandlungen des Reichstags, 291, p. 6187.
[18]Ibid., pp. 6186-6188.
[19]Ibid., pp. 6188-6192.
[20]Ibid., p. 6194.
[21]Ibid., pp. 6192-6196.
[22]Ibid., p. 6197.
[23]James W. Gerard, My Four Years in Germany (New York: George H. Doran Co., 1917), p. 86.
[24]Ibid.
[25]Wolff, The Eve of 1914, p. 342. The hat referred to here is that which Schiller in his William Tell referred to as belonging to Gessler the bailiff of the Austrian Emperor Albert I and which the former had put on a pole in the central square in Altdorf for those who passed to salute.

William Tell refused.

[26]See above, pp. 65-66.

[27]The Eve of 1914, p. 342.

CHAPTER V

AFTERMATH OF THE VOTE OF MISTRUST

The main issues crystallized during the third and fourth of December, 1913, were not long kept from the public. An immediate change in Zabern was brought about by the transfer of the regiment stationed at Zabern, the 99th, to training grounds at Hagenau and Bitsch. There were some objections to this from Zabern, where a large part of the income of local store owners came from the permanent market of the army soldiers stationed there, but assurances were soon given that another regiment would replace the 99th and the fears of the people of Zabern that they would be deprived of trade were assuaged. The removal of the garrison was taken to mean that the Emperor wanted peace between the civil and military authorities and that this was to be the first step in solving the problems of Alsace-Lorraine. Indeed, it was more than that. It was an attempt to placate the civil authority in Alsace-Lorraine and, at the same time, to salvage the reputation of the Reichs-Chancellor by a show of support. There was no doubt that Bethmann-Hollweg needed support. Rumors in Berlin at this time maintained that he might resign. The National Zeitung said that the Reichs-Chancellor would resign only if General von Deimling had his way with the Kaiser, which would of course mean the discrediting of the Statthalter, Count von Wedel, and the indirect discrediting of the Reichs-Chancellor who had supported him in the introduction of the Alsace-Lorraine Constitution of 1911. Thus any attack on that Constitution would also be an attack on the Reichs-Chancellor. The National Zeitung suggested that Bethmann-Hollweg's staying in office was dependent on the Kaiser's government showing respect for him, and indirectly for the Reichstag, by the removal of the Ninety-Ninth Infantry Regiment from Zabern.[1] The fact that this had occurred seemingly gave him renewed strength of voice and decision. There actually began, therefore, on the fourth and fifth of December an

91

attempt to salve the wounds of the Reichstag, preserve the reputation of the Reichs-Chancellor and the Emperor and at the same time to preserve the feeling that the government was at least acting less dictatorially than before in blind support of the military and in keeping with the spirit of the constitution.

While the Reichs-Chancellor was at Donaueschingen on the fifth of December, his subordinates in Berlin were propagating the view that a great deal of the speech that Bethmann-Hollweg had planned to give on the third and fourth of December had been omitted due to the Reichs-Chancellor's illness and due to the continued interruptions by the members of the Reichstag during the speeches. The part omitted, said subordinates of the Reichs-Chancellor, would have explained more fully the nature and extent of the Emperor's actions.

The Frankfurter Zeitung's reporter said that Herr Wahnschaffe, whose function as Under Secretary to the Imperial Chancellor was to act as a channel of communication between the government and the Reichstag, had had conversations with the Reichstag Conservative Oertel, Radical Payer, Centre Prince Carolath, and National Liberal Bassermann. The morning papers had had reports of what had been said and the gist of this was that, as Gerard had reported,[2] the Chancellor had been indisposed at the debate, and that long before the Reichstag debate the Emperor had expressed his views and wishes to both the civil and military authorities. The Communique expressing these views appeared on the sixth of December in the Nord Deutsche Allgemeine Zeitung. According to it, full understanding of the Chancellor's speech had been prevented by the emotional excitement that had prevailed in the Reichstag. The Communique described in perfunctory fashion the events in the Zabern Affair up to the twenty-eighth of November, when it indicated that reports of the events were being sent to the Emperor and to both the Statthalter von Wedel and General von Deimling, and that it was the Chancellor who had arranged that the War Minister should meet with the Emperor at Donaueschigen. Again it was the Chancellor in conjunction with the Minister of War who had proposed that a General be sent immediately from Strasburg to Zabern in order to bring about order and establish the authority of the civil administration and good relations with the people. At the same time according to the Communique, orders had been sent from the Emperor to the Statthalter and the Commanding General telling them to provide for full cooperation between the civil and military authorities. His Majesty had instructed General von Deimling to make sure that the military stayed within the confines of the law. The Kaiser had further required that the General who had been sent to Zabern submit a precise report. Statthalter Von Wedel had sent an official from the

Ministry to Zabern to clear up the facts. The requisite investigations had been taken in hand by the civil and military authorities.

The Communique gave a summary of the Reichstag events according to the spokesman, Herr Wahnschaffe. On the first of December the Chancellor in a preliminary communication had said that the authority of the laws would be protected, as well as public order and the authority of the Executive. On the third and fourth of December he had given an account of the events and of the measures taken, leaving no doubt that he had regarded the military proceedings from the time of the clearing of the Schlossplatz at Zabern onward as illegal, and the wrong committed had to be expiated. As, in the meantime, further arrests by military patrols had taken place, the Emperor had commanded the Statthalter and the Commanding General, as well as the Imperial Chancellor, who had already applied for permission, to make a personal report to him.

Herr Wahnschaffe's Communique ended with the announcement of the removal of the garrison from Zabern and the remark that further decisions could not be taken until the proceedings under military law had been concluded. The "facts" presented by this Communique were not in accord with the speeches in the Reichstag, especially those of the Minister of War to which the Chancellor had given his full support.[3] This Communique had emphasized that Civil law would take its course and this contradicted the War Minister's insistence on the jurisdiction, solely, of military authority.

This change in the Reichs-Chancellor's statements was not denied by Bethmann-Hollweg when he came back from Donaueschingen, even though he did discredit Herr Wahnschaffe's feeble attempts to explain away his deficiencies by theorizing that the Reichs-Chancellor had been unwell. Thus, the question of why he was weak and inarticulate had not been satisfactorily explained. Dr. George Weill, who had been present in the Reichstag on both the third and the fourth of December, speaking before his constituents in Metz on the seventh of December, attributed the Reichs-Chancellor's confusion to an attempt to reconcile the Kaiser's wishes for peace in Alsace-Lorraine with the desires of the Crown prince, whose nationalistic views had been voiced before Bethmann-Hollweg in a visit on the third of December, just before Bethmann-Hollweg's poor speech.[4]

Whatever the reason for this speech, it was quite clear that the Reichs-Chancellor had raised a furor on all sides. The conservative Post had asserted that he had aroused such party difficulties that when the time came for the budget to be considered, no matter how firm the support given him by the Kaiser, "his resignation must be anticipated early in the next year."[5] Indeed, there were even suggestions made that Admiral von

Tirpitz, the Kaiser's cohort in trying to convince the Reichstag of the need for a strong navy, might be the next Reichs-Chancellor. It was noted that Tirpitz's point of view was quite opposed to that of Bethmann-Hollweg's for during the debate he absented himself from the Reichstag because he did not share the cabinet's opinion.

Despite all of the rumors, it seemed that the people of Germany and Alsace-Lorraine, had adopted a "wait-and-see" attitude concerning the possible outcome of the inquiry concerning the events in and around Zabern. There was good reason for hoping for a judicious settlement of the disputes, as the Reichs-Chancellor seemed to have been successful in his talk with the Emperor, General von Deimling, and the Statthalter, Count von Wedel. Indeed, within the Centre Party there was already a reaction taking place against the determined, radical attitude of the last few days, and the party press was, on the fifth of December, already beginning to qualify its previous remarks. Further evidence of possible compromise was found when it became generally known that the concluding remarks in the Reichs-Chancellor's speech of the previous day were based upon a Cabinet Order to General von Deimling and other express commands of the Emperor. These remarks involved maintaining the law and strict obedience by both military and civil authorities to the law as well as guarantees that the wrongs committed would be redressed. As far as Zabern was concerned there seemed to be cause for some small amount of satisfaction and a general belief that a temporary solution there would prevent any further outbursts.[6]

On the other hand, the issues of constitutionalism and parliamentary authority were not so easily settled. A great deal of praise from the majority of the parties was heaped upon the Reichstag and phrases such as "proved itself to be the true representative of the people" and "maintaining freedom and civil rights" were common in the newspapers of the fifth of December.[7] In South Germany, particularly, the Imperial Government attitude on the Zabern Affair in the Reichstag had made an ominous, foreboding impression. In Bavaria, the Lower House of the Diet at Munich was especially condemnatory of the Imperial government but also of Prussia whose value system was held responsible for the Zabern Affair. Dr. Pichler, the Centre Party leader, who was considered the blackest of reactionaries, was cheered by the whole house on the fifth of December when, while he was trying to establish that the Centre Party was not a Catholic ultramontanist party and was quite liberal like most of Bavaria, he stated that no Bavarian Minister would for a moment have adopted the attitude of Reichs-Chancellor Bethmann-Hollweg. On the contrary, said he, an entirely different conception of freedom and civil rights existed in Bavaria from that which was shown by the Imperial official. Representative Quibbe, a Progressive Party member, fully agreed with Dr. Pichler on the Zabern subject. He condemned the value system of Prussia which produced such men as Lieutenant von Forstner who had to be barons before becoming diplomats. He was here denouncing a view that there was a natural aristocracy which, no matter what their training or abilities, must lead the state in every capacity. This Prussian attitude, he said was one which did not exist generally in Bavaria, although at times it was advocated.[8]

The question of whether the Reichs-Chancellor would remain in the government after the vote of mistrust and also if, indeed, he did resign whether by his resignation the Reichstag would gain additional power and in essence change the constitution was settled decisively on the ninth of December when the Social Democrat, Herr Scheidemann, interrupted the debate on the Estimates to deliver a speech against Bethmann-Hollweg and to demand his resignation. He attacked the Chancellor in a quietly effective manner and rather mercilessly denied that Bethmann-Hollweg was the man to lead the German Empire. He attempted to prove this by enumerating the political failures of the Chancellor, the most glaring of which was the failure of the bill to amend the Prussian franchise law, and stated that the few bills which had been passed, such as the bill giving Alsace-Lorraine a real constitution, had been carried only with the help of the Social democratic Party. He then went over the events of the Zabern Affair and related the reaction to them by the Chancellor and the Emperor who, he said, had evidently been too busy with hunting and festivities to devote time to such trivial matters as the Zabern Affair. He said that a man of honor would not want to continue in office but that if the Chancellor refused to resign then the only possible conclusion from the vote of the 293 Reichstag members, who were certainly not influenced by personal feelings against the Chancellor, was that the Chancellor must be sticking to his post only because of the mistaken idea of the Emperor's authority and because he must believe in the fetish of personal government. Scheidemann begged that the same majority which had passed the vote of censure should now follow it up by voting down the Chancellor's salary and thus force him out of office and that the Reichstag should withhold supplies by not discussing the budget.[9]

The Chancellor replied that he would take care of his own honor and needed no help from Herr Scheidemann and that when the government had agreed to the change whereby the Reichstag was allowed to make a resolution of disagreement after an interpellation he had expressly reserved the authority either to regard or disregard any such resolution. It had further been agreed at the time that such resolutions could have no binding effect either upon the government or any member of it. Nobody had ever dreamed that by a mere change of business rules the whole constitution of the Empire would be changed and authority given to the Reichstag to dismiss ministers at will. In France and Great Britain conditions were different, but that, unlike in the other countries, parliamentary government did not exist in Germany. It was the constitutional privilege of the Emperor to appoint the Chancellor without any assistance or advice from the Reichstag. He, the Chancellor, would resist with all his might every attempt to change this system and therefore refused to resign because the resolution had no other effect than to make it evident that a difference of opinion existed between the Reichstag and the government.[10]

Dr. Spahn for the Centre Party and Herr Bassermann, for the National Liberal Party promptly disassociated themselves from the Socialist suggestion made by Herr Scheidemann that the parties which passed the vote of censure on the fourth should on the ninth of December refuse to vote supplies as long as the Imperial Chancellor remained in office. Dr. Spahn simply stated that the Reichstag did not pass either estimates or laws for an Imperial Chancellor, or a Minister of War, but devoted its activities to the Empire and the people.[11]

Herr Bassermann refuted Deputy Scheidemann's theories about the constitution and said that the vote of censure referred solely to the Zabern Affair. This vote condemned the Imperial Chancellor for not punishing the guilty immediately and for the conflict between the military and civil authorities, and that this should not be extended to an attempt to change the constitution by unconstitutional means. He, like the Chancellor, seemed devoted to opposing every attempt to diminish the constitutional rights of the Emperor and to subject the Imperial power to Socialist compulsion.[12]

Until Saturday, the sixth of December, the Social Democrats had soft-pedaled their condemnation of the government in the Zabern Affair and had allowed the other parties to "carry the ball" as they well knew that active leadership in the affair on their part would be the best possible excuse the Reichs-Chancellor could use to drop the whole mess by shouting "Red Herring." Yet, the waning of the outcry against the Zabern "culprits" in the newspapers at the end of this week and the beginning of the next, and the failure of the party to gain any answer from other parties when Herr Scheidemann and others passed secret notes asking for solidarity of the censure coalition in demanding the Imperial Chancellor's resignation brought about a desperate attempt to apply the coup de grace to Bethmann-Hollweg by what would have amounted to a coup d'état if it had succeeded and overturned the constitution.

The quick denial on the part of both the Centre and National Liberal

Parties that they would have anything to do with the Social Democrats attempt to further weaken the government showed the multiplicity of views that had led to the censure vote and also the fear of the advantage that might be taken by foreign countries of Germany's weaknesses. Characteristic of this fear are remarks made by Prince Philip Eulenburg in his memoirs:

> Small blame to the Reichstag for its vote of want of confidence in the Chancellor, though in general it is wiser, if one has no gun, not to talk about shooting people--but only an utter lack of political common sense could have afforded urbi et orbi such a spectacle in connection with such a show of itself. That serious politicians should have babbled, for Europe at large to hear, about Zabern and the military and civil antagonisms there, shows so great a lack of political sagacity I should not have thought possible, despite my low estimation of our political abilities.[13]

This attitude was one which was responsible for the middle-class reaction that began to take place as early as the ninth of December and was given further impetus by the extremely light sentences given to three of the "informers" of the "instructions hour" on the eleventh, and by the continuing middle-class fear of the Social Democrats as anti-Government nihilists, a condemnation which had been expressed by both Bethmann-Hollweg and Count von Westarp in the Reichstag on the tenth of December.[14] The latter called this "socialist terrorism" while the former said that the Socialists used last week's censure only as a vehicle to attack the Emperor as supreme War-Lord and "at this point the Socialists stood alone, as he hoped they always would."[15]

This was not quite true. Dr. Wiemer, representing the Progressive People's Party, was still in agreement with the Social Democrats on many points, including that of favoring parliamentary government over the existing constitutional system.[16] He was quite opposed to the East Elbian methods of Count von Westarp, which he said could not work because the goal was to persuade people to act in a certain way, not to alienate them. As far as this was concerned he agreed with Bethmann-Hollweg that all parts of the Empire had to be treated differently and the relationships with the Imperial Government had to differ to some extent for each part due to special circumstances or environments.[17] On the other hand, Dr. Wiemer did not think that the Chancellor should resign. There would be no government to replace the present system if it were to be destroyed and the resignation of the Chancellor would be a first step in that direction.[18]

Dr. Wiemer's view concerning parliamentary government stated above was one which a Frankfurter Zeitung writer maintained was a general outcome of the Zabern Affair, which was notable also for producing the beginning of an understanding of the Alsatians and the development of a new type of citizen, the German-Alsatian. In his article of the tenth of December, he stated that "the birth of German-Alsatian citizens and the beginning democratization of Germany from Alsace outward was taking place: for such a price we would lead gladly again a campaign like that of Zabern."[19] This was written on the eighth of December, two days before it was published, and was headlined "The Victory of Zabern."[20] It revealed the excitement during these days between the fourth and tenth of December. Dr. Wiemer's reason for not wanting the Chancellor to be replaced was also symptomatic; it revealed one of the main reasons for the middle-class reaction and thus also for the conservative reaction. The weakening of the stand of the Centre and the middle-class National-Liberals indicated lack of resolve against the conservative reaction which began at this time and gathered momentum until reaching its peak after Lieutenant von Forstner was convicted and sentenced on the nineteenth of December. The fear of the prospects of an unknown new government and the distrust of the Social Democrats left no room for change. The conservative reaction's most eloquent spokesman was Dr. Jagow.

The turning point at which the conservatives began to declaim against the Social Democrats and any form of liberalism in an organized manner seemed to have occurred on the tenth of December when even Bethmann-Hollweg's remarks seemed to bear a conservative tinge. To show the difference between the Chancellor's later views, Professor Lamprecht of the University of Leipzig published a letter which had been written to him in the previous June by the Reichs-Chancellor. A portion of this letter was printed in The Times on the thirteenth of December, with comments on the anxiety the letter aroused in the militarist and chauvinist press and their suggestions that Bethmann-Hollweg would do better as a university professor than as an Imperial Chancellor. The Chancellor's letter stated that "the Germans are a young people with perhaps too innocent a belief in force and too little appreciation of the finer methods, and they do not yet know that force alone has never yet been able to maintain what force has won..."[21]

The Chancellor said that the people must awaken but that this could not be accomplished by the German government without the aid of the educated classes. The Times journalist quoted Dr. Wiemer as saying that "for at least twenty years past any attempt to say what Bethmann-

Hollweg had said so admirably had been branded in this country as nothing short of anti-Germanism and <u>hetzerei</u>."[22]   This attitude compared to that of the Reichs-Chancellor on the fourth of December was diametrically opposed to that unqualified support for the militaristic attitude of the Minister of War. The difference could again be seen on the tenth of December when he condemned the Social Democrats for using the vote of censure as no more than a vehicle to attack the position of the Kaiser as supreme war lord. This attack was for the military the greatest of all sins for not only did it question the chain of command and assert the domination of the military by civilians, but above all it was the Social Democrats, the agents of revolution, the arch-enemies of the conservative, order-loving army man who were committing this horrendous attack. Thus was Bethmann-Hollweg appealing to all who feared change, to all who loved order, to all who feared an indeterminate future, to the conservatives and the army. Now he used this conservative view as a tool. At other times, when he had attempted and failed to reform the Prussian electoral laws or when he had successfully brought about a new constitution for Alsace-Lorraine, he had opposed exactly these tendencies, this same philosophy of conservatism. Now he used this to support his own position of authority and stability, which he had attempted to re-establish by refusing to resign.   He linked the censure vote with destruction of authority, stability and order. Those who had voted for censure were now associated with revolutionaries, with those who would refuse supplies to the army and thus put the German Empire at the mercy of her enemies. In this way he alarmed the timid who, now that the crisis was over, had second thoughts of fear for the government, of fear of having gone too far, of fear of the enemy. Reinforcement for his position of authority and stability as well as for the weakening of his enemies, those who voted his censure, came from his forceful and determined reminding of the German people that the foreign policy of Germany was an executively determined matter, that there were enemies outside the borders more dangerous than those within, and that the Reichstag with its various divisions and degrees of ineptitude as well as ignorance could not hope to cope with a diversified and complicated subject as this. The budget for the army and the foreign policy which had to have the support of that army were linked inseparably. For any man to question one or the other, he declared, was to question both and this would mean the end of the German Empire.

It was a combination of this type of demonstration of reasoning, fact, action, as well as the natural boredom over the continuous rehashing of events of the Zabern Affair, as Representative Erzberger pointed out in the Reichstag on the eleventh of December,[23] that led to a gradual diminution of the intensity of the fervor against the conservatives and the army concerning the events of the Zabern Affair on the part of all parties other than those of Alsace-Lorraine and the Social Democrats.

On the other hand, the conservative views of Count von Westarp stated on the tenth of December did not go uncriticized on the eleventh. Indeed, outside of his own party his ultra-reactionary opinions had little support. It was, however, not his views concerning the events of Zabern that on the eleventh were discussed, as the subject was no longer the center of attention, but his conceptions of the position of the officer in Imperial society and of what the Reichstag could do about that position if it needed to be changed or modified. Yet the issues were those that grew directly out of the controversy over the Zabern Affair. Concerning this issue, of the position of the officer in Germany, Dr. Ricklin from Alsace-Lorraine stated:

> Count Westarp has put before us yesterday a theory of self-help which to any of us was unheard of before this time. To me at least it was not known that a state within a state was being built by the military, and that the officer has the right in all cases to take measures of self-defense. Such a view has no basis.[24]

He was aware of the theory earlier stated by Deputy von Gamp (Massaunen) that the military command in Alsace-Lorraine had an entirely different program or set of rules from that which applied in the other German Federal States, that was, that the military in the former had the general supervisory right over the civil population. According to the theory the rationalization for this supervisory right was that the interests of the military authority must be above all other because Alsace-Lorraine was a frontier land. To Dr. Ricklin this theory was nothing other than the famous theory associated with Bismarck at the inception of the Alsace-Lorraine governing program in the early 1870s. This theory had been called the "mirror theory" (Glacis theorie) and was a brutal theory that the people of Alsace-Lorraine could be made to become just like Prussians by a transplantation of Prussian officialdom and institutions to that province, and a repression of all native Alsace-Lorraine customs, traditions, and talented or intelligent individuals. An example of this could be found in these Reichstag debates when Count von Westarp and Herr Representative von Gamp-Massaunen directed their anger against the Kreisdirektor Mahl. Why? Because he was one of the few Alsatians to reach that office. The statistics Dr. Ricklin had cited to support his views showed that out of the twenty-four Kreisdirektors of the province in the forty-two years of German Imperial domination, only three had been born in Alsace-Lorraine.

Not only did he condemn the Prussian militarism that had made Alsace-Lorraine no more than a military state, but he also condemned the aristocracy of Prussia who had disregarded the express wishes of the Emperor William II to allow the civil authority to take care of riots and who had introduced the military government. He claimed that the nobility of Prussia followed William II only when he acted according to their will:

Und der Konig absolut
Wenn er uns den Willen tut[25]

Deputy Ricklin condemned Westarp's attribution of fault for the past riots in astonishment that such should be attributed to the nationalistic newspaper press of Alsace-Lorraine and the 1911 constitution. The speaker claimed that the conservative East Elbian was merely trying to shift the blame from its proper source in order to protect it, namely the military authority. The policy, called "Himmeldonnerwetter policy," by Herr Ricklin, that Westarp would apply was one of military repression and Dr. Ricklin compared it with the policy of the French under their rule in Alsace-Lorraine and such comparison showed that the French policy was less repressive. He stated that the speeches of both Herr Westarp and Herr Gamp-Massaunen were taken straight from the pages of the National Liberal Rheinisch Westfälische Zeitung.

In his concluding statement, he remarked that what the people of Alsace-Lorraine wanted was sovereignty like that of the other federal states. He said that the first act of this tragi-comedy called the Zabern Affair was now over with the Reichstag's impending adjournment. The second act would begin when the Zabern Affair went before the Landtag. He concluded with the statement that although the people of Alsace-Lorraine had lost faith in the German government, the German people had, as a result of the Zabern Affair gained a new faith in Alsace-Lorraine.[26]

As a deputy from Alsace-Lorraine, Dr. Ricklin was not as influential as others who might have been considered less closely associated with the events. His lack of influence might also be due to his rather poor delivery and the fact that he had had little to add to what had been said formerly by his colleagues and others within the house. He did reveal, however, that the Reichs-Chancellor was not the only one to threaten resignation if he did not get his way. He revealed that there existed on the day that the Reichs-Chancellor had given his speech, the third of December, a crisis concerning the Statthalter which had been resolved only by the conference at Donaueschingen. Count von Wedel had flatly stated that he would resign if he had to give in to the military.[27]

The pressure for the removal of the troops from Zabern, then, came from two directions. The change of views by the Kaiser concerning this removal came after the third of December, when the War Minister having just returned from Donaueschingen, and seemingly echoing the will of the Kaiser, was adamantly pro-military and no changes were considered in the location of the troops. The change in the Kaiser's views must have come on the fourth of December when the Reichs-Chancellor and Statthalter von Wedel at Donaueschingen both threatened resignation and thus the decision to move the troops had been made in opposition to the desires of the military and in support of the civil administration of the Statthalter von Wedel. Thus these threats must have caused the decision rather than, as Erzberger suggested had been said, that the cause had been the mistrust vote in the Reichstag.[28]

Perhaps the reason for the lack of interest in Dr. Ricklin's speech of the eleventh of December was that the parties of the Reichstag were more interested in the position of the Reichstag in the German Empire as a power-governing unit and the problem of the constitutionality of such a position than in the actual attitude of Prussianism in Alsace-Lorraine or the already well-debated problem of the position of the army in that province. In other words, the vote of mistrust against Bethmann-Hollweg had brought up other issues more directly related to the German Empire; the Empire had become foremost in the minds of the deputies. Indeed, Prussianism and its possible consequences became even more important now as they were related to Imperial issues.

It was the Social Democrat, Herr Hoch, who set the stage for the debate of that day by summarizing the debates of the previous days and stating the issues in a logical form. The question of whether the military authorities were subject to law and justice in their actions, just as the civil authorities were, he said, had led to the decision that they were not and the action of the Reichs-Chancellor had led to a vote of mistrust which had led to a question of ministerial responsibility or not and involved the question of the power of the Reichstag which ended in the question of what should be done to the Constitution in order to bring about ministerial responsibility and an increase in the power of the Reichstag.

On the issue of whether the army officers should be subject to the law, Deputy Hoch was emphatically in favor of this subordination. He stated that if anything had been made clear in the debate of the previous days it was that an officer had been illegally and unconstitutionally assaulting the people and that this could not be denied by the Reichs-Chancellor and the Minister of War. The whole world was aware of this fact.[29]

Yet, the Centre Party Deputy, Herr Erzberger, denied that this fact had been made clear to the Reichs-Chancellor and to Count von Westarp. On the contrary, he stated, both of these conservative-minded gentlemen had pushed this whole main point of strife onto a side or dead track and it was against this endeavor that the Centre Party had to sharply protest. He asserted that according to the Reichs-Chancellor on the third of December, the Commanding General of the Guard Corps had the power to imprison everyone on the Wilhelmstrasse. Like Hoch and echoing the former speech of Deputy Fehrenbach, his Centre Party colleague, Herr Erzberger stated that the military had to be under law and justice. He did not demand that, as Westarp had said, either the military or the civil authority had to win in this case. He emphasized that justice and law must win regardless of the parties to the dispute. Tongue-in-cheek at this point, he stated that he was quite willing to allow the Conservative Party to exist but that it could not be an all German party representing all the Empire. A South German, he declared, would not be able to comprehend a single leading article in the Kreuz Zeitung; his implied meaning was, justice and law and the Conservative Party were contradictions in terms and the latter could not be understood in that center of justice and law, South Germany.[30]

The Progressive People's Party Representative in the Reichstag, Herr Haussmann, was generally in agreement with Herr Erzberger that the Reichs-Chancellor had ignored the major issue and that he had attempted to cover up this attitude by indecision and the making of unclear statements.[31]

On the other hand, the Conservative Party Representative, Dr. Oertel, believed that Colonel von Reuter handled the Zabern Affair as it should have been handled insofar as he had any right to handle it at all. But even he could not contradict Representatives Hoch, Erzberger, and Haussmann on the subject of whether the legal right of Colonel Reuter to handle the affair at all existed. He even went so far, unlike his conservative colleague, Count von Westarp, as to say that the military authority was not right on all points. However, rather than condemn this authority, he left the question open as to whether Colonel Reuter had any right at all to deal with the problem.[32]

Dr. Paasche, representing the National Liberal Party, was just as condemnatory of the illegalities of the army in Zabern as Herrs Hoch and Erzberger and he related that he could not console himself with the supposition that this was a single case. It was not important whether the military regime in Zabern should be abolished eight days earlier or later. What was important, and here he was echoing his Party colleague, Dr.

Calker, was the spirit reflected in the whole proceeding. He stated that in Germany the army was a people's army, in which not only unripe recruits served, but also in case of need reservists and men of the Landwehr served. These would follow their leaders willingly if they were able to respect their efficiency, but would not do so just because they knew that a leader was ready to send his sword through the body of any civilian who chanced to insult him.[33]

The issue of just exactly what the vote of mistrust meant was one which Deputy Hoch found of great significance. To this Social Democrat the significance of the vote of mistrust lay in the fact that a coalition declared it would no longer accept a passive role in the government. Despite the fact that the Reichs-Chancellor viewed the vote as meaning nothing, it was the people who now realized that the Reichstag was united.[34]

Deputy Erzberger represented the Centre Party view when he opposed both the view of Bethmann-Hollweg that the mistrust vote meant nothing and the view of Herr Scheidemann that the Reichs-Chancellor should automatically resign or else no business should be conducted by the Reichstag. The Centre Party leader suggested that the truth lay between the opposing points of view. He condemned not only the misconceptions on the left, but also those on the right. For instance, the conservatives, represented by Dr. Oerter,[35] said that even the fact that the coalition vote had occurred, was unconstitutional, but Herr Erzberger denied this as well as the view of Bethmann-Hollweg that it was just a count of votes expressing a difference of opinion. He also denied that it brought the Imperial Minister under the power of the Reichstag. As did the Progressive Herr Haussmann,[36] Herr Erzberger condemned the Reichs-Chancellor for not treating the mistrust vote as a vote of mistrust, and like Dr. Paasche who spoke for the National Liberals,[37] he could not agree with Herr Scheidemann or Herr Hoch of the Social Democrats.[38]

To Herr Hoch the mistrust vote was the first step toward ministerial responsibility and he did not regard it or the actions of his party as intended to bring about a change in the constitution. The mistrust vote to him meant that the Imperial Chancellor must resign. The Reichstag must have a man as Chancellor who would maintain a strong stand and with will power proceed against excesses. Bethmann-Hollweg was not a responsible minister. He was not called to the Kaiser, but the War Minister was. He had become merely a royal lackey and this was intolerable for an Imperial Minister in this important office. His irresponsibility was shown clearly by the fact that before he had a chance to offer one word regarding the interpellation on the Zabern Affair, two notes had gone from the Kaiser to General von Deimling and the

Statthalter without any regard for the constitution. The Reichs-Chancellor knew absolutely nothing about them. How could such a man be responsible to the Reichstag?[39]

Herr Erzberger's remarks concerning ministerial responsibility pointed to the experiences of the past as examples of what Imperial Ministers should do in the present. The man who had shown the way in this regard had been Prince Bulow, the former Imperial Chancellor. He had declared that he would not remain as Imperial Chancellor if the National Liberals would not support his financial reforms, namely inheritance taxes. They had not, and he had resigned. Since that day in 1909 a great many state secretaries had left because they had not had the majority confidence of the Reichstag; Herr Dernburg, Herr Wehrmuth, and many more in the past had done so, and many in the future would follow these examples. Erzberger confessed that there were no legal means by which to bring this about; neither had law givers in other states the means but they resigned as a matter of course when there was no majority. He believed that if this did not take place in Germany there could be no effective government and that with such a lopsided vote against the Imperial Chancellor, that he should not want to remain. Regardless of its effects, he believed that the vote did bring about calm in the provinces. The people of Alsace-Lorraine were heartened by the Reichstag's protection of them and the people of the German Empire realized that this body cared for the preservation of justice. He said, "The advantage is that the German people know that when justice and law are brought into question, the representation of the people stands like a wall."[40]

On the other hand, like Dr. Wiemer, Erzberger refused to follow Herr Scheidemann and the Social Democrats because they had no responsibility to the government and this was shown in their consistent opposition to the budget for forty-two years. He cited the 1910 Party Conference when Bebel had said that regardless of any reason to the contrary or any circumstances, it was the duty of every Social Democrat to oppose the budget. He asked how any man could be a leader who was chained in such a way as was Herr Scheidemann.[41] Despite this opposition to the views of the Social Democrats he was not totally opposed to them and in the same speech agreed with Herr Hoch that a general reform of the higher echelons of the army was needed in order to eliminate the clique that rule it.[42] He was also in general agreement with the Social Democrats as to the importance of the vote of mistrust and he stated that "what has happened in the Reichstag during the previous eight days is not an insignificant small part but the soul, the main point, of our whole interstate political relationship. One cannot lightly regard the mistrust vote."[43] Still, he was reluctant to advocate action. He wanted to await the reaction of the Reichs-Chancellor in the new year and insisted that the world would not end today or tomorrow and that the Reichstag would still exist in the coming year as it had in the past.[44] In truth, he seemed not to know what to do or just exactly what the mistrust vote should mean. The Constitution could not be broken and there could be no remedy outside of the Constitution and traditional practice. In this view, Erzberger agreed with the Progressive, Herr Haussmann.[45]

The Conservative position was in keeping with that of Bethmann-Hollweg as was shown by Dr. Oertel's statement that all the power that the Imperial Chancellor wanted should be given to him[46] and that the Constitution should be maintained strictly without change.[47]

Dr. Paasche was in basic agreement with Herr Erzberger. He too wished to maintain the constitution but he also stressed that the Reichs-Chancellor should not ignore the mistrust vote but should instead take it into consideration for the future, not just for one case in Zabern but for all the Empire generally. He regarded this vote as fulfillment of duty by the Reichstag and not as an evil deed as suggested by Count von Westarp.[48]

Representatives Hoch, Erzberger, Haussmann, and Paasche were in agreement that the powers of the Reichstag had to be expanded. Social Democratic leader Hoch stated that the middle-class and its party had complained over the lack of power of the Reichstag. "The Reichstag has the power which the parties in the Reichstag want it to have; its power lies only in the parties. Zabern has taught us what we can do together. We must protect civil rights. We must make the Reichstag strong."[49] His appeal to the middle classes to cooperate with the Social Democrats was made only after he had condemned them as strike-breaking capitalists who were represented by such evil men as Herr Ballin, the very good friend of the Kaiser, and Herr Krupp. He stated that the man sitting beside Herr Brandt at the Second Krupp trial would have received a good many years in prison if it had not been for the fact that he had been a Krupp official. Yet he turned around and asked for cooperation from them in order to preserve justice, freedom, and progress when he had just condemned them for a lack of exactly those attributes.[50]

Dr. Paasche's National Liberal Party view was exactly the same as that of the Centre Party view of Herr Erzberger as far as the expansion of the powers of the Reichstag was concerned. He paraphrased Erzberger when he stated that the Reichstag was not a house of stone but a living thing which dealt with life and in time would grow larger.[51] Also, like Erzberger, he would not tolerate an unconstitutional parliamentary rule; yet at the same time he wanted, like Progressive leader Haussmann, a strong parliamentary leadership in the government.[52] Both the Conservatives, Dr.

Oertel and Count von Westarp, were opposed on principle to parliamentary rule in Germany, but cited the Constitution as a safeguard against it.[53] Dr. Paasche was, however, apprehensive of the future. There had to be an end to the two-headed battle within the army officership; one battle against the law and the other against the individual's religious conviction within the army. This latter point referred to the anti-Catholicism found among the officers and noncommissioned officers as was noted in the Affair in Zabern, but which was general for all Germany.[54] On this latter point there was much applause from the predominantly Catholic Centre Party. He received repeated applause of great amounts from both the Centre and Left throughout his speech and seemed to reflect the opinion of a large number of the representatives.

The Minister of War gave a short speech in which he did little but condemn all that had been said by all parties other than the Conservatives. Herr Ricklin, in a personal remark, ended the debate with a note of despair in observation that the War Minister seemed not to have learned anything in the previous few days.[55]

On the eleventh of December, the military court of the thirteenth division at Strasburg passed light sentences upon three of the recruits of the 99th regiment at Zabern. These three had been responsible for the publication in the Zaberner Anzeiger newspaper of a signed declaration regarding the language of Lieutenant von Forstner. The sentence passed was that the three were to be confined to prison from one to six weeks and to barracks for two to three weeks.

Colonel von Reuter had testified at the trial that he had warned everyone as soon as the publications about Lieutenant von Forstner had begun that giving information on about what happened in the barracks or on the drill square was giving away official information and that all who did so were liable to courts martial. Nevertheless, the court was lenient and found the three guilty only of disobedience and considered it a special case in which the three being very young and inexperienced with military discipline (twenty years old), could not foresee the effect of their disclosures.They also had not expected publication as they had been promised by the reporter that the information would not be published. Moreover, they had been convinced of the accuracy of what they had said and all three agreed that Lieutenant von Forstner had referred to the French Foreign Legion as good enough for German deserters, and had added what von Calker had termed a barnyard term, which was grossly offensive, about the French flag. Two other recruits called as witnesses were not sure that the barnyard term applied to the French Foreign Legion or to the French flag. Nevertheless, it was evident that the military court was criticizing the actions of Prussian officers by the lightness of the sentence and the refusal to consider the offense more grave as had been suggested by the testimony of Colonel von Reuter.

An even greater criticism of the military actions occurred on the nineteenth of December when the military court of the Thirtieth Division at Strasburg sentenced Lieutenant von Forstner to forty-three days' imprisonment, not detention in a fortress but imprisonment, for the assault and wounding of a lame cobbler and for the unlawful employment of weapons.

According to Lieutenant von Forstner, people from the village had been mocking the troops and he had made unsuccessful attempts to catch them. He had caught the cobbler, who had resisted arrest and had tried to jump at him and strike him, as he had threatened he would. The Lieutenant had drawn his sword and in self-protection had struck him over the head. When asked why he felt justified in arresting the man, the Lieutenant said that the military had to act vigorously against any abuse or insult on the part of civilians; that this was what he had been ordered to do and that these orders had come from the office of the commanding general and from the regimental commander. He had stood no nonsense from Shoemaker Blank in resisting his efforts to arrest him; if Blank had not resisted he would not have used his sword but would have handed the shoemaker over to the Burgomaster and that would have ended the whole affair. The fact that Blank had struggled, suggested the defense of Lieutenant von Forstner, was sufficient evidence that he intended to use the knife found in his pocket. Blank, on the other hand, said that he had resisted because he had done nothing and had not wanted to be late for work.

The testimony of Lieutenant von Forstner's commanding officer, Colonel von Reuter, was that he had warned the officers against tolerating insults. There had been many insults of late, newspapers had published unfounded statements and he had himself received "dirty" letters form anonymous individuals and Lieutenant von Forstner had also received such letters. Under these circumstances he had believed it to be necessary that energetic action be taken and had advised Lieutenant von Forstner, a frequent target for such insults, to carry his pistol or his sword at all times and in case of need to use it. He had gone so far as to suggest that allowing the military to be insulted was such an offense that it warranted bringing the officer who allowed it without reacting against it before a court of honor. He had informed the Burgomaster of Zabern that his officers meant to compel respect from all civilians and that his non-commissioned officers were instructed to act, if necessary, to knock down any assailants just as his officers were so instructed.

The civilian witnesses said that Blank had not acted belligerently, but had said that he would strike Lieutenant von Forstner on the nose if he was not left alone. They also gave evidence that the soldiers were marching through the village singing indecent songs and many objected to this. They emphasized that the cobbler was lame and would not had been a threat to an army officer. The trial ended with Blank walking the length of the courtroom to show how lame he was.[56]

The judgement of the court satisfied the great mass of the population but this satisfaction was not enough to end the Zabern Affair. This premature satisfaction that the Affair was ended was immediately surprised by the immediate, vociferous condemnation by all militarists and ultra-nationalists. The highest military authorities refused to accept the judgement and at once countered with the announcement an appeal would be made against it. They insisted that the sentence would just about end the career of Lieutenant von Forstner, and the fact that he was convicted of the unlawful recourse to arms would make him subject to civil law, and Colonel von Reuter, an accessory. The Colonel's trial was to come about next, and the indictment against him might be not merely unlawful arrests as anticipated, but incitement of a subordinate to have unlawful recourse to arms.

This hostile opposition of the Conservatives, particularly of the Prussian antipathy, was shown most clearly in a letter to the Conservative Kreuz-Zeitung by the police president of Berlin, who signed himself Doctor Juris von Jagow. In this letter the actual underlying antagonisms of the Zabern Affair were brought out with great clarity. The letter stated that military exercises were acts of sovereignty, and if obstacles were placed in the way of their performance, as at Dettweiler, the obstacles had to be removed in the execution of this act of sovereignty. He continued that prosecution because of an act of sovereignty was not permissible according to an obvious principle of law, which in Prussia was expressly defined. Lieutenant von Forstner, therefore, ought not to have been prosecuted, much less convicted, and, if the position in law were different, it would require the most speedy amendment. He continued:

If our officers, and even those who are stationed almost in an enemy's country run the risk of custodia inhonesta because they clear the road for the execution of the King's service, shame is brought upon the most distinguished profession. In that case a protective law of the Empire, copied from the Prussian law, would be an urgent political necessity.[57]

This letter produced a storm of indignation in the entire press with the exception of the conservative journals, which were jubilant. Doctor von Jagow revived the nearly dead popular feeling over the Zabern Affair and expanded the subject. The Berliner Tageblatt called Doctor von Jagow's remarks simply incredible, brutal, ruthless intervention in Imperial affairs. The Zabern Affair was bad enough, said the author, but to renew the controversy over sabre dictatorship at such a time as this when the Reichstag, the Kaiser, and, to a certain extent, the Chancellor, were doing their utmost to eliminate the painful impression left by this sabre-dictatorship was incredible. The author condemned the president of the Berlin police, whose authority was restricted to preservation of law and order in the capital of the Empire, for now opening all the wounds afresh and at one stroke nullifying the attempts at conciliation which had been going on for almost a month. "Doctor von Jagow has thrown down the Imperial gauntlet to Alsace-Lorraine and to an overwhelming majority of the Reichstag."[58]

The Kölnische Zeitung declared that of all the incredible things that had happened in the Zabern Affair, Herr von Jagow's proclamation was the most incredible. He had violated the principle that criticism of royal proceedings should be withheld while sub-judice. He had not only cast suspicion on the justice of the verdict by the courtsmartial, but had also done something designed to reinflame the passions in Alsace-Lorraine. The journal said that action by the superiors of Doctor von Jagow would be inevitable and that he had to be put back within the limits of this office in both words and deeds.[59]

On the twenty-fourth of December, the Nord Deutsche Allgemeine Zeitung, the organ often used by the Imperial Government, announced that although Doctor von Jagow had written to the Kreuz-Zeitung as a private citizen, the political importance of the affair, of course, made it necessary for the Prussian Government to decide whether and to what extent his free expression of opinion exceeded those limitations which were incumbent upon a public official even in his private capacity. It was added that when this question had been thoroughly investigated, "the necessary corrective measures would be taken."[60]

The Frankfurter Zeitung said that the whole world was astounded when Doctor von Jagow called Alsace-Lorraine "almost enemy country" and that this had done a great amount of harm for the reputation of Imperial Germany in foreign countries.[61] The next day this journal printed the comments of other newspapers and maintained that everywhere these comments come to one conclusion, that Doctor von Jagow was wrong about the law.[62] The Centre Party press was especially vitriolic in its condemnations of this "Prussian attitude." The Kölnische Volkszeitung, the most important voice of this party, said that a disavowal of the police president must be expected," if only in order to destroy the idea that his opinion represents in any way the attitude of official headquarters in Berlin." The same journal said that many people regarded Herr von Jagow's letter as a pronouncement on the part of those who would like to see him made Imperial Chancellor, but that the result, might be different than was expected, and might show that Herr von Bethmann-Hollweg was the stronger man.[63]

It seemed obvious from the tremendous amount of public feeling stirred up by this letter that the Zabern Affair would continue to influence the nature and subject of political affairs in Germany for a long time to come. The conservatives and the army regarded this letter as an expression of what they had been urging half-heartedly up to this time. Theodor Wolff, the pre-World War I editor of the Berliner Tageblatt and an astute observer of the Zabern Affair, wrote in his autobiographical Eve of 1914, that the action of police president von Jagow was met with great happiness by the conservatives, that the general staff invited him to a banquet, the Crown Prince gave a dinner in his honor, and at the Liebesmahl (officers' banquet) of a regiment of the guards the officers carried him around in triumph and set him on the table like a birthday cake amid cries of "Hoch," and that the Crown Prince, not to be left behind by this hero of the hour, sent to Colonel von Reuter and to the commanding General, von Deimling, telegrams of which one contained the brief message: "Immer feste druff!" ("Give it to them!")[64]

For the conservatives, Herr von Jagow had summarized their position very clearly. He had said that they had maintained that the soldier carried the king's authority and that this was above the law and therefore the military could do no wrong outside of its own disciplinary rules and especially could not be subject to civil authority. He had said that the Prussian law should be applied to the Empire and had intimated that Prussia should control the Empire. His intimation that the French were the enemy and that the Alsatians were almost enemies was a reflection of the point of view said to have been stated by Lieutenant von Forstner on the drill-square. The Zabern Affair had turned full cycle.

It was on this note that the year 1913 came to an end. It was also on this note that the Court-martial proceedings were to begin on the fourth of January against Colonel von Reuter for the actions he had committed at Zabern.

NOTES

[1]National Zeitung, December 4, 1913.
[2]James W. Gerard, My Four Years in Germany (New York: George H. Doran Co., 1917), p. 86-87.
[3]Nord Deutsche Allegemeine Zeitung, December 6, 1913.
[4]Frankfurter Zeitung, December 8, 1913.
[5]Die Post, December 5, 1913.
[6]Frankfurter Zeitung, December 6, 1913.
[7]Ibid., December 5, 1913.
[8]Nord Deutsche Allgemeine Zeitung, December 6, 1913.
[9]Verhandlungen des Reichstags, 291 (1913), 6286.
[10]Ibid., p. 6290.
[11]Ibid., p. 6294.
[12]Ibid., pp. 6297-6298.
[13]Johanne Haller, Philip Eulenburg: the Kaiser's Friend, trans. E.C. Wayne (New York: A. Knopf, 1930), pp. 275-276.
[14]Verhandlungen des Reichstags, 291 (1913), p. 6320.
[15]Ibid., pp. 6344-6345.
[16]Ibid., p. 6323.
[17]Ibid., p. 6234.
[18]Ibid., pp. 6326-6327.
[19]Frankfurter Zeitung, December 10, 1913.
[20]Ibid.
[21]The Times, December 13, 1913.
[22]Ibid. (Agitation)
[23]Verhandlungen des Reichstags, 291 (1913), p. 6360.
[24]Ibid., p. 6348.
[25]Ibid., p. 6349. And the King is absolute
        If he does what we want.
[26]Ibid., pp. 6349-6350. The condemnation of the Alsace-Lorraine constitution is anticipated by Prince Eulenberg in his Erinnerungen, when, on the day Bethmann-Hollweg visited the Kaiser, the Prince wrote in his

memoirs that he could visualize the scene at Donaueschingen which was well known to him and that the Kaiser would threaten to snip off the Alsace-Lorraine Constitution if they didn't stop. This indicates that this attitude of personal government is one common to the Kaiser. See Haller, Prince Eulenberg, p. 275.

[27]Verhandlungen des Reichstags, 291 (1913), p. 6349.

[28]Ibid., p. 6368.

[29]Ibid., p. 6351.

[30]Ibid., p. 6362.

[31]Ibid., p. 6378.

[32]Ibid., p. 6385.

[33]Verhandlungen des Reichstags, 291 (1913), p. 6391.

[34]Ibid., p. 6352.

[35]Ibid., p. 6382.

[36]Ibid., p. 6390.

[37]Ibid.

[38]Ibid., p. 6362.

[39]Ibid., pp. 6355-6356.

[40]Ibid., p. 6365.

[41]Ibid., p. 6366.

[42]Ibid., p. 6370.

[43]Ibid.

[44]Ibid.

[45]Ibid., p. 6381.

[46]Ibid., p. 6382.

[47]Ibid., p. 6388.

[48]Ibid., p. 6390.

[49]Ibid., pp. 6359-6360.

[50]Ibid., p. 6360.

[51]Ibid., p. 6390.

[52]Verhandlungen des Reichstags, 291 (1913), p. 6379.

[53]Ibid., p. 6388.

[54]Ibid., p. 6392.

[55]Ibid., p. 6394.

[56]Frankfurter Zeitung, December 20, 1913. See also, Schulthess, Deutschegeschichtskalendar, December 20, 1913.

[57]Kreuz-Zeitung, December 21, 1913.

[58]Berliner Tageblatt, December 23, 1913.

[59]Kreuz-Zeitung, December 23, 1913.

[60]Nord Deutsche Allgemeine Zeitung, December 24, 1913. The journal article very pointedly does not link von Jagow's article with the Zabern Affair itself.

[61]Frankfurter Zeitung, December 24, 1913.
[62]Ibid., December 25, 1913.
[63]Kölnische Volkszeitung, December 22, 1913. See also The Times, December 22, 1913.
[64]Wolff, Eve of 1914, pp. 342ff.

PART II

THE CONSERVATIVE REACTION

CHAPTER VI

THE TRIAL

The "conservative reaction," which was composed mostly of members of the Conservative Party and of some recalcitrant or deserting National Liberals, used von Jagow's official position and his well-known close friendship with the Emperor despite his statement to the contrary, to oppose the outcome of the von Forstner trial. It approved the proposition that the law of Prussia should govern the Imperial troops; that if it did not then the Imperial law should be changed to conform with the law of Prussia.[1] The Conservative stand revived a spirit of Prussian particularism that was to grow in succeeding months into an organized movement extending to all parts of Germany. The militaristic Wehrverein and the newly formed Prussian nationalist movement, the Preussenbund were to expand in numbers and influence. People from the Centre and National Liberal Parties of a very conservative persuasion would be drawn in and evoke the ethos of von Moltke and von Roon and would call themselves Prussians in spirit although they might live as far away from Prussia as Munich. Yet, this Prussian particularism would be faced with a reaction that was endemic in such places as Bavaria, which was enraged against the military and the civil government during December and was to be enraged even more by the outcome of the von Reuter trial, by the Preussenbund speeches and by the anti-Bavarian attitude expressed in the Centenary of 1813 speech of General von Kracht. The issues discussed in January of 1914 were virtually the same ones of German divisiveness and fragmentation that were so thoroughly examined in the preceding month. But, there was now a major difference in that the Conservatives had taken the offensive, and the forces of opposition to the government seemed to be retreating like Matthew Arnold's Sea of Faith, with a "withdrawing roar."[2]

At the beginning of January the strength of the conservative reaction was not a vital threat to the parties of the mistrust vote and, indeed, the Munich Allgemeine Zeitung stated that liberal journals such as the Strasburger Post at that time were publishing rumors in a suggestive manner that the Reichs-Chancellor was soon to retire into private life, but that this would occur only after some face-saving measures were taken such as the settling of the Baghdad railroad problem. This Munich National Liberal journal also reported that the liberals were not the only ones questioning the leadership of Bethmann-Hollweg; rightist journals like the Kreuz-Zeitung, Deutsche Tageszeitung and Berliner Post had indicated that a feud existed among the leading officials of the German states. They had suggested that this had only happened once before in German history, in the time of Reichs-Chancellor Caprivi. The Allgemeine Zeitung writer stated that the only party to support the Reichs-Chancellor at that time had been the National Liberal Party, but now, even that Party had joined the radicals in the storm against the Chancellor. Yet, said the writer, the monarchical and nationalistic groups considered what happened in Zabern an occurrence not likely to be repeated and having no importance outside its locale. They even insisted that the events would not have had any significance if the Chancellor had taken action against the well-planned French agitation in Alsace-Lorraine and, indeed, if such action were not taken immediately, the security of the Empire would be put into jeopardy. An article that reflected these views in the Nord Deutsche Allgemeine Zeitung went so far as to state that Reichs-Chancellor Bethmann-Hollweg was not the man to put through these decisive measures.[3]

As the confidence of the Conservatives waxed, however, the democratic tide waned. Evidence of this was found in the Munich journal, the Allgemeine Zeitung, on the tenth of January, 1914. On this day that newspaper reported that Reichstag representatives Naumann and Haussmann, the latter in an article in the Vossische Zeitung, stated that the democratic force aroused by the Zabern Affair was declining. The Social Democratic journal Vorwärts stated that the freedom war of 1913 that had begun with so much fanfare was petering out in a running fight.[4] A division within the National Liberal Party was found by the conservative Deutsche Tageszeitung, early in January when the National Liberal journal Goester Kreisblatt commented that what seemed to have been forgotten in the Mistrust Vote of the fourth of December was that the army in Zabern had been in difficult circumstances due to the French sympathies of the population. It stated that for the second time the Left-Liberal faction in the Reichstag served as a stepping stone to social democracy. It went on to avow that good national-spirited Germans could not support nor understand this.[5]   On the other hand, the Tägliche

Rundschau as well as the Munich Allgemeine Zeitung were of the opinion that Germany would have to bear the effects of the Zabern events "still longer," although they castigated the Social Democrats for terrorism and an international outlook which was not patriotic and nationalistic.[6]

In summary, here we have the seeds of why the democratic freedom-fight waned: the fanfare of the "freedom war," the fact that it was in its latter stages being conducted most vitriolically by the Social Democrats, the rather tired-of-it-all attitude shown in Tägliche Rundschau's "still longer" and the age-old castigations of the Social Democratic party which was by definition against the government and hence could not be trusted as a partner in any new government. What, of course, defused this freedom-fight bomb was the fact that the Social Democrats held a greater membership in the Reichstag than any other party and therefore any future government would have to include members of this group who would be opposed to the government on all issues that were not oriented toward a socialist state. These reasons seemed to reflect a general feeling of futility as basic to the subsiding of interest.

Yet, there were other reasons. The law-abiding traditions and tendencies of the German people inclined them to consider the von Reuter trial decision as the final word on this subject and therefore to regard it and its attendant issues as closed subjects. The promise of the Reichs-Chancellor that the law regarding the actions of troops in emergency situations and the prevention of illegal activities by the military would be considered by the Kaiser seemed to placate some. Bethmann-Hollweg's suggestion that the problems could be solved and the controversies settled to the satisfaction of all concerned seemed to satisfy many even though the appointment of a committee by the Reichstag to give recommendations to the Kaiser on this subject showed the lack of faith that anything would be accomplished without Reichstag pressure. At the same time this appointment reasserted the view that the Reichstag intended to have a hand in the government of the German Empire and that that participation included the regulation of troops, even though the Reichstag jurisdiction based upon budgetary controls was highly questionable considering the fact that the Constitution stated distinctly in Article sixty-four that "All German troops are required unconditionally to obey the Emperor. That obligation is to form part of the military oath of fidelity."[7] According to the Constitution, then, the power of the Emperor over the army was unlimited.[8] The Emperor's orders regarding the army did not have to be countersigned by the Chancellor as they did in civil matters even if these orders should in some way touch upon budgetary matters. The fact that this Zabern committee reached no conclusion and, indeed, that having accomplished nothing it fell apart on its second meeting, was not as important as that it was formed in the first place. Those who voted for its formation, a majority of the Reichstag, knew full well that it was an unconstitutional bid for increasing the power of the Reichstag. This was even more significant for this appointment had occurred after the Zabern Affair had seemed to be settled on the twenty-third and twenty-fourth of January, when representative Fehrenbach's appeal that Germany must pull itself together rather than tear itself apart fell, upon willing ears, despite the tirades of the Social Democrats.

The three factors of great importance in causing the democratic pressure to wane were: the acquittal of Colonel von Reuter and Lieutenant von Forstner, the increased criticism that the Conservatives made of the Reichstag and Chancellor Bethmann-Hollweg in the Prussian Landtag, and the criticism that began to be widespread in French newspapers of the Crown Prince and of Germany in general, rather than of Prussia.

The courts martial of Colonel von Reuter was reported in great detail by most of the major newspapers in Germany, by the journals in France, the major dailies in England and publications throughout the world. There was no significant difference in the factual account of these trials because the reporting was very thorough.

The trial began in Strasburg on the fifth of January, 1914. Both Colonel von Reuter and Lieutenant Schad, who were the accused, had civilian council. The indictment by the prosecution against the Colonel was in three parts: first, unwarranted assumption of police functions; second, the incarceration of twenty-seven individuals overnight; third, violation of the clauses of the military penal code referring thereto. Lieutenant Schad was charged with the unjustified arrest of civilians, with bodily coercion by hitting a civilian on the head and with repeated violations of domicile.

The Defense of Colonel von Reuter against these indictments was that he had acted with good will toward the people of Alsace and, indeed, had come there of his own choice; yet he had been forced into a position of self-protection. He took upon himself the responsibility for everything done by his subordinates, stating that he had ordered these actions in order to protect himself and the officers under his command. Although he had tried to establish friendly relations with the local press, he had soon become the object of published satirical condemnation in poems and articles that were insulting. He did not condemn all Alsatians for this, as some had insisted, but only civil and, particularly, the judicial and police authorities who refused to take any counter measures. The judicial authorities, in particular, had been at fault because they were biased in favor of the Alsatians. An example of this biased judgment, he insisted, had occurred when a fight had taken place in the street between the soldiers and the natives, and the court had exonerated Alsatians of all charges and punished the soldiers. In opposing this decision he had written to the Burgomaster asking that the police protect his soldiers rather than the natives. Because it was so difficult to determine who the assailants were, he commanded his troops to protect themselves vigorously so that these assailants would not get escape. When Lieutenant von Forstner's remarks had been published in the local press, he had inquired into the accusation that the Lieutenant had used the word "<u>Wackes</u>" and had found that the Lieutenant had not acted with good forethought, but that nonetheless, his action had not been punishable. However, the publicity had caused a great amount of excitement and had caused him to feel he had been too patient already with the insulting postcards and "dirty" letters he had received. Furthermore, the crowds had gathered in the avenues and had howled like Indians. He had heard a noise in the barracks, and had ordered Lieutenant Schad to catch one of the noisemakers and establish his identity. The Lieutenant had caught two but they had been freed by the police and his authority made to look foolish. At this point he had decided that his patience had lasted long enough and that all this nonsense had to stop.

In justification of the actions that he had taken, he cited a portion from a Prussian Cabinet Order of 1820, which commanded the military authorities if there was need, to take over control of the public order. At this point the Colonel was asked by the military assessor of the court whether he considered this order to be valid, especially in the province of Alsace-Lorraine. Colonel von Reuter indignantly stated that he was a Prussian officer in the service of the King commanding Prussian troops and that he had carried out the orders of his King. When he was asked if he had said that, "It would be good if blood were shed," he said that this was a situation of great urgency; not only was there a question of protecting military prestige, but there was also the problem of restoring some semblance of government authority. On the other hand, he insisted, he had actually prevented bloodshed because he had locked up the natives in the cellar and had thus protected them from bodily harm.

The defense of Lieutenant Schad consisted of his insistence that people were laughing at him and although he could not catch them at it, he suspected that they were; this was sufficient reason for teaching the civilians the gravity of the situation by arresting them. He had also arrested the Judges of the civil court of Zabern because they had refused to follow his orders and move on, and, indeed, one had stated that the military could not order him around. He denied the charge that he had hit a civilian on the head, asserting that he was so far above the civilians that he would not stoop to such low tactics as brawling in the streets. He was also charged with breaking and entering a person's house, but to this accusation he merely replied that this was in pursuance of his duty of arresting those who had laughed.

The statement of the civilian officials, a policeman and the Burgomaster of Zabern revolved around the point that the actions of the civilians had been provoked by the younger officers. The Kreis Direktor of Zabern, Herr Mahl, when asked what action he had taken to avert the crisis, said that at first he had been informed that there was no crisis of any moment and then had been offended when Colonel von Reuter, whom he personally disliked, had not called upon him to solve the problems that had arisen. He insisted that he had intervened as soon as the street strife commenced. His instructions at that time had been that this strife had to cease and that the military were to be given adequate protection, and he ordered the Burgomaster of Zabern to instruct the police accordingly. He said that he next heard from Colonel von Reuter when the police reported to him that they had received a letter threatening to proclaim martial law. He had replied that he had done his duty as far as protection was concerned and that Colonel von Reuter had no right to proclaim martial law, as this could only be done by the Kaiser. The Colonel had answered that he knew full well the extent of his duties and his rights and that there was a new crowd in front of the barracks. Kreis Direktor Mahl had then called the Burgomaster and had gone to observe the crowd. They had found that it consisted of approximately seventy-five percent women and children and that the police had been doing their duty; about twenty arrests had been made.

After this the Kreis Director had not seen Colonel von Reuter for some time, but on the next encounter the Colonel had greeted him coldly. As far as the disturbances were concerned, he had heard two sides: on the one hand, the people had been continually annoyed by the patrols passing through the streets with fixed bayonets and by Lieutenant von Forstner's provocative attitude when he stood on the balcony outside his rooms and smoked cigarettes; on the other hand, he had been informed that the natives had been whistling the forbidden Marseillaise and had cried "vive la France," but these accusations by the military had led to his investigating them and he had found that no evidence existed that "vive la France" had been uttered by people. Colonel von Reuter had sent messages asking him to come to see him on several occasions regarding these incidents, but he had refused on the orders of Statthalter von Wedel of Alsace-Lorraine, who had commanded him to wait for the Colonel to come to see him and that if he had wanted anything important he would have done so. He had been informed that the Statthalter had taken precautions that incidents would not happen in the future by strengthening the police and by asking for cooperation of the owners of business and industry to calm their employees. The Statthalter had also commanded him to request that the young officers not appear upon the streets more than was necessary and he had done so.

The Kreis Direktor maintained that all seemed to be going on rather smoothly until the twenty-sixth of November when as a result of a party given by a number of officers there occurred an incident which was due to the drunkenness of Lieutenant Schad who at that time, leading a four-man patrol on the streets, had come upon a bank official named Kahn and had attempted to arrest him. Herr Kahn had resisted arrest by stating that the Lieutenant had no authority to arrest anybody and that if he was to be arrested he demanded, as the law stipulated, to be delivered to the police.

Then, on the twenty-seventh, came the famous disturbances. Kreis Direktor Mahl was at that time at dinner with Under-Secretary of State Mandel, General von Deimling, and one of the highest officials of the local railway. During the dinner word came from Zabern of the disturbances. According to the testimony of Herr Mahl, he had wanted to leave for Zabern but was dissuaded from leaving by Herr Mandel, who had said that he would never get there in time anyway even if he left immediately, and by General von Deimling, even though the local railway official had offered him a private railway train that would have sped him there immediately. He then said that he had warned Colonel von Reuter on the twenty-ninth that his actions in usurping the powers of the police were illegal, that he had had no right to impose police rule upon the civilian population. However, his warning had not been heeded, and on the following day more arrests had been made by the military. When Colonel von Reuter's lawyer asked Herr Mahl what could have been the reason for the arrests, this official said that he could not say; he did not know; he would not attempt to explain why Colonel von Reuter did anything.

The twenty-seven persons who had been arrested and incarcerated overnight in the coal cellar were examined thoroughly as to what possible reasons could have existed for their incarceration and why they had been arrested in the first place. According to them, they had done nothing of a provocative or illegal nature or anything that might be interpreted as having criminal intent or could in any way have justified the actions of Colonel von Reuter. The counsel for the defense had contradicted the testimony of the witnesses who had been incarcerated by having several soldiers deny the truth of these statements. This witnesses were faced with the men who had arrested them, who were asked why they had done so. "The laughter and hooting of the crowd, estimated at from fifty to eighty men, women, and children," were the reasons given by the military for the arrest and incarceration of the civilians. This contravention did not have the consequence, however, of changing the testimony of the witnesses. One witness declared that Lieutenant Schad had even gone so far as to draw his sabre and had chased the children away. The Lieutenant insisted that the children had cheered in an ironic manner when he had arrested a workingman whom he had suspected of having laughed. He had also arrested three boys of age fifteen, sixteen, and seventeen who had hidden behind a fountain and had whistled at the patrol. It was established that these boys had been struck and pushed into the coal cellar. Colonel von Reuter was accused of having called one of these boys a rascal, an actionable insult in Germany. To this accusation Colonel von Reuter had stood before the court and replied that the boy had passed by him without taking off his hat and that this was no way for a well-behaved boy to act before a Prussian colonel.

The charge of rowdy behavior made by Colonel von Reuter was denied on the sixth of January by the police sergeant at Zabern, who said that there had been curiosity and excitement and that he too had been excited due to the brandishing of machine guns by the military and obvious ready-for-a-fight attitude on the part of the military, but that if there had been any rowdiness on the part of the civilian population it would have devolved upon him to stop it; none had occurred.

Colonel von Reuter had considered the situation dangerous and had therefore set up the machine guns. He had said that the civilians should not walk around in front of the barracks and that if they stood around and laughed, he would open fire on them. The testimony of the police sergeant was that when this was said to him he had replied that it was impossible to prevent the people who lived in the town from walking through it.

Those who gave evidence in favor of the military contentions were closely associated with the army. A woman who had sold cigars to the officers had said that she had always found them to be polite and unprovocative in their behavior. A school teacher of Prusso-German descent said that he had been uneasy at the crowds and was highly satisfied when the troops had cleared the square. A governess brought from Prussian for the family of an officer stated that the police had been inadequate and that the military intervention had been necessary.

On the same day, the seventh of January, testimony was heard from the chief public prosecutor of Zabern, a retired army officer who had served the Kaiser for thirty-two years. He emphatically denied the testimony of Colonel von Reuter; first, that there had not been adequate police protection for the military due to the civil authorities neglecting their responsibilities, and second, that evidence of the police at this trial had been changed or influenced by the coercion of their civilian superiors. It was apparent from the testimony that there had been animosity between the military and civil authorities for some time due to Colonel von Reuter's excessive sensitivity to any affront or suspected affront to the military. The testimony of the public prosecutor, Judge Beemelmans, and Judge Kalesch concerning the arrest of the latter because of his unwillingness to take orders from Lieutenant Schad supported this point of view. As a result of the interview with Colonel von Reuter in the barracks after their arrest, they had found him totally unwilling to admit for an instant any question of his authority or any criticism of his actions. The colonel had excitedly exclaimed that the military had been acting according to orders. When the judges were questioned as to what orders he had meant, his own or someone else's, they would not hazard a guess.

The court martial judges questioned the civilian judges as to the legality of their own actions in refusing to obey the commands of the military in exercising police functions. The civilians refused to retreat from their position; they stated that the military had no right to exercise police functions, that their conduct was entirely legal, and that they would act in the same way in similar circumstances in the future. They were decidedly critical of Colonel von Reuter's actions and stated that no siege had been in process, a state of war had not existed and the civilian authorities had been functioning; therefore there had been no reason for the exercise of police authority by the military. The major issue in the trial was here brought up and the two opposing sides stated their opinion; the military judges in their suggestions of illegal civilian action in the face of military acting as police and the civil judges in stating the law and firmly adhering to it and suggesting that the military whims had dictated military action and that the military pride could not supplant the law. On the other hand, Colonel von Reuter cited as legal justification for his military intervention a cabinet order of Frederick William dated 1820 which allowed such action.

On Thursday, the eighth of January, the prosecutor delivered a speech that was very mild in its accusations against Colonel von Reuter and Lieutenant Schad. Indeed, at times he suggested that the officers had been victims of circumstances beyond their control and that the police had not carried out their duties, although this was not the Kreis Direktor's fault. The scum of the town with the aid of the Zaberner Anzeiger had been to blame and the actions of the military had been well taken or at least unavoidable in the situation. His proposed sentence was that Colonel von Reuter should be acquitted of the charge of assumption of police functions, and sentenced to seven days' imprisonment for unlawful incarceration of civilians.   Concerning Lieutenant Schad, prosecutor Oslander withdrew the charge of violations of domicile, and asked that he be given three days' imprisonment for physical assault.

Of course, the defense asked for complete acquittals. Colonel von Reuter spoke after the pleading as if he had done nothing illegal and had acted rightly as a good soldier should to prevent worse things from happening to the civilians. His counsel had said that they ought not send to prison a man who had served the Kaiser for thirty-five years just for defending the honor of the German army. In fact, he predicted that after the trial was over there would be a complete change in public opinion. The German Empire had to maintain a strong fist in Alsace-Lorraine and if it did not, then those borderlands would be lost and it would serve the German Empire right to lose them, at least in spirit.[9]

The trial of Colonel von Reuter and Lieutenant Schad was now over except for the decisions of the military judges as to guilt or innocence. These decisions, however, were postponed two days until Saturday when the court martial, having carefully gone over a difficult legal problem in the interim, would give the decision. However, it seemed more than just coincidental that this date, the tenth of January, was also the date upon which was scheduled the decision on the appeal of Lieutenant von Forstner by the superior military court of the army at Strasburg.

Would the military court render a severe judgment against officers? The question was answered on the tenth of January, 1914. There could hardly have been a decision other than that of guilt or innocence. The issue had been clearly stated; there had been no compromises, nor had the testimony of any of the witnesses wavered or hesitated in the least. Germany had read in the newspapers that the Reichs-Chancellor had considered that some minor illegalities had taken place and that these would be rectified. No one had considered that Colonel von Reuter and Lieutenant Schad would receive stiff sentences or be cashiered from the army. Everyone had thought a token punishment would be given; enough to show the displeasure of the army with two of its members and enough to show the disturbed general populace of the German Empire that the army abided by its laws. However, even this was too hard a judgment for the army to make of itself; the verdict was not guilty on all counts. The military court of the thirtieth division at Strasburg acquitted both Colonel von Reuter and Lieutenant Schad of all the charges brought against them. Three hours later the earlier verdict against Lieutenant von Forstner was reversed and he was acquitted. The conservative reaction had won!

An important stimulus to the conservative reaction was the support given by the Crown Prince to the actions of Lieutenant von Forstner, Colonel von Reuter, and General von Deimling in the Zabern Affair and in the trial.   Whether the support was known at first hand by the Conservatives and moderate Centre and National Liberal party members was not important.   Far more important was that they heard that he had given support and even more important was the source from which they had heard this, namely, the French and the Social Democratic newspapers. Condemnation by these papers, if for no other reason, made the Crown Prince the Conservatives' hero.   The French journal L'Autorité was the first to mention the action of the Crown Prince.   Then the Frankfurter Zeitung fully reported it on the fourth of January.   This newspaper stated that during the Zabern debates of third and fourth of December, the Crown Prince had congratulated both Colonel von Reuter and General von Deimling on their conduct during the troubles of the previous three weeks in Zabern.   The writer was not sure that this was true but stated that because of the Crown Prince's political views the report could not be completely discounted.   According to this report, the reason the Crown Prince was suddenly transferred from Danzig to Berlin and to office work was that the Kaiser had heard of his telegraphing "good luck" to the two military men.[10]

Simplicissimus on the second of January, the day after the Crown Prince arrived in Berlin, published a cartoon on the front page showing William II seated in an armchair remarking to the Empress, "I'd just like to know where that boy got that damned habit of telegraphing!"   The title of this cartoon was an ironic comment on the Kaiser's own telegraphic activities; it read, "Not true to type."[11]

In the Deutsche Tageszeitung, a conservative paper, there appeared on the fifth of January the remark that the French press of late have been talking of the Crown Prince's telegrams, but that the German national press, except the Frankfurter Zeitung, have ignored it.[12]

On the sixth of January the Strasburg correspondent of the Frankfurter Zeitung, stated that there had been two telegrams from the Crown Prince: one on the twenty-eighth and one on the next day, both sent to General von Deimling.   The first telegram was said to have exclaimed, "keep doing the same," while the second telegram merely exclaimed "Hurrah."[13]

The Deutsche Tageszeitung of the seventh of January commented upon a long leading article of the previous day published in the French journal Le Temps.   The article had reflected on the conflict of evidence at Strasburg and the actions of the Crown Prince and had as its most important point the polarization of Germany into two groups corresponding to the two positions of whether there was to exist within Germany a constitutional or a military government and whether Germany was to divide between the law and the sword, between a liberal Germany and Pan Germanism, between civil authority and the army authority and between the authority of the Kaiser and the opinions of the Crown Prince. The comment by the Deutsche Tageszeitung was typical for the Hamburger Nachrichten, Die Post and the rest of the conservative press on the subject at this time. They all held that the actions of the Crown Prince, if he had committed them, were the actions not of the heir to the throne, but of a private individual and had no meaning other than that in the eyes of the military concerned with the Zabern Affair. Furthermore, it stated without equivocation that the Crown Prince was not transferred to the general staff in order to keep him quiet and to prevent him from sending any more telegrams, that the plan for his training in connection with the general staff had existed long before.[14] To Die Post, the fact that the report on the Crown Prince concerning his encouragement of the military in the Zabern Affair was first printed in a French newspaper and that it was then repeated in the Frankfurter Zeitung was enough to question its credibility and to render it virtually worthless.[15]

The Crown Prince, himself, denied the report according to the Deutsche Tageszeitung of the eighth of January. He stated that officers must protect themselves against insults but not by illegal means, and that he was shocked that his views as a private citizen should be interpreted as interference with a case before the courts and as an expression of autocratic views which he did not support. It was noted that the Crown Prince had an interview with the Reichs-Chancellor the day before.[16] It was perhaps due to the view that the Crown Prince did not support autocracy that there was abroad a general tendency to discredit all questions of the Crown Prince supporting the military in the Zabern Affair. On the ninth of January came the explanation for his transfer published by the Tägliche Rundschau, that General von Mackenson and the Crown Prince's commanding officer, Count Schmettow, requested the transfer because they were unable to carry out the wishes of the Kaiser with regard to the education of the Crown Prince in military affairs.[17] This completely explained the whole incident of his transfer, the paper declared, and he had denied sending the telegrams of a congratulatory nature and thus there was no foundation for the French and Frankfurter Zeitung view that he represented either the official army or the Pan-German view of the Zabern Affair.[18]

Yet the consequences of this revelation concerning the Crown Prince's interference in the Zabern Affair showed quite clearly the issues at hand. His action undoubtedly influenced the outcome of the trial. Proof of this was found in the report of the telegrams of a judge at the trial, Pelet-Narbonne, sent to the Crown Prince, Berlin police president von Jagow and Oldenburg-Januschau, who did not even dignify the Zabern Affair by mentioning it in his memoirs. Whether the telegrams from a military judge after the trial really existed or not was not important. What was important was that the story was reported in the newspapers and people believed it.[19] There was also implied that a link existed between the Crown Prince, police president von Jagow, and Oldenburg-Januschau, but more than this the incident showed that these were the heroes of the conservative reaction along with Colonel von Reuter, the victor of Zabern.

A further result of the revelations concerning the Crown Prince was the excitation of the French press to do more than merely "report" the day-to-day events of the Zabern Affair. According to the French press, the actions of the Crown Prince revealed that there was an official Germany trying to solve the problems and issues brought up by the Zabern Affair consisting of the Reichstag, the Reichs-Chancellor, to some extent, and the Kaiser, and then there was another Germany as indicated above which sought to retain autocracy, military rule, and, by this, belligerency toward foreign countries such as France, which was often mentioned by conservatives such as Berlin police president von Jagow as enemy country.   In addition to the polarization mentioned, the French journal, Le Temps criticized Colonel von Reuter and attempted to show that all his actions had been planned in advance by a Pan-German element represented by a coalition-pact between the army and the educational profession at the professor level. According to Le Temps Colonel von Reuter's praise of bloodletting as a good thing was just a characteristic expression of Pan-Germanism and this was an example of the new Germany which was being bred from the primary schools to the university level through the educational system. According to this French newspaper, the planned militarization of Zabern by Colonel von Reuter was unsuccessful in its first stage because he was unable to impose martial law and because of this he had resigned. The second stage of the plan was a renewed attempt by more forceful measures to carry out the intention of the moribund first stage. This time Colonel von Reuter had returned with his resignation refused and changed into a leave of absence in order to give him a reason for having left Zabern. This was considered support for his actions and therefore he was met at the railway station, band playing, by General von Deimling who had only recently received the "Immer feste druff" telegram from the Crown Prince and who now had considered it to be reason enough to employ force in Zabern. The French newspaper insisted that at that time Zabern was quiet but during that day the Colonel had had the coal removed from a cellar which he had intended to use as a prison that evening. The local shop owners were warned to stay off the streets because of a possible excitation in the evening. At seven o'clock, Colonel von Reuter found out that the subprefect Mahl was at Strasburg and fifteen minutes later his troops appeared on the streets with bayonets fixed and charged the crowd, which had been drawn by the drums to the square, and the arrests began. Replying to protests from the city officials, Colonel von Reuter had said that he had acted on orders from his superiors. This, said the writer of the French article, was a great maneuver of Pan-Germanism and reflected the attitude that would welcome an incident which might provoke a war between Germany and France. The author asked whether this attitude, which was not widely accepted at this time, might not be the majority view in the future if the educators and military men in revolt against the pacifism of William II continued to dominate in Germany.[20]

It was impossible to judge whether the views of Le Temps had any influence on the outcome of the trials of Colonel von Reuter, Lieutenants Schad and Forstner, but these views were reported in the German newspapers[21] and could very well have created antagonism toward those who criticized the army, the protector of Germany. Indeed, it was perhaps questionable whether the outcome of the trials was not already decided before the trials began. The "coincidence" of rendering the verdict in Colonel von Reuter and Lieutenant Schad's trial on the same date as the verdict in the appeal-trial of Lieutenant von Forstner and the same decision being rendered in both trials seems too coincidental not to have been arranged. Indeed, Abbé Wetterlé, who at that time was a member of the Reichstag from Alsace and rabidly anti-German, said in his autobiography that the verdict had been ordered by War Minister von Falkenhayn.[22] However, this accusation was not supported with factual proof and therefore was questionable. Nevertheless, the coincidence mentioned and also the very coincidental action of the Prussian upper house while the verdict was being delivered in the trials could be considered as evidence that the conservative reaction had reaching its fruition.

NOTES

[1]Nord Deutsche Allgemeine Zeitung, January 15, 1914.
[2]Matthew Arnold, "Dover Beach," from Our Heritage of World Literature, ed. Stith Thompson and John Gassner (New York: Dryden Press, 1942), p. 1333.
[3]Allgemeine Zeitung, Munich, January 3, 1914.
[4]Ibid.
[5]Deutsche Tageszeitung, January 9, 1914.
[6]Allgemeine Zeitung, January 10, 17, 1914.
[7]"Constitution of the German Empire," in Walter F. Dodd (ed.), Modern Constitutions: A Collection of the Fundamental Laws of Twenty-two of the Most Important Countries of the World with Historical and Bibliographical Notes, Vol. I, Art. 64 (Chicago: University of Chicago Press; London: T. Fisher Unwin, 1909).
[8]Ibid.
[9]Deutsche Tageszeitung, January 4, 1914.
[10]Frankfurter Zeitung, January 4, 1914.
[11]Simplicissimus, January 2, 1914.
[12]Deutsche Tageszeitung, January 5, 1914.
[13]Frankfurter Zeitung, January 6, 1914.
[14]Deutsche Tageszeitung, January 7, 1914.
[15]Die Post, January 7, 1914.
[16]Deutsche Tageszeitung, January 8, 1914.
[17]Tägliche Rundschau, January 9, 1914.
[18]The Crown Prince of Germany, Memoirs of the Crown Prince of Germany Here he admits that he had sent telegrams to Colonel von Reuter and General von Deimling encouraging them to use strong measures in Alsace-Lorraine, but denies that he had said "Immer feste druff."
[19]Strasburg Post, January 10, 1914. Berliner Tageblatt, January 10, 1914. Frankfurter Zeitung, January 11, 1913.
[20]Le Temps, January 6, 1914.
[21]Deutsche Tageszeitung, January 7, 1914.
[22]Wetterlé, Behind the Scenes in the Reichstag, p. 235.

CHAPTER VII

THE REACTION TO THE VERDICT

Was it merely coincidental that, although the Prussian upper house had been meeting since the seventh of January, it had not discussed the position of Prussia in the German Empire, nor the democratization of the Prussian army, nor the growth of power of the Reichstag and the condemnation of Bethmann-Hollweg for having allowed this? Was it also coincidental that it chose the tenth of January, the day that the pro-Prussia, pro-Prussian army, anti-Reichstag verdict of the Strasburg trials was delivered to debate these matters? Such a combination of attacks on the liberal forces which had plagued the conservatives for the preceding twelve months was not likely to be a coincidence.

One hour after the final session of the trial began, the protest of the upper house was initiated by Graf Behr-Behrenhoff who stated that it was the right and duty of the Herrenhaus to warn against the danger of a weak Prussia and to protect the position of Prussia within the Empire. This sally was picked up by Count Yorck von Wartenburg, who elaborated upon the motion made by Count Behr-Behrenhoff that Prussia be assured a position within the Empire commensurate with her past leadership and that there should not be changes made in the constitution that would alter that position. Count Yorck condemned the Reichstag for not showing a spirit in keeping with the spirit of glorious victory of this centenary year. He invoked the spirit of Bismarck shown on the fifteenth of March, 1884, when the great statesman had delineated the boundaries of each branch of the government of the Empire using Montesquieu's example in the Spirit of the Laws whereby there were independent executive, judicial, and parliamentary branches. Bismarck had reiterated this position on the twenty-sixth of November of that same year but admitted that some changes might be made but only within the lines of the constitution. Graf

Yorck von Wartenburg accused the Reichstag of seeking to destroy the work of this great Prussian Chancellor. According to the Count, the deputies in the Reichstag were trying to add to their powers at the expense of the Emperor, the Federal Council, which was the true representative of the people, and the separate states within the Empire. The Reichstag was attending to matters outside its surveyance and had even presumed to censure the Minister President of Prussia. Imperial laws were being passed and Imperial authorities were being created whereby the King of Prussia lost more than the German Emperor gained. The Reichstag was trying to change the constitution without the constitutional right to do so. It was trying to: change the uniforming of the army, replace active officers by inactive officers, change the ways of advancing and pensioning officers, reduce the number of man-servants for officers, and eliminate barter between fixed officer-corps. The Reichstag budget commission now had gone one step further. That commission now made motions concerning the length of furloughs granted and concerning the elimination of strong detention as disciplinary punishment. Wasn't this impinging on the authority of the Kaiser's supreme command which was guaranteed to him by the constitution, he queried? Furthermore, the Reichstag sought to eliminate states-rights. The members wanted to change the military-law code book of Prussia. They wanted to subordinate the army to the parliament and install a parliamentary government in Germany. The Reichstag was trying to do this through a change in procedure and was interfering with the Emperor's military power. Count Yorck emphatically stated that the army and the state must not be democratized, because the result would be a state like England which had a president for life at the head of a Republic.[1]

In his capacity as Prussian Minister-President, the Imperial Chancellor Bethmann-Hollweg replied to the conservative criticism by stressing that the special position of Prussia within the Empire made the relations between it and the Empire difficult and that this problem was one that would always be present. At the time of the German Empire there had been protests that Prussia would take advantage of her power and exceed the limitations of her position as an equal among the other federal states and impose her power as the source of the army and the Emperor upon the others, but she had not done so. The result of her abiding by the constitutional limitations she set upon herself was that the other dynamic states had had confidence in her and supported her in the federal council and that this created the strength in solidarity of the German Empire.

Concerning the criticism that Count Yorck von Wartenburg had made of the 1911 constitution initiated by von Bethmann-Hollweg for Alsace-

Lorraine, the Imperial Chancellor had said that Prussia still maintained power of control over it. The procedural power to which Yorck von Wartenburg had referred, according to the Chancellor, was the new power of members of the Reichstag to ask the government short questions and to him, this meant no more than that a difference of opinion existed. He would do everything he could to prevent the Reichstag from encroaching in any way upon the prerogatives of the executive branch of the government. The passing of resolutions such as the recent vote of censure concerning Zabern was of no consequence whatever as the Reichstag had no constitutional powers of coercion. Regarding the armament inquiry committee which had been set-up as a result of the revelations of the Krupp affair that possible influencing of the military by such large industries as the Krupp industry had taken place, he declared that the Reichstag had no power whatsoever and thus the committee had no constitutional right to do anything.

Concerning the relationships between the Reichstag and the Prussian Landtag, Bethmann-Hollweg declared that there had been a steady increase of Imperial hostility against Prussia since the centenary celebration had revived the memories of the national struggles and of what the Empire owed Prussia, which had been pushed into the background by the more material interests of present-day Germany. The disparity between the conditions ruling the two parliaments, of the Empire and of Prussia, because of the different electoral laws, had increased steadily, and the government, which had to work with both legislatures, had found it increasingly difficult to do so due to the entirely different problems and persons that it had to face in each.

As far as Zabern was concerned, the Chancellor followed the precedent set by Yorck von Wartenburg and did not discuss it, but he did state that law (Recht) would remain law there as elsewhere in the Empire. He showed satisfaction that the heart of the entire Prussian nation had been stirred to the quick by the recent questioning of the honor of the army. The letters he had received from all classes, mainly from the simple people, had shown him their interest. The people of Prussia saw in its army the embodiment of its power and strength, and this was the strongest support of law and order. The great desire of every Prussian was to preserve this army, which was led by the King, against all attacks and to prevent it from becoming a parliamentary army, just as Count Yorck von Wartenburg had said and he regarded it as his major responsibility to do just this.

He was most laudatory toward the exploits of the army in the past and emphasized that all Germans owed it a great debt. The Prusso-German military system was the cornerstone of the power and strength of

Prussia and of Germany and neither he nor anyone else could face posterity if any aspect of the army system was in any way changed to its detriment. He emphasized throughout his remarks concerning the army that the Reichstag's differences of opinion, as in the Zabern events, were no more than that and that he would and could maintain the honor of the Prussian army.

These remarks seemed reason enough for Prince Hatzfeld to move closure of the debate and he did so. Nevertheless, the conservatives wanted to record a lasting impression of their displeasure by voting what was called a "division." They explained that they did not mean to vote an expression of mistrust, a measure taken in the Reichstag and one which they had condemned, but merely wanted to show a difference of opinion over the way Bethmann-Hollweg had carried out his duties as a Prussian official. If the Reichstag could vote a difference of opinion, so could the Prussian Landtag. The motion was carried by a vote of one hundred eighty six to twenty. Now, all parts of the political spectrum had voiced "a difference of opinion" with Bethmann-Hollweg.[2]

The judgments of the Strasburg trials did as much if not more than anything else to consolidate and strengthen the conservative reaction. The decision in the case of Colonel von Reuter and Lieutenant Schad went into detail on the incidents at Zabern and the evidence given on the both sides in order to show that the civil authorities did not act to quell the anti-military disturbances and that therefore the army had no choice but to assume the role of the police. Concerning the incarceration of the twenty-eight civilians in the coal-cellar, the evidence was re-examined with the decision made, in contradiction to the civilian testimony, that the police authority had not existed. The Cabinet Order of 1820 that had been invoked by Colonel von Reuter to justify his actions was declared by the court to be applicable to the Imperial army due to the inclusion of this order in the Imperial Order of 1899. Since it was at that time countersigned by the Minister of War, there could be no doubt as to its authority in 1914. The military judges considered that the major cause of the military's having to take action in Zabern had been the failure of the Kreis Direktor Mahl to act upon the warnings given to him by Colonel von Reuter, and because of this failure Colonel von Reuter had no choice but to intervene. The court declared that if these grounds were not sufficient for the exoneration of Colonel von Reuter from all charges, the fact that he had not believed that he was acting illegally was enough to acquit him.

The court made the point here as well as in the case of Lieutenant Schad that an officer was guilty of an infraction of the civil law only if he thought he was guilty and committed the act anyway. In the case of

Lieutenant Schad, the court declared that he had not willfully acted in an illegal manner and that if he had he would have admitted it. It found no evidence that he had hit the civilian who had lost a tooth.

In the case of the reversal of Lieutenant von Forstner's sentence by the Superior Military Court of Appeals at Strasburg, the court insisted that before the young Lieutenant had struck the cobbler, Blank, on the second of December, the civilians of Zabern had harassed the young officer continuously to a point at which he felt victimized by dangers which perhaps never existed. Concerning the striking of Herr Blank, the court decided that the Lieutenant in the midst of the tussle had thought that the cobbler might be going to strike him, that although the cobbler was being held by a number of soldiers, the Lieutenant had felt threatened and had struck Herr Blank in self defense. According to the court, the cobbler was an extraordinarily strong man, and thus the Lieutenant had the right to protect himself. Furthermore, there had been, unbeknownst to Lieutenant von Forstner, a knife in Herr Blank's pocket which might have been used against the Lieutenant, and one had the right to protect oneself. All of the action including the cut made by the Lieutenant's sword occurred in an instant and even though there might not have been any intent of assault on the part of the cobbler, the accused had thought there had been and therefore this justified his deed. Regarding the plea of self-defense, the court declared that the action was unpremeditated; it had been done in a heated tussle and the young Lieutenant had not had his sword especially ground for the occasion. The damage to Herr Blank had been of a minor nature and no stitches had been required although he had bled profusely. The cobbler had been able to return to work after eight days and his work had not been seriously impaired. Because of this the court granted the convicted Lieutenant von Forstner the legal protection specified in the Penal Code, paragraph fifty-three, and the decision of the lower military court was reversed. He was acquitted.[3]

The reaction of the newspapers in Germany to the judgment in both trials was mixed. The Radical journals responded to the decision as if stunned, whereas, on the other hand, the conservatives were almost gleeful in their self-congratulation. The immediate opinion of the democratic Frankfurter Zeitung was muted but nevertheless condemnatory. The Centre papers were also mild but attacked point by point the logic of the Strasburg military courts in a thorough manner.

The Deutsche Tageszeitung on the eleventh of January gave a very good synopsis of the views of various sides on the outcome of the trials: the Kreutz-Zeitung greeted the judgment happily as the right one and stated that the excitement and anxiety aroused by the first decision in the Forstner case needed to be toned down and the second decision had done that.   The equally conservative Reichsbote said that the courts martial finally had given a clear picture of the whole scandalous incitement in the Affair and the mischief involved.   The propitious result was that now the air was clear so that one knew what was fair and what was foul.   Die Post greeted the judgment with satisfaction: no other decision had been expected.   Colonel von Reuter was an honorable man and stood for all that the Right thought best in the army.   However, the civil authority in Zabern was morally condemned and was now on trial; Die Post hoped that justice would be meted out as quickly to this authority as it had come to the military.   In Der Tag Otto von Gottberg wrote that he was happy to see that the officers sent into danger in the Zabern Affair were not sent into a dishonorable conflict.   He would not like to have had his sons put behind bars with rogues for a mistake in carrying out an unwanted service.   What was most remarkable in reviewing the reaction of the conservative journals was the fact that the verdicts of the trials and even the reasoning used by the judges were found in the predictions of the Hannoverscher Courier of the few days before the verdict was given.   The Tägliche Rundschau reported that a different picture had come out of the trial from that of the wildly worded accusations of militarism and soldier brutality, that this was seen that very day in both the Centre and liberal journals where especially the fear of Colonel von Reuter as a man-eating werewolf was dispelled.   The democratic and comic strip press had been shown to have been wrong.   This Tägliche Rundschau journal had much praise for the honorable, dutiful Colonel von Reuter who had followed the King's commands as ordered in the Cabinet Order of the seventeenth October, 1820 and repeated in the Order of 1899; "The Colonel is no jurist, and if the 1820 order is repeated in the 1899 order, then he deserves to be freed."   However, it stated, that this did not entirely dispose of the spectacle of Zabern.[4]

The Deutsche Tageszeitung labeled these accounts and comments on the trial reasonable and just.   On the other hand, the comments of what it called the "mass press" it considered in comparison with the conservative views to be "disgusting howls of rage."   The Berliner Tageblatt was indeed greatly disturbed by the decision and declared that the actions of the military were still illegal despite the outcome of the trial.   The fact that people laughed did not warrant brandishing machine guns, nor did the laughter justify jailing two dozen people in a cellar. "The King's cloak had become a Gessler's hat, before which all must have reverence, and the army that wears it must also be reverenced and so can do no wrong," it stated.   " No one is safe from the coal cellar or the bayonet thrust if he does not throw himself down before the King's cloak," it continued.   The ridiculous assumptions of the court could not be justified. Just because people were allowed to laugh did not mean that civil authority had broken down in Zabern, nor did this justify the actions of Colonel von Reuter which, according to the court, proceeded naturally from these laughs. According to this journal, then, the Zabern Affair was far from ended by the judgment of the trial.[5]

The Berliner Börsencourier was somewhat conservative before the verdict in that it considered, in an article published the day before, that there was no doubt that the agitation of the military in Zabern was understandable and that also the position of the civil authority was not irreproachable but seemed too irreproachable and seemed too irresolute in its actions. However, from this comparison of the pro and con about the circumstances and behavior of the military and civilians, from this calm and considered standpoint, on the next day it turned full circle by declaring that there was no bridge to the militaristic one-sidedness with which the courts martial had now decided the verdict according to its best knowledge and understanding.[6] The Deutsche Tageszeitung ended this section on the voices of the press with a carefully planned effect in illustrating its own views by paraphrasing an article written by Fritz von Briesen in the Hamburger Neuesten Nachrichten. The author told a story of a boy who was seasick and ill-clad for the cold foggy weather aboard ship. The man who gave this poor shivering waif his cloak was not the ogre pictured in Simplicissimus but the kind-hearted Colonel von Reuter.[7]

On the twelfth of January the Berliner Tageblatt pictured Colonel von Reuter as an antediluvian phenomenon, basically an honest man, but out of place in a modern democratic, bourgeois, constitutional state.[8] The state that the Berliner Tageblatt envisaged here was not at all the state wanted by the Deutsche Tageszeitung. Indeed, just such a state had been condemned heartily two days before in the Prussian upper house. Nor was it what the National Liberals wanted, at least according to one of their outstanding spokesmen, Herr Bassermann. More vitriolic in his criticism, however, was Fritz Bley in an editorial in the Deutsche Tageszeitung. He linked the Zabern Affair, the German democratic press, and the French in a subversive collaboration in planning the whole Affair. He stated that from beginning to end the Jewish-democratic press affected the events. He specifically condemned the Frankfurter Zeitung for viewing the affair with iron rocks in the heads of its writers, and accused Abbé Wetterlé and the rest of Alsace-Lorraine of following Clemenceau and France.

A good deal of what had been said by the Prussian speaker Yorck von Wartenburg in the Herrenhaus on the tenth of January was reproduced here repeating the paramount fear of the increasing emphasis of the Reichstag on parliamentary-democratic government. The Deutsche

Tageszeitung even went so far as to insist that democratization would mean the end of King and constitution.[9] The conservatives had stated, the article said, that the first step toward this goal was the weakening of the position of the Reich-Chancellor by a vote of mistrust and had condemned the participants in this vote for so doing. Herr Bassermann of the National Liberal Party had been among those condemned.

There was no doubt that Bassermann had supported the nonconfidence vote, but he had insisted as late as the ninth of January that although this vote should not be disregarded by Reichs-Chancellor Bethmann-Hollweg, it should be made clear that his position as well as that of the National Liberals was that the vote dealt only with the clear illegalities for which Colonel von Reuter had been responsible and the lack of action by the Reichs-Chancellor to remedy the situation produced by these illegalities.[10] Evidence that the military verdict of the Strasburg trials had a great effect upon public opinion was seen by the change of position of Representative Bassermann after the verdict. At the Wurttemburg National Liberal Party conference, Herr Bassermann went over the entire Zabern Affair and questioned whether the whole affair might not have been nipped in the bud by the early transfer of Lieutenant von Forstner. He put the question rhetorically before the representatives of the party whether or not the real trouble that lay before them was that the German people had failed in the construction of constitutional rights and had failed in the relationships with foreign language speaking areas in the German Empire in general? The government had now felt the consequences, but it had been too late for it to have proceeded against the nationalistic elements in Alsace. Nonetheless, he said, with reference to the letter of police president of Berlin, von Jagow, "from which it does not follow, however, that we were almost in enemy's country" in Alsace.[11] This was especially true in Zabern, where the Alsatian nationalists were not in the majority and from which progressives had been elected to the Reichstag. He then went on to say that the mistrust vote in the Reichstag was contrary to his position which did not concern itself with the whole policy of the Imperial Chancellor; conservatives wrongly accused the National Liberals of setting in motion an attempt to overthrow that minister, he said, and this brought up the question of whether or not the foregoing events of the Prussian upper house against the Imperial Regime were not a much sharper expression of disapproval of the whole policy of the Imperial Chancellor than the mistrust vote of the Reichstag. According to Herr Bassermann, the National Liberals believed that Bethmann-Hollweg was the man best suited for the position of Imperial Chancellor even if he were not a man whom the conservatives liked; his policy was more in line with that of the National Liberals. Bassermann then stated that he was opposed to a parliamentary type government because it would be an impossibility considering the variety and multiplicity of parties existing in Germany. What the National Liberals wanted was a strong Reichstag which would have equal powers in law-making with the other branches of the government. Of course he wanted a strong executive branch led by the Kaiser. Again he referred to the question put forth by Yorck von Wartenburg "whether Prussia was to remain strong in the Empire," when he stated that Prussia must be entitled only to the same rights as the other states within the Empire, particularly those of South Germany, whose citizens could well ask the same question that Count Yorck von Wartenburg posed concerning their state. Coming to the position of the National Liberals concerning the recent verdicts at Strasburg, he said that the trial concerning Colonel von Reuter proved completely the validity of the position of the National Liberals in the Reichstag that the civil authorities had failed in their duty so that the military had been forced to take over. This, however, had not been the position of the National Liberals in the Reichstag, nor even that of two days before.[12]

The Deutsche Tageszeitung was quite scathing in its criticism of the National Liberals and at the same time showed the complete acceptance of the trial decision. The journal denied that the views of the National Liberals before the trial were supported by the decision, as Herr Bassermann claimed at Wurttemburg. The beginning of the Zabern Affair, it held, was caused by elements who used Forstner's actions as an opportunity (excuse) to bring other issues to the fore. If Bassermann believed that the transfer of Lieutenant von Forstner would have nipped the Zabern Affair in the bud, then he must also believe that the outcome of the trial at Strasburg decided only an extraordinary case and had no general meaning. The leader of a great party should not interpret the information with such stupidity. According to this journal, Bassermann was trying to explain away the blameable error that his party made in the December debate. Bassermann was not happy with the outcome of the trial because the mistrust vote against Bethmann-Hollweg was predicated on the assumption that Forstner and Reuter had done something wrong and that Bethmann-Hollweg had not acted quickly enough to stop it, but now it had been proven that nothing had been wrong with the military actions in Zabern, and so that therefore the attempt by Bassermann to show that the no-confidence vote had been limited in its scope revealed only more clearly that it was wrong to begin with.[13]

Like the German reaction to the trials, the French reaction reported in the newspapers was mixed. The great daily newspapers such as the Matin and the Journal satisfied themselves by reporting the Trial without any special condemnation. Their reaction was probably due to the pressure of the French government which, according to Freiherr Eduard von Schoen, the German Ambassador to France, was trying to repress any outspoken animosity toward Germany in the press at the time when negotiations for an economic alliance were being considered between France and Germany.[14] On the other hand, the small newspapers and weekly journals were not so easily repressed. The Radical said that the trial was held on the intent rather than the actual actions of Colonel von Reuter. He had not intended to do anything illegal and therefore was not guilty, although he actually committed illegalities. The Lanterne wrote that the trial proved the scandalous victory of an army over a nation. The events of Zabern offered an example for the whole world of what happened when one allowed Soldateska[15] to take over power; the time had come, said the journal, for France to show more pity toward its eastern neighbor than animosity and distrust. The journal stated that in the Strasburg trial not only justice but the whole people of Germany had been dishonored. The Petite Republique philosophized that the freeing of the officers by the trial at Strasburg was more the result of the doctrine of the state, Prussia-Germany, than it was due to the leadership of an officer corps. According to this journal, the doctrine of Prussia-Germany was a mixture of authority, obedience to dogma, and absolutism, which constituted the foundations of state power.[16] According to Le Temps, a military state might be the future of Germany, but it hoped not. It compared the Germany of 1913 with the France of the time of Louis XIV and said that modern day Germany was based upon a monarchy very similar to that of the "Sun King" in its emphasis on divine right and military right. In this way Germany belonged with a different set of values in a different world and was inaccessible to the liberal and humanitarian dreams that had led both France and England on their paths to power. Thus the Germany with which France had to compete in armaments was one between which and France there could be no understanding and the appeals of the French socialists to France that Germany was composed of people who could be understood, from the view of both politics and practical affairs, could not be reassuring and must fall upon deaf ears.[17]

Indeed, excerpts from French accusatory opinion were published in journals throughout the world; and the old statement that Mirabeau had made during the French Revolution that "Prussia is not a country that possesses an army, but an army that possesses a country" was revived and applied to the German Empire. Le Temps proclaimed the "triumph of the mailed fist" as early as the seventh of January. The London Times of the eleventh of January contrasted the Germany of the mistrust vote of the fifteenth of December with that of the military-caste dominated Germany of the Strasburg trials. Le Temps of the eleventh of January, accused the military judges of intentionally ignoring the evidence of witnesses to the Zabern incidents because of Imperial pressure. The Literary Digest of the seventeenth of January published excerpts from the clerical-aristocratic Parisian Le Soleil condemning the "Teutonic Jailers of Alsace." The American Review of Reviews published excerpts from La Revue de Paris, a bi-monthly literary review, condemning military brutality. Again The Literary Digest, on the thirty-first, in an article entitled "Triumph of the Sabre in Germany" published excerpts from Le Temps and Le Figaro declaring that the militaristic Pan-German spirit as evidenced in the trials was meant by Germany to provoke France into declaring war.

The Allgemeine Zeitung of Munich summed up what many Germans thought of the French reaction to the Zabern Affair in the statement that the French showed the greatest satisfaction when everything went wrong in Germany. It was stated here that in general the French believed that the outcome of the Zabern trial showed what elements ruled in Germany and that these Pan-German elements would lead to a Franco-German war. According to this journal the French rightist elements and the monarchists such as those writing in the Action Francaise were most vociferous concerning the Zabern Affair and the latter group took the lead in publishing in its newspaper, le Gaulois a comparison of the Zabern Trial with the Dreyfus Trial. It also reported a "Revanche Festival" at which the very-ill Paul Deroulade gave the cheering crowd his blessing in the forthcoming Revanchist war against Germany. Concerning this demonstration,the National-Liberal Munich Allgemeine Zeitung stated that the Zabern demonstrations showed such closeness to the "enemy" position that one suspected that a French chauvinist clique was at work in Zabern. This journal summarized one opinion, and perhaps the German majority opinion, of the attitude of France during the Zabern Affair and, indeed, in all political relations with Germany, by stating that the French radicals called the outcome of the trial proof of the decadence of German militarism and furthermore stated that "All in all the French see our political relations only with the spectacles and in the light of the French position."[18]

On the thirteenth of January in the Prussian House of Representatives, Imperial-Chancellor Bethmann-Hollweg as Minister President of Prussia was faced with the criticism of the conservative, Deputy Winkler. Herr Winkler criticized the weakness of the Reichs-Chancellor during the previous June when the Reichstag passed the, to him, infamous Army Budget Finance Bill and Bethmann-Hollweg had not opposed it, as Herr Winkler had assumed that he should have done. The result, of course, had been the passing of the bill to the detriment of the present and future fortunes of the conservatives of Prussia, and as far as he was concerned, for the future of all of Germany.

Herr Bethmann-Hollweg protested against the accusations of not having had the energy to resist the socialists in his attitude toward the problems in the provinces, especially Alsace-Lorraine, and his attitude toward the Reichstag in general. He said that he had explained his position concerning the provinces of the Empire in the Prussian Upper House two days before and also his protection of the rights of the individual states against the encroachments of the Reichstag. Concerning the Army Budget Bill he had to emphasize again that the situation was such that extraordinary measures were necessary. Indeed, the conservatives in the past had stated that support of both a material and spiritual nature would be given in such a time of crisis; he cited the exclamation of Herr Heydebrand in 1911 that the conservatives would support the government not only with their blood but with everything they owned when the time came for this necessity of sacrifice on the altar of the Fatherland. But, the Chancellor said, this promise had not been fulfilled; now that the time had come for such a sacrifice the conservatives had reneged. This had been shown very clearly and succinctly when Count von Westarp had declared in the Reichstag that the army financial contribution must not be paid in property taxes and had asked for deletion of those property taxes voted by the Bassermann-Erzberger bill. Furthermore, he said, he had tried to introduce a "government financial proposal" into the Reichstag but had been entirely unsuccessful. Therefore he had been forced to accept the Reichstag bill whether he wanted to or not because of the absolute necessity of having an army bill for the protection of Germany. If the conservatives had supported the original mild financial proposal of the government finance bill regarding a tax on the increment of fortunes, then possibly the Reichstag might have considered this, but since the conservatives did not, the Reichstag had gone on to a much more radical measure. Instead of the mild one which all parties had opposed, it had passed the one now in force, the Bassermann-Erzberger Bill. He said he had regretted having to accept this finance bill including the tax on increment of fortunes, but he had had no choice since it had been necessary to approve the most serious sacrifices in order to guarantee the strength and independence of the German people.[19]

Concerning the National Liberal Representative Rochling's question on Bethmann-Hollweg's position on the foregoing events in Zabern, the Minister President of Prussia stated that any criticism of his actions as Imperial-Chancellor could not be accepted from the Prussian House of

Representatives, but that concerning the events of the twenty-eighth of November he had supported the report of the military.[20]

In answer to the accusations made in the upper house and again brought up in the lower house, that he was not statesmanlike in his reply to the Reichstag Interpellations of the preceding December, he declared that everyone had learned something from the revelations of the Strasburg decisions, including those who had expressed the opinion that the civil authorities had been right and the military authorities had been wrong and that Soldateska ruled. He asked rhetorically, who could know on the third and fourth of December whether the civil authorities were guilty or not? When Representative Adolf Hoffman answered this same question with the name "Rochling," it was obvious that Bethmann-Hollweg became angry when he said emphatically that no one could have known the outcome. In a rather petulant manner he then reiterated what he had said in the upper house three days before and what he had said earlier that day, that it was not the right of the lower house to criticize his position as Imperial-Chancellor of the Empire; they could only criticize him as Minister-President of Prussia; Imperial affairs were not under their jurisdiction. He then appealed to them not to question his competence. It was easy to criticize. They must understand that the Zabern Affair was a very delicate subject to handle because of the serious effect this affair would have upon the government in the future.

Bethmann-Hollweg then changed the subject and turned to the question of reform of the three-class electoral system in Prussia, which had been criticized annually and against which this year the criticism had been especially heavy. The King had promised in his January opening-day address to the Prussian Landtag in 1908, he stated, that there would be a change in the voting system; this promise had not remained unfulfilled as they suggested but had been fulfilled by the Franchise Reform Bill of 1910, which the Landtag had not passed. The government would decide when to introduce such a measure again, but now was not a propitious moment because of the fact that this was the first session of the newly elected Landtag, and certainly no franchise bill could yet be introduced.[21]

As in the Reichstag and in the upper house of the Prussian Parliament, so also in the lower house of that Parliament, the larger issues involved in the Zabern Affair were magnified out of proportion to the usual reaction to them by the passions aroused by and the clarifying effect of the Zabern Affair. Thus Herr von Zedlitz, a conservative, on the fourteenth of January, 1914, said that under all circumstances they must prevent the Reichstag from gaining power over the Kaiser, and thus over the Imperial Command power over the army. He displayed fear of

Liebknecht, and of the general strike and socialism as destroyers of Germany. He said that the Representatives must protect Germany against this danger and stated that they must have an army to prevent it. Herr von Zedlitz declared that the soldier must be free to interfere and also obedient, for he might have to protect the Fatherland by shooting his own mother, father, sister, or brother. Only in this way could the terrible crisis be averted. He offered an example of this necessary military behavior in the workers' strike in the Ruhr District in March, 1912, in which the military in attacking the strikers killed four and thus broke up the resistance. These were the tactics proper for Alsace-Lorraine.[22]

Thus again on the fifteenth of January, as had happened two days before, the Minister President of Prussia, Bethmann-Hollweg, faced hostile criticism of his actions as Imperial-Chancellor by the Prussian House of Representatives Conservative Deputy Dr. Heydebrand. The deputy declared that the Minister-President's denial on the thirtieth of January of the Landtag's right to criticize his position as Imperial-Chancellor was wrong; the members of this House of Representatives did have this right. He claimed that in Alsace-Lorraine there had taken place a constitutional change which could not have come into being without the Prussian votes in the Bundesrat having been heard; the House of Representatives was partially responsible for these votes. Dr. Heydebrand held that they had asserted in 1911 that the constitution of that year for Alsace-Lorraine was fraught with danger because of the lack of close control over the people by the Prussian administration. Now this could be clearly seen in pro-French tendencies that had grown in the past few years in Alsace-Lorraine. Another example was the Zabern Affair; if a strong Prussian authority had been in existence instead of a weak civil authority, then the episode would not have reached the dimensions it had. He further condemned the Imperial-Chancellor for the property tax bill that would be so detrimental to the conservatives and for the development of last summer concerning the taxation of earned increment in wages and the introduction of inheritance taxes, all of which had not been necessary. In proof of this lack of need, which was a need that had been justified by Bethmann-Hollweg in order to meet the great expenditure necessary for the development of the military, he cited a statement of Secretary of Treasury Kuhn of November, 1913, to the effect that the Bassermann-Erzberger bill went beyond what was necessary in making the expenditures of the bill as it stood; therefore, asserted Dr. Heydebrand, the Imperial-Chancellor had been wrong concerning the expenditure needs. Furthermore, he condemned the Imperial-Chancellor for his statement that the conservatives had opposed the finance bill all the way; this was not true. Bethmann-Hollweg had said that the conservative representative in the Reichstag, Count von Westarp, had opposed the bill as totally unacceptable. What the latter had said was that the government bill was unacceptable as it was, but that it could stand as a base for further reports with which conservatives would work. This was not the same as being unacceptable. The Imperial-Chancellor gave up too easily on the government bill. Why had he not dismissed the Reichstag instead of surrendering to it? It was little wonder that the government bills were rejected when the Imperial Chancellor gave the impression that he did not believe in them himself.

The deputy considered the property tax to be a great danger to Germany. Indeed, it would be so great a danger that its future utilization would have accomplished what the Social Democrats had tried and failed to do for generations and continued to insist upon for the future. Notably, they wanted to tax property out of existence. Thus this would do just that and bring about an end of the whole culture. Therefore, this bill threatened the very future existence of Germany. According to Herr Heydebrand this fate of Germany could very well come about if the individual states lost their independence and the Empire took over power from the states. Already, he says, the Empire was encroaching unconstitutionally upon the rights of the independent states, and the culprit behind the encroachment was the Reichstag. He ended his speech with the statement that it was the duty of the conservatives to put the Prussian state-regime as well as the Imperial regime right if they wander, and thus he again emphasized the right of his Conservative party to criticize not only the Prussian Minister President, but the Imperial Chancellor as well.[23]

Both the Centre Party speaker, Dr. Bell, and the National Liberal speaker, Dr. Schiffer, agreed with Herr Heydebrand that the Prussian lower house had the right to criticize Bethmann-Hollweg as Reichs-Chancellor. Dr. Bell stated that the Zabern case had brought out important questions for the future: one, what were the rights of the soldier and officer and, two, when and under what circumstances could military authority take over police-power? There also had to be uniformity of law; for instance, in the Zabern Affair there had been Bavarian contingents in Alsace-Lorraine and the Prussian Cabinet Order of 1820 could not apply to them. This situation could not be maintained in the future. As far as the position of Prussia within the Empire was concerned, the Centre Party had in 1871 made its position very clear and this still applied: the interests of one state must not dominate the whole Empire.[24]

The National Liberals shared these views. Representative Schiffer explained that the problem had several aspects, one of which had been stated by Centre Deputy Dr. Bell, who had asked whether states- rights or Imperial power should dominate.[25] However, he introduced one which had been brought up by the Imperial Chancellor concerning whether in his position as the Prussian Minister-President he should represent Prussia in lieu of his position as Imperial German Chancellor when affairs in the Empire affected Prussia.   Deputy Schiffer supported the attitude of Bethmann-Hollweg expressed in the upper house of the Prussian Diet on the tenth of January and in the lower house of the Diet on the thirteenth, that this situation of one position's blocking the other could not be endured.   Deputy Schiffer condemned Prussian particularism, and, with regard to the increasing animosity and opposition between the Prussians and the South Germans, he condemned the former for their one-sided "Borussian" attitude and the latter for wanting to eliminate all Prussian influence in the Empire.   He foresaw for the future of Germany the iron fist of Prussia and its strong will being complemented by the cultural superiority of South Germany in a bond that would unite the right mixture of Prussian iron and German blood.[26]

Bethmann-Hollweg was at a disadvantage when he answered the charges of Herr Heydebrand because he had been elsewhere during much of that deputy's speech.   His reply, therefore, was couched in rather general terms and was more in the nature of an appeal to the representatives to soften the condemnations of him as weak and vacillating and without strength of purpose.   The events and the decisions regarding them, he said had cost him many sleepless nights due to his anxiety over the question of whether he had been serving the best interests of the people of the German Empire.   When the countless newspapers had condemned Prussia and Prussianism he, just as they, had been very annoyed for he too was Prussian.   He insisted however, as he had on the tenth and thirteenth of January, that bringing the Imperial affairs before this <u>Landtag</u> was a serious business and improper.   It also was serious and improper for the members of the House of Representatives to bring an Imperial official, Imperial Secretary of State Kuhn, into the controversy over the property taxation because of the possible damage that the remarks made by such an official might have upon his future usefulness to the Empire.   He could not believe that Herr Kuhn had criticized the Bassermann-Erzberger bill in a derogatory manner.

Concerning the property tax dispute, he acknowledged that his former statement that "the Conservative Graf von Westarp had declared the government finance bill for the army budget unacceptable" had been incorrect.   "Unacceptable" was a word, he says, that he had used in the heat of argumentation.   It was true, just as Herr Heydebrand had said, that the Conservative Count von Westarp had stated that the government bill would be a basis for further work by the Conservatives.   On the other hand, the fact that the Conservatives had not given him the support when he had needed it made him despair of future support. His assumption at that time had been reinforced by the memory of what the Conservative Dr. Oertel had said on a former occasion that "with us, the point of view is always the same when it comes to a property tax--"no"--and he had assumed that this would be the case in the property tax government bill of 1913. The fact that not one party came to the support of the proffered government bill had been very discouraging, and it had been tactical error on the part of the Conservatives in the Reichstag that, when they had seen all other parties aligned against it, they had not supported it.

With regard to his acceptance of the Bassermann-Erzberger Bill, which gave tremendous strength to the army through the provision of much money and new divisions of soldiers, he said that he believed this to be far too important in a national German Imperial sense to have given it up. The element of time had been too important for him to have rejected all that army finance bill which had been supported by every party except the Conservative Party, for if the army bill had not been put through by the first of October of 1913, then at least a half if not a whole year would have been lost and in the circumstances of that time, he had believed it absolutely necessary for the security of Germany that he accept it as it was.[27]

Among the myriad of protests coming from all over Germany in opposition to the application in Zabern of the 1820 Cabinet Order of Prussia, which allowed the military the right to intervene in the jurisdiction of the civil authorities, were those of Free Conservative Dr. Moyna. Delivered in the Prussian House of Representatives on the fifteenth of January, these protests were that he and his colleagues of the Reichs Partei hoped that a Cabinet Order from a pre-Constitutional time, which did not even agree with the Prussian Constitution in spirit or in sense, would not have legal validity. Thus Dr. Moyna stated the party opinion that denied the right of Prussian Army to have adopted this Cabinet Order as part of the service orders in 1851 when the Prussian Constitution had gone into effect.[28]

Statements in newspapers had indicated that the Interpellations that were to come up on the same day as Dr. Moyna's speech would be at least equally condemnatory of the application of the 1820 Cabinet Orders to the Zabern crisis as well as to any other crisis in this time. They had been placed first on the agenda of the Reichstag, but discussion had been postponed by the Secretary of State for the Interior because the Imperial Chancellor could not have dealt with them until the proceedings against the officers had been settled. There remained at that time still a right of appeal to a higher court, and this either had to be made or abandoned; in the latter case there had to be time allowed for the judgements to go into effect.[29]

On the fifteenth of January, the Nord Deutsche Allgemeine Zeitung published some of the many criticisms of the Cabinet Order of 1820. An example of this was the speech given in the Bavarian Chamber of Deputies by Dr. Mullerhof, a National Liberal, the arguments of which showed his complete opposition to this Cabinet Order which could no longer be applicable once the German Empire had been formed. He stated that in this void Imperial law-making had to step in and Bavaria had to propose a legal change so that Prussia's laws would not be accepted without comment or opposition. The Bavarian Minister of War equally disapproved the Cabinet Order of 1820. He declared that in Bavaria, at least, there could not be the slightest authorization for military action which might in any way interfere with civil authorities.[30]

South Germany was especially insistent on the illegality of the Cabinet Order. In the lower house of the Alsace-Lorraine parliament, Herr Knopfler and Herr Mahl on the fourteenth of January declared use of the Cabinet Order in the Empire without justification.[31] Vorwärts as early as the tenth of January printed an account of an interview with a staff officer, who had said that any officer knew that the 1820 Cabinet Order was no longer valid.[32] Indeed, from not only the south but from all over Germany came letters, newspaper articles, and other expressions of opinion indicating to the Emperor, the Imperial Chancellor, and other members of the government rejecting the Cabinet Order of 1820 as an Imperial service order.

The effect of pressure on the Emperor and the government was seen on the fifteenth of January when the Nord Deutsche Allgemeine Zeitung published a more or less official announcement concerning the verdicts of the Strasburg courts martial. The announcement was that the verdicts of the courts martial of acquittal for Lieutenant von Forstner and Colonel von Reuter would not be appealed by the Commander of the Strasburg Military District, General von Deimling, because of the very slight chance that such an appeal would succeed illegally in view of the fact that, in the case of Lieutenant von Forstner, the accused had not gone beyond the limits of self-defense, and therefore the law did not allow a reconsideration of the evidence. In the case of Colonel von Reuter, according to the court he either had been acting in good faith or believed he had been so acting according to the Cabinet Order of 1820, which had given him the right to interfere, and therefore he had been acting according to an acknowledged principle of the law and could not be punished. There could be no appeal against the verdict of the court on the basis that the 1820 Cabinet Order was Prussian because it had been included in the service order of 1899 for the Imperial army concerning the usage of weapons by the military and had been reprinted in all service orders since having been included in the Prussian service orders of 1851. There never had been in the years since that time any question concerning these orders. However, because there had been aroused during and after the Zabern Affair some doubt as to whether the order of 1899 defined the power of the civil and military authorities, the Emperor-King ordered a re-examination of the service orders in 1914![33]

The decision of the commanding officer at Strasburg, General von Deimling, not to appeal, was a justification of the actions of the military in the Zabern Affair in the past, while on the same day, the fourteenth of January, the Emperor announced that the future would be taken care of as far as the future application of the service orders were concerned by his statement published in the Nord Deutsche Allgemeine Zeitung that he intended to have the service orders re-examined. For the present what was achieved by the combination of justification of the past and provision for the future was that the government hoped for a period of quiet and calm in which the inflamed passions of public opinion would cool down. In his remarks in the Prussian House of Representatives, the Imperial-- Chancellor emphasized that there had been too much criticism of him and the government and stated that as of this date, the fifteenth of January, he had the support of the King and Emperor for his actions and when he did not or when he felt he could no longer serve the Empire, he would resign.[34]

An important factor in calming the passionate public opinion was the replacement of the Zabern Affair as the most important issue in the news-papers by other events.   Dr. Moyna in the Prussian House of Representatives on the fifteenth of January and many conservative newspapers had stated that what was causing trouble, generally, and what had caused the trouble over Zabern were the newspapers.[35]   It was perhaps with this in mind that Bethmann-Hollweg refused to answer the Reichstag Interpellations and postponed them three times until the twenty-third of January, ten days after they had been introduced. In the interim he could "persuade" the leaders of the parties, except for the parties of the Left, that considering the tremendous disruption that occurred and the great criticism both foreign and internal that had been engendered, it was in the interests of Germany and all concerned that the Zabern Affair be dropped.

It is possible that all of this might have been planned or at least explained to all concerned at the fourteenth of January meeting of the Emperor, the Imperial-Chancellor, the Minister of War, the Chief of the General Staff and the head of the Imperial Military Cabinet.   The speeches in the Prussian House of Representatives seemed to express a new approach which might have been formulated at this meeting. The change was obvious. Conciliation seemed to be the new tack of the Imperial regime. The Emperor had stated he would re-examine the service orders, the Reichs-Chancellor had admitted being wrong concerning Count von Westarp and had shown his deep concern as a Prussian for Prussian and Imperial affairs with an almost pathetic appeal to the Prussian House for sympathy and understanding of the difficulties. He had pled for a sense of responsibility which would make it impossible, however much they might have differed in their views, for them to produce a state of affairs which, in times of anxiety like the present, could imperil the Fatherland. Conciliation was definitely the thought of the Imperial regime. In his remarks in the upper house of the Prussian Diet on the tenth of January, and in his speech in the lower house on the thirteenth of January Bethmann-Hollweg had shown that the mood of the government had been antagonistic to criticism, that the Landtag had not even the right to discuss Imperial affairs. In his speeches in the Reichstag, as well as in those of the Minister of War, the mood of the government had been antagonistic to criticism. Indeed, antagonism had steadily increased since the fourth of December. The one exception to this had occurred in the early speeches before the Chancellor had been in consultation with the Emperor and before he had been informed of the governmental position. At that time he had said that the injustice in Zabern would be rectified.[36]

The attempt of Bethmann-Hollweg and the government to placate the conservatives did not achieve much success. As early as the eighteenth of January, one of the worst and most offensive examples of Prussian particularism erupted in the form of an organization which called itself the Preussenbund. It was established in Berlin as part of the reaction against both the Zabern Affair and anti-Prussianism that had developed throughout the German Empire. Its formation was a result of the Zabern Affair. The Preussenbund sent telegrams to Colonel von Reuter, the Prussian Minister of War, and the Emperor announcing its formation and its particularist goals of Prussian nationalism and Prussian domination within the Empire. It showed dislike of the Imperial-Chancellor and Prussian Minister President, von Bethmann-Hollweg, by omitting him from the list of those to whom it sent telegrams.

The speakers at this first meeting included such avid Prussian conservatives as Herr Heydebrand, who gave an inflammatory speech condemning both Bethmann-Hollweg and the Reichstag for attempting to lessen if not to eliminate the power of Prussia within the Empire through weakening its army. Retired officers and Evangelical clergy joined the chorus with resounding condemnation not merely of Bethmann-Hollweg,

THE REACTION TO THE VERDICT   157

but of the socialist-dominated Reichstag.[37]

In an open letter published in the <u>Allgemeine Zeitung</u> of Munich on the seventeenth of January, Dr. W. Freiherr von Pechmann explained why he wanted to join the <u>Preussenbund</u>. He joined not because of the particularism but because the Bund embodied the ethos of <u>Preussentum</u>, the party of history, of Bismarck, Moltke, and Roon, and because the democratic and socialist elements were polarizing Germany. Even his own party, the National Liberal, no longer represented his beliefs but was associated too much with the Social Democrats.[38] The latter point of Dr. Pechmann's very likely referred to the Old National Liberal Party of Bavaria, which, under Dr. Quidde, who had given the antimilitarist-Prussian speech in the Bavarian Landtag on the first of December,[39] and with Herr Casselmann had linked the party with democracy for the next Landtag election with the statement that the National Liberal Party would no longer be placed on the firing line against Social Democracy.[40] On the other hand, there had been much condemnation of the National Liberal Party by some of its members for Social-Democratic tendencies like those exhibited by Herr Bassermann in the Reichstag in December. Dr. Pechmann might, therefore, have been referring to the National Liberal Party in Bavaria itself. An example of this criticism was reported in the <u>Deutsche Tageszeitung</u> as early as the ninth of January. It quoted the Westphalian National Liberal Journal, <u>Goester Kreisblatt</u>, as saying that the army had been in difficult circumstances in Zabern and that for the second time the liberal faction in the Reichstag had served as the stepping stone to social democracy. The author condemned the National Liberals for not being national spirited Germans in the no-confidence vote of the fourth of December.[41]

In the same issue of the Munich <u>Allgemeine Zeitung</u> with Dr. Pechmann's open letter, appeared an article called "new Goals of State Development, Political Study." The author, Dr. Walther Schucking, Professor of Law at the University of Marburg, condemned Prussian particularism as its own worst enemy. By placing this article right after the letter of Dr. Pechmann, the National Liberal Munich <u>Allgemeine Zeitung</u>, in effect, replied to that letter. Dr. Schucking urged the people of Germany to put aside their apathy and express their political convictions. He stated that he was not a political dogmatist, that all citizens should participate in the political life of the country.[42]

One of the most important results of the speeches given at the <u>Preussenbund</u> Conference was the antagonism it engendered throughout all Germany outside Prussia. The speech given on the eighteenth of January by General Kracht especially aroused anger. According to the conservative <u>Deutsche Tageszeitung</u>, the Prussian general spoke of the

Battle of Orleans where the Bavarians had run away from the enemy in the Franco-Prussian War of 1870, and said that it was only when the Prussian army had come and saved them that the Bavarians had finally recovered their courage and returned. This derision of the Bavarian army was not taken lightly by the people of southern Germany. The Deutsche Tageszeitung criticized the radical press for making so much of the speech, but the account of the speech by this journal itself showed clearly that General Kracht had spoken contemptuously of the army of one of the federal states of the German Empire.[43] Such remarks could not be taken lightly in Bavaria and they were not. The Munich Allgemeine Zeitung protested strongly against the statement with a letter from one writer asserting that there had been no Prussians at all aiding Bavaria and that the only Germans present had been Hanoverians and Saxons.[44]

The Bayerische Staatszeitung, the Bavarian government organ, published a formal protest. The Bavarian House of Representatives and the Reichsrat (upper house) of Bavaria as well were filled with stormy protests not only against General Kracht's insult but also against Dr. Pechmann's assumption that one was not born Prussian but could become Prussian in heart, an assertion that the leader of the Preussenbund, Dr. Rocke, said illustrated the Prussian spirit even if Dr. Peckmann had, unfortunately, not been born in Prussia.[45]

General Kracht, in an attempt to smooth over the ruffled feelings brought about by his Preussenbund speech, wrote a letter to the Prussian Minister of War in which he explained that he had not meant to insult the Bavarians at all but merely sought to bring out the comradeship and good feeling between the Prussian and Bavarian armies. Although published in the Bayerische Staatszeitung, this letter did little to abate the storm of antagonism which had developed in Bavaria. Indeed, in the lower house of the Bavarian Diet representatives of all the parties condemned the whole spirit of the particularist movement and the language used by General Kracht in front of the Preussenbund meeting which questioned the loyalty and courage of the Bavarian army.[46]

Just as important in maintaining the surge of conservative reaction was the speech of Herr Schwerin-Lowitz at the Conservative Party Conference at Stettin on the twenty-second of January. This speech contained a formal conservative condemnation of the growing democratic tendencies, established as the first task of the conservatives a battle against the development of democracy in Germany and stated that this could only be accomplished by a battle-ready governmental regime.[47] The speaker emphasized the need for readiness on the part of the Kaiser and his regime to fight democracy, and he implied that the regime was not ready. He made quite clear that the peace-making attitude of Bethmann-Hollweg in the Prussian House of Representatives had not been accepted on the terms and under the conditions offered.

NOTES

[1]Stenographische berichte uber die Verhandlungen des Preussischen Hauses der Herren, hereafter cited as Verhandlungen des Herrenhaus, Session 1914/1915, p. 25.

[2]Ibid., pp. 38-45.

[3]The report of the trials and the judgements is from a number of newspapers which do not differ in great detail. These report on various dates from January 10 to 12, 1914. These include conservatives - Deutsche TagesZeitung, the Norddeutsche Allgemeine Zeitung; the National Liberal Allgemeine Zeitung from Munich; the liberal Berliner Tageblatt; and the equally liberal Frankfurter Zeitung.

[4]Deutsche Tageszeitung, January 11, 1914.

[5]Berliner Tageblatt, January 10, 1914.

[6]Deutsche Tageszeitung, January 11, 1914.

[7]Ibid.

[8]Berliner Tageblatt, January 12, 1914.

[9]Deutsche Tageszeitung, January 12, 1914.

[10]Allgemeine Zeitung of Munich, January 10, 1914.

[11]Deutsche Tageszeitung, January 12, 1914.

[12]See above, pp. 106-107 for Reichstag position of National Liberals. Here he refers to the clear illegalities for which Colonel von Reuter had been responsible.

[13]Deutsche Tageszeitung, January 12, 1914.

[14]Documents relating to the Origins of World War I, ed., E.T.S. Dugdale (New York: Harper and Bros., 1931), XXXIX, pp. 305-307.

[15]Soldateska means militarism, soldier brutality and forceful and egotistical dominance of soldiery over civilians and subordinates among the ranks.

[16]Deutsche Tageszeitung, January 11, 1914.

[17]Le Temps, January 11, 1914.

[18]Allgemeine Zeitung, Munich, January 12, 1914.

[19]Verhandlungen des Preussische Hauses der Abgeordneten, I, 118-123.

[20]He had expressly declared in the Reichstag on December 4 that he had not followed the military report. See above, pp. 69.

[21]Verhandlungen des Preussische Hauses des Abgeordneten, I, p. 122.

[22]Ibid., I, 140ff.

[23]Ibid., pp. 247ff.

[24]Ibid.

[25]Ibid., pp. 266-283.

[26]Ibid., pp. 283-309.

[27]Ibid., I, 309-314.

[28]Ibid.

[29]Verhandlungen des Reichstags, January 15, 1914, p. 6517.

[30]Nord Deutsche Allgemeine Zeitung, January 15, 1914. The provision for Bavarian independent army control is in the 1871 Constitution, Article No. 68, the King of Bavaria must agree to army use and change. Some other states including Saxony have similar provisions.

[31]Allgemeine Zeitung of Munich, January 17, 1914.

[32]Vorwärts, January 10, 1914.

[33]Nord Deutsche Allgemeine Zeitung, January 15, 1914.

[34]Verhandlungen des Preussischen Hauses der Abgeordneten, pp. 306-9.

[35]Ibid., pp. 309-314. See also the conservative Deutsche Tageszeitung, January 10-15, 1914.

[36]See above, pp. 68-69.

[37]Deutsche Tageszeitung, January 19, 1914.

[38]Allgemeine Zeitung, January 17, 1914.

[39]See above, pp. 123-124.

[40]Deutsche Tageszeitung, January 12, 1914.

[41]Ibid., January 9, 1914.

[42]Allgemeine Zeitung of Munich, January 17, 1914.

[43]Deutsche Tageszeitung, January 19, 1914.

[44]Allgemeine Zeitung of Munich, January 19, 1914.

[45]Schulthess, Deutsche Geschichtskalendar, p. 41, January 19, 1914.

[46]Ibid., January 19, 1914, p. 40.

[47]Schulthess, Deutsche Geschichtskalendar, January 22, 1914, p. 51.

CHAPTER VIII

THE ZABERN INTERPELLATIONS IN THE REICHSTAG

The Interpellations about Zabern were placed in the Reichstag by the Radical, Social Democratic, and Alsatian deputies on the fourteenth of January. Generally, they dealt with illegal military action in Zabern, questioned the legality of the Strasburg trials and condemned the attitude toward the Reichstag and the German Empire of both Houses of the Prussian Landtag. Indeed, on this latter point, the President of the Reichstag, Herr Kaempf, had opened the proceedings of that body in 1914 by formally protesting against the accusations of the Prussian Upper House deputy Count Yorck von Wartenberg which had been made on the tenth of January. President Kaempf stated that the Diets of the States of the German Empire had just as much right to criticize the proceedings of the Reichstag as the Reichstag had to criticize the proceedings of the Diets. To charge the Reichstag, however, with having no national spirit, was an insult, especially when such a charge was made concerning the "levy" which had been adopted by an enormous majority in the Reichstag in order to promote the good of the Empire. To this insult he objected most strenuously.[1]

It was expected that the Interpellations would be answered soon but this was not to be the case. Each day that the Reichstag met, the Interpellations were postponed until finally, nine days later, on the twenty-third of January, the Imperial Chancellor heard and answered them. In the meantime, it was said,[2] he sought out all the leaders of the parties in the Reichstag and asked for cooperation in dropping this subject so dangerous to the tranquillity of the internal as well as external relations of the German Empire. That he was successful in getting the cooperation of all the parties except the socialists is demonstrated not only by the outcome of the debate on the twenty-third of January, but also from his speech on that date in answer to the Interpellations before any of the parties had discussed them. He stated that the path for the future of Germany and of the Reichstag was not to go on digging into the wound left by the Zabern Affair but to heal it.[3] With this, all parties except the Socialists applauded him. Their reaction pointed to the assumption that he had consulted and reached agreement with all but the Socialists before the debate began; nine days earlier, as was shown in the preceding chapter, not one party would have agreed with him. On the other hand foreign opposition and vitriolic condemnation of Prussian-German militarism had not been greeted with acceptance throughout Germany. Such criticism had weakened some of the more strident opposing arguments voiced against Prussian elitism.

Deputy Frank began the Social Democratic Interpellation about Zabern. The significance of Frank's remarks went far beyond his mere repetition of what every Social Democratic journal in the German Empire had been saying since the Strasburg trials, namely, that those trials had been a farce of the military judging the military; none other than a prejudiced decision had been expected from the outset. He offered a careful and logical argument based on history. In discussing the Cabinet Order of 1820, he pointed out that it was the fruit of the most debased period in German history, when the princes had been determined to destroy any vestige of liberal or democratic feeling left over from the Napoleonic revolutionary era. In order to do so, they had first made laws severely restricting students in 1820 and then had issued this Cabinet Order to enforce these restrictions whereby the military could step into a town or area in which authority was weak and assume the executive authority. Both sets of orders had been acts of oppression and both had been negated by the Constitution of 1850, which had created a new Prussia with the intention of establishing a limited representative government.

Dr. Frank represented, so he says, the Social Democrats who were imbued with the spirit of sacrifice of the War of Liberation and because of this spirit had passed the army finance bill in honor of its Centennial celebration last year. However, he mentioned that the Centennial celebration of 1913 offered a sad commentary on what the heroes of the War of Liberation had gained; the 1820 Cabinet Order was typical of the repression of that time, and the fact that it was still in use today was an equally sad commentary on the present. He continued with the suggestion that illegally and without any right whatsoever the military had included the 1820 Cabinet Order in the Service Orders of 1851 in order to maintain a strong-arm control for the possible destruction of that limited representative government which the military had opposed since its inception.

Furthermore, Dr. Frank continued, the inclusion of the 1820 Cabinet

Order in the 1899 service orders had been absolutely unwarranted since the Empire had more than one army; this order could only be imposed upon the Prussian Army; it was not Imperial in jurisdiction and especially could not have been applied in Alsace-Lorraine where the civil authorities had expressly stated that no military interference was wanted or needed. He denied that any civil disturbance of sufficient significance existed to warrant introduction of martial law unless one would interpret whistles and cat-calls as civil disturbance.

Dr. Frank asserted that the point made by the trial-jurists that the law of the army went in the knapsacks of the soldiers was equally unwarranted. Many of the soldiers in Alsace-Lorraine were not Prussian and did not belong to the Prussian army. Should they have to obey a non-Imperial order which was not accepted by their state? No![4]

Yet, Representative Frank's remarks extended to issues beyond the Zabern Affair although they were aggravated and made more important by that Affair. One such issue that he most adamantly addressed was that concerning the constitutional rights of the people. Would the Constitution of the German Empire rule that Empire or would the military rule? If the latter, Germany would regress instead of experiencing the progress that had been anticipated with the former. This question was to him more important than whether culprits were imprisoned or decorated.[5]

As a member of the Social Democratic party he represented the anti-revolutionary revisionist wing that dominated the party at this time. Of course the doctrine of "revolution" was not completely repudiated by his emphasis on working within the Constitution for more power for the Reichstag. When Representative Frank was speaking of the Crown Prince's telegram to General von Deimling and the one to Colonel von Reuter in which he supposedly said "Immer feste druff," meaning "continue forcefully in the same way," he did threaten action of a revolutionary nature. He was not sure that the Crown Prince could have written that; according to content and style it was worthy of Herr von Oldenburg-Januschau, politically without meaning although politically unhealthy and intolerable. For the Social Democrats, however, the telegram was beneficial for it would awaken hundreds of thousands of Germans out of their lethargy who would say that if the future German Kaiser continued in intimate friendship with those who condemned the Constitution and the haters of the free state, it would be necessary for the people themselves to take their fate into their own hands.[6] Even here, however, Dr. Frank did not refer directly to the Social Democrats leading a revolution but to a spontaneous revolution which would be advantage-ous to the goals of the Social Democrats. Throughout his speech he played down the Socialist part of the cognomen Social Democrat and emphasized his party's democratic role. While showing that the middle class parties were afraid of conservatives, he quoted Herr Scheidemann's statement that the conservatives were no longer secure and could only continue to exist by marrying into the middle class for money. The President of the Reichstag interrupted and told him to relate his remarks to the Interpellation on Zabern as this was, he assumed, the subject of that Interpellation. The Dr. quickly countered with the remark that the President was very much deceived if that was what he thought; his Interpellation concerned what Zabern represented, what both the Social Democrats and the Progressive People's Party most wanted, constitutional rights. What they wanted was the application of the majority will against such injustice that the Zabern Affair represented and against the unconstitutionality of applying the defunct Cabinet Order of Prussia to the German Empire. They wanted the representatives of the people to stay on the floor and fight for justice.[7]

Dr. Frank, who spoke for the Social Democrats and the Progressive People's Party, did not consider Bethmann-Hollweg as the primary enemy or as a threat to the constitution but as a neophyte who had been knowingly or unknowingly exploited by the real government of the German Empire, the officers and high military authorities who constituted the military Cabal. Thus Bethmann-Hollweg's actions, according to him, came as a result of political necessity, not from any thought of justice, which was an ideal alien to the members of the Cabal. He cited as evidence the advice of Herr Witting to Bethmann-Hollweg to this effect in the Krupp affair and, more recently, the advice of Herr Rochling. This advice along with pressure from Potsdam had led to the latest attempt to placate the angry but hesitant middle classes, who shrank from earnest battles, by announcing in the Nord Deutsche Allgemeine Zeitung that the Kaiser would re-examine the 1820 and 1899 army regulations.[8] Although, he predicted that nothing would come of the re-examination but a gain of time for the government, he was equally condemnatory of the conservative reaction to the re-examination, one of terror. The conservative aristocracy had raised cries in the Kreuzzeitung, and in the Deutsche Tageszeitung, that even to consider such a step as that of modifying the Cabinet Order of 1820 or the service regulations of 1899 would automatically put an end to Prussia.[9]

Dr. Frank adduced evidence from the history of past such "re-examination" that nothing would be done about the army regulations. This was evident, he says, in the promise of the Kaiser in his King's speech of 1908 that the Prussian Electoral system would be reformed; today the aristocrats laughed and stated that history was in no hurry. Another example could be found in the request of the Reichstag just after it had passed the greatest army bill of all time last year that the army practice of creating officers be examined in order to determine why all officers were aristocrats. The answer had been "no." When the Reichstag passed a resolution against continued proliferation of guard-corps, the government answered that any such change would require that political and economic interests be taken into consideration.[10] Certainly no illusions could be held that anything could be accomplished in attempting a change in the Constitution although, he said, the Social Democrats were quite willing to cooperate in an attempt.[11]

Concerning the particularism resulting from the Zabern Affair and the recent division of opinion in Germany which had resulted therefrom, Dr. Frank pointed to the origin of this feeling in the encouragement of the Conservatives in the Prussian Landtag by Herr von Jagow and by the Crown Prince. As a result, he said the Landtag had raged against the Alsatian Constitution, against the property tax in the Empire, against the reform of the Prussian electoral rights, and had demonstrated that they wanted to continue the conservative gentleman-class society. The members of the Landtag had asserted, according to Dr. Frank, that they had sought to protect the control of the Kaiser over the Empire, but in reality they had wanted to perpetuate their own privilege.[12] Regarding the insults to the Bavarian army by the Preussenbund and the program of the Preussenbund for curbing the actions of officials of the Empire, for insulting the South Germans, and attacking the Imperial Constitution, he asked the Reichs-Chancellor what he intended to do to prevent the destruction of the unity of the German Empire. How would he prevent some other North German Reuter, Forstner, or Schad from committing similar encroachments on Imperial interests when he had already promised to both houses of the Landtag that he would manage Imperial politics in the spirit of Prussianism? Dr. Frank stated that these promises would do no good for the aristocrats wanted more; they wanted someone who would chase the Reichstag to the devil, they want someone who would force the conflict to a head, they wanted someone, as Herr Heydebrand had said, who would make a revolution that could be put down bloodily.[13] With regard to the tendencies toward dividing Germany, he insisted that the only way that the Empire could remain united was by the unified action of the Reichstag under the Constitution, and that this could only come about if the middle class forgot the defeats of the last fifty years by the Conservatives in the Prussian Landtag and regained its faith in itself. The Conservatives had become increasingly weaker and the middle class increasingly stronger, thus unity could only be maintained if the middle class gave up its defeatist attitude and stood up within the Reichstag for justice and the constitution.[14]

Here, Dr. Frank was trying to counter the attempts made in the preceding ten days by the Imperial-Chancellor to placate the National Liberals and the Centre Party and to dispel fear among these parties of the potential revolutionary activities of the ultra-conservative Preussenbund and the equally divisive activities of the Landtag of Prussia. He pled for the parties under the constitution to cooperate and thereby to weaken what would naturally be the argument of the opposition, that the Social Democratic party was the party of revolution, of anti-monarchy, of anti-constitutional government. His goal was to show that the Conservative Party was the party of revolution, not the cooperative Social Democratic Party.

Concerning the constitutions of both Prussia and of the various Federal States, Dr. Liszt, a member of the Progressive People's Party from Glogow, made a very careful and professionally legal study of the relationship of army regulations, including the taking-away of the executive authority from the civil authorities by the military, and the provisions for such abdication of executive authority within these constitutions. He stated that his purpose was to avoid repetition of what has been said by his colleague, Dr. Frank, in his own speech for the Interpellation of Payer and associates regarding the maintaining of unity within the German Empire. He did so in order not to stir up but to heal the wounds and make possible the future advance of peace within Germany.

Dr. Liszt began by emphasizing the enormity of the problem which faced Germany at that time. A trivial occurrence in the town of Zabern had released a flood which was drowning all of Germany. The triviality of its origins, however, had not in any way cast doubt upon the gravity of the vote of no confidence by the Progressive People's Party on the fourth of December. He stated that this party was just as ready and even more ready to cast the same vote as it had in December. The outcome of the trials and indeed the whole course of events since the fourth of December had convinced his party more than ever that the vote it had given in 1913 had been correct then and was just as valid now in 1914.[15] Yet the affair that had begun in Zabern and had spread to Alsace-Lorraine no longer was isolated to that area but had engulfed the whole Empire. In the Landtags of Baden and Wurttemburg Interpellations had been registered concerning the Affair and its repercussions. In Bavaria everyone had involved himself in the Affair and in the Prussian Landtag it had been extensively discussed. The Prussian Upper House had even insulted the Reichstag over the Affair and the Reichstag President, Dr. Kaempf, had rejected these insults in a calm and dignified manner.[16]

Dr. Liszt, even more than Dr. Frank, abandoned the purely party viewpoint on the Zabern Affair. He said that if it had followed its principles his party would have been very happy over the proceedings of the <u>Preussenbund,</u> but that his party did not assert itself on that standpoint and indeed went so far as to state with deepest regret and vivid pain that what had never happened before in the time since the founding of the Empire had now occurred. The boundary line[17] between North and South Germany had been deeply underlined through the opposition which had been aroused over the insults to South Germany; in general relations between North and South had been embittered and poisoned by the developments during this great war-anniversary year. The result had come, he said, from the failure of the military authorities to discipline a little lieutenant. The feelings of the whole population had become inflamed. Indeed, the conflagration was no longer confined to Germany alone, for outside her boundaries the foreign press had reacted to the waves of agitation within the Empire, and his party had seen with deep pain its foreign friends mourn, and its enemies with unconcealed malicious joy point to the events of Zabern and to the divisions among the Germans.[18]

Dr. Liszt's central thought for the future concerned how to prevent such a catastrophe from recurring. He believed that the military regulations had to be examined and rewritten. He therefore had as the main theme of his speech the military law. He examined in detail all the related cabinet orders and laws in Prussia, Baden, Wurttemburg, Bavaria, and found no basis for military intervention in civil affairs without the consent of the civil authorities as long as they existed. He stated that although the military regulations might be changed they could be changed again and the only way to prevent a recurrence of another Zabern Affair was to give to Alsace-Lorraine the status of independent federal state within the Empire of Germany.[19] In pursuance of the goal of changing the military regulations he presented to the Reichstag a bill to define the circumstances under which the military could take over civil authority; they had to be requested to do so by the civil authority.

Dr. Liszt's bill was actually unconstitutional; the Emperor as King of Prussia had complete control over the army. It was also unconstitutional in that a bill could not be introduced into the Reichstag, by any party within the Reichstag. By introducing the bill he was emphasizing that the Reichstag had the right and the power to determine the laws under which the military act, and thus he was shifting the center of authority over the military from Prussia, Bavaria, and other privileged states and their rulers to the Reichstag and promulgating a new constitution that would have to be adopted for this parliamentary government which he was introducing.

Dr. Liszt and his party directed their Interpellation not against the Imperial-Chancellor, with whom he and his party expected to work in cooperation in the future, nor against the army or the country's nobility insofar as it was a people's nobility serving to protect the people with self-sacrifice and devotion, although the party emphasized the necessity of regulating that army to prevent mistakes and to rectify injustices. His Interpellation was not against Prussia; his party wanted a strong Prussia but a Prussia that realized the equal rights and equal value of the other members of the Federation of States. Indeed, concerning Prussia's importance, he condemned the Preussenbund as unrepresentative of the Prussian spirit. This spirit could be found in the words of King Friedrich William IV, "Prussia will henceforth rise in Germany" and, the deputy continued, not in the swaggering miles gloriosus who rattled his sabre and distorted the true spirit of Prussia that arose in 1806 when the people's militia had been drawn into the War of Liberation and had produced the great Prussian spirit that had conquered in 1813. The Interpellation was also not aimed against the commanding power and the rights of the Crown, a claim so often brought forward in the past as a favorite trick of the aristocracy to confuse issues. In this manner they often played off monarchy against democracy and vice-versa. He stated that anyone who had any logical sense or who had studied the development of the monarchy knew that it had not been democracy that had offered the prime opposition to the monarchy; it had been the aristocracy. There had been constitutional democratic monarchs many times in history. The aristocracy had used the supposed threat of democracy to the monarchy as a pretense to fight for their own power and economic privileges and right. His Interpellation was against domestic unrest and the resulting division of Germany; he and his party wanted peace and surcease from the Zabern Affair and all of the trouble which threatened and deranged Germany creating a gulf between the civil and military authorities and between the North and the South of Germany.[20]

The Reichs-Chancellor's reply to the Interpellations began with the observation that it was obviously necessary to establish very clearly in what cases the military should intervene in disturbances. He agreed with the findings put forth by Dr. Liszt that the principle that, as a rule, the military could intervene only upon the demand of the civil authorities was the constitutional law as far as he knew in all states and at any rate in Prussia. The Prussian Constitution specifically stated that in exceptional cases a demand from the civil authorities was not necessary. Otherwise the Constitution would not have reserved the subject for special legislation. As Dr. Liszt had said, he, Bethmann-Hollweg recognized that this legislation had never been passed, and the question therefore arose whether the military was always and in all circumstances unable to intervene on its own initiative except in cases of self-defense, war or declaration of martial law, in cases where they had to remove obstacles to the performance of military duties, and finally in cases in which the civil authorities were overpowered or were for other reasons unable to appeal for help. According to him, these military rights were recognized and based on the principle that a state could not renounce the right to defeat all menaces to the foundation of the state by any available means. The military orders regarding the use of arms and the cooperation of the military in the suppression of disturbances had been formulated in 1899, and there had been no possible doubt that it had been the responsibility of Colonel von Reuter to follow these instructions without examining their legality.[21] Throughout these remarks the Reichs-Chancellor had received enthusiastic support in the form of repeated shouts of "Quite right" from the National Liberals.

Concerning the Cabinet Order of 1820, he stated that criticism had been directed solely to the fact that the instructions of 1899 in certain of their provisions lacked the necessary basis in law, and especially where they adduced the Cabinet Order of 1820. It had not been the whole of this Cabinet Order that had been subject to criticism by Dr. Liszt and others, but only the clause of it which had laid down the right of the military to intervene if the civil authorities were too slow in requiring their assistance and in cases in which their own forces no longer sufficed. This then was the real matter of dispute between him and Dr. Liszt. Since 1820 the only case in which this provision had been applied was the Zabern case. The military court at Strasburg had regarded it as beyond question that the service orders of 1899 had been binding upon the military. It was not their business, he said, to consider whether the Cabinet Order of 1820 had legal sanction or not. However, considering the doubts about whether the Cabinet Order was well founded on the principles of the Constitution, in the statute book, and in the general principles of law, the Emperor had commanded that there should be an inquiry. He said, in a rather terminating-the-whole-thing manner, that everything therefore had been done that could be done at the present. He hope it would be possible under the service regulations for the different contingents belonging to units from the various Imperial states to have uniform regulations on all vital points throughout all the Imperial provinces.[22]

After this rather perfunctory dealing with the future of the military authority, the Chancellor turned to the political results of the conflict over the service orders. He said that the service orders had been described throughout the country as monstrous and as proof that Germany lived under sabre rule. This allegation was not true because the only case in which the provisions had been applied had been in the Zabern case. He hoped that the country would refuse to exaggerate and generalize from a case which had aroused stormy seas enough to drown a whole nation. It was evident that a great deal had to be done in the provinces to restore normal conditions, but he had to protest against the accusations that the Zabern case was typical of relations between the military and the civil authority. The Zabern case had been a local event which had arisen in the first place from personal differences. This had been brought out clearly in the Strasburg trials. There ought not to be drawn any other conclusion from the events than that the provinces could not flourish except under a calm, uniform and just, but at the same time firm, policy. The recent attempts to create differences between the North and the South had to be nipped in the bud. Not one of the federal states could exist outside of the united German Empire. The Empire was entitled to the best that each state had to give; their fathers had shed their blood in loyal comradeship-all of them with the same enthusiasm, the same devotion, and the same courage.[23]

The Imperial-Chancellor then turned to the pressing problem of placating Bavaria over the recent insults of the Preussenbund. He paid a tribute to Bavaria by his declaration that the Imperial idea was just as strong there as elsewhere. The battle fields of Worth, Weissenberg, Bazeilles, the bloody fights around Orleans had proclaimed what Bavarian soldiers in the year 1870 had accomplished, just as all battles of that year had reflected the united courage of all German states.[24]

This plea for unity having been made, he now turned to attacking those whom he thought had opposed such unity. He emphasized that it was senseless to continue digging in the wound that had been created by the Zabern Affair. It was imperative that this division in German unity be healed. The Social Democratic Party had disagreed with him, and he turned upon its members with seemingly fresh enthusiasm, condemning them as the destroyers of Germany in the future and citing as proof a recent article from their newspaper, Vorwärts, which had given as the Social Democratic program: elimination of the military courts, revolutionary democratization of the whole army, removal of the Imperial power of command, institution of a democratic militia army.[25] He went on to condemn the Social Democrats for these revolutionary goals as well as their misuse of the faith that people of the nation had in law and order as a means to stir up agitation over their claims that lawlessness and disorder had characterized the Zabern Affair.

Another scapegoat for the troubles of the last few months the Chancellor found in the foreign press and the use of that press as a weapon against the government by the Social Democrats. He said that the foreign press characterized Germany as a country of outworn, decaying conditions where the sword suppressed the peaceful citizen. The foreign journalists, he said, were too smart to level these accusations at Germany without having had some direction from others. In fact, they had received their information from the Social Democratic press and also, in a large part, from the Radical press.[26] The Social Democratic newspapers printed the remarks of the foreign newspapers as a lever for changing the present situation. He stated that he followed the foreign press very closely, but he knew of no foreign country in which the opposition in its struggle with the government used the foreign press comments to strengthen their position against the government.[27]

Thus he initiated his plea for nationalistic love of Germany and he concluded his speech by strongly praising the sacrifices of the German army under which Germany had become a bulwark of European peace for a whole generation and had made such enormous progress. He emphasized German pride and belief in a people's army, keeping the nation young and healthy by absorbing the whole German youth and filling it with a sense of duty, loyalty, pride and love of the Empire. These virtues, he emphasized, would be needed if Germany was to maintain its place in the world. They should not be abandoned because in a single place in the great Empire things had happened which every one of them hoped would not happen again.[28] His speech brought forth lively applause from the conservatives and from the National Liberals, while hisses from the Social Democrats and Radicals.

NOTES

[1]Verhandlungen des Reichstags, 292, p. 6490. The "levy" is the Army Budget Finance Bill of June, 1913.

[2]Paul Lensch, "Schluss mit Zabern," in Neuezeit, 32 Jg., 1913/14, I, p. 641ff. As cited in Kurt Stenkewitz, Immer feste Druff: Zabern Affare, 1913 (Berlin: Rutten und Loening, 1962), p. 140.

[3]Verhandlungen des Reichstags, 292, p. 6751.

[4]Ibid., pp. 6732-6734.

[5]Ibid., p. 6738. The decoration mentioned above was that of the Red Eagle given to Colonel von Reuter on January 21 by the Kaiser as one part of the traditional yearly decorating of those who have served a certain amount of time in the army and reflected more the value of medals than it did a conscious decoration for valor or good service.

[6]Ibid., p. 6736.

[7]Ibid., p. 6739.

[8]Ibid., p. 6731.

[9]Ibid.

[10]Ibid., p. 6732.

[11]Ibid., p. 6733.

[12]Ibid., p. 6736.

[13]Ibid., p. 6738.

[14]Ibid., p. 6739.

[15]Ibid., p. 6740.

[16]Ibid., p. 6741.

[17]Mainlinie is translated boundary line.

[18]Verhandlungen des Reichstags, 292, p. 6741.

[19]Ibid., p. 6747.

[20]Ibid., pp. 6748-6749.

[21]Ibid., pp. 6749-6759.

[22]Ibid., p. 6750.

[23]Ibid., p. 6750.

[24]Ibid., p. 6751.

[25]Ibid., p. 6751.

[26]This is rather a "stock" condemnation of the Social Democratic and foreign press responsibility for disruption. It could be called the "official explanation." The Reichs-Chancellor's remarks seem almost as if they had been copied from the Deutsche Tageszeitung of January 11, 1914.

[27]Verhandlungen des Reichstags, 292, 6752.

[28]Ibid., p. 6752.

CHAPTER IX

REACTIONS TO THE INTERPELLATIONS

In the discussion of the Interpellations, Deputy Fehrenbach of the Centre Party spoke first. He stated emphatically that what he had said against the Reichs-Chancellor on the third of December he still maintained. However, what the Imperial Chancellor had said this day concerning the healing rather than digging into the wound created by the Zabern Affair had received the approval of his friends and he too agreed. He assumed that the government would do all in its power to help heal the sick body that was Germany at that time.

Although he agreed with Bethmann-Hollweg in theory that the wound should be healed instead of irritated, Fehrenbach's practice seemed quite opposed to the theory, especially concerning the insults that had been aimed at the Reichstag. However, his acid criticism extended to other fields as well and, although he spoke of the great disruptions that had struck Germany and said that they must be stopped for they were tearing apart the basic fibre of the people, yet he managed to condemn the military and the military court system, Prussia, the Preussenbund, Alsace-Lorraine-nationalism and its sometimes lax civil administration, and generally all critics of the Reichstag and particularly those of the no-confidence vote of the third of December. He first castigated Professor Roethe of Berlin University for having said "What an Imperial Diet we have been forced to watch! This Reichstag had the nerve to hand out votes of no confidence based on newspaper flummery and demagogic talk, and now it would take these votes back begging on its knees." He went on to say that Professor Roethe was quite mistaken if he thought that he would retract one word of what he had said on the third of December in the name of his friends.[1] Indeed, there had not been restitution to Alsace-Lorraine since that time, as there should have been, and also the military court trials had given the false impression that the

177

tumultuous scenes and riots in Alsace-Lorraine had happened out of the blue without any military provocation. This had not been the case. All the circumstances that he had described in detail in December had been preceded by serious insults of all of the people of Alsace.[2]

He had much to say on the actual events of the Zabern Affair including the trial at Strasburg in January. From his investigation he had concluded that there had been no inner unrest in Zabern, as the military had claimed, but that the actions of the people had been knavish pranks on the part of a few individuals. On the other hand, he criticized Zabern because he believed that either the will of the people or the civil power could have prevented the situation from developing as it had. Particularly with regard to the civil authority, it had been admitted by Herr Mahl at the Strasburg trial that he had had dinner with General von Deimling when on the twenty-sixth of November news had come that there had been trouble in Zabern and he had refused to leave despite the fact that a special train had been offered him. This, Herr Fehrenbach considered inappropriate behavior. He also condemned the biased verdict of the courts at Strasburg, although he was quick to point out that such a generalization as that of Dr. Frank, "that all military courts would be easy on the military," was wrong. He, himself, had served as counsel for the defense at several trials which he was sure would have gone much easier on the officers if they had been held before civil judges instead of military judges.[3] He tried to explain away the mistakes of the Strasburg trials by saying that these had happened in civil trials as well. On the other hand, he was quite in agreement with both Dr. Frank and Dr. Liszt that self-defense had been an impossible justification for Lieutenant von Forstner to have taken during the second trial and the verdict wrong and obviously political. He pointed out that Colonel von Reuter had been an honorable and courageous man to have accepted the blame for everything that had been done by his subordinates, but that Dr. Liszt had been right in condemning von Reuter for his accusations against the civil-judicial persons and against the postal administration. As for the verdict he said that it had the force of law, although this was regrettable and that there was nothing that could be done without giving up all respect for law. He hoped in the future that there would not be the predictions by the court of "verdicts of not guilty" and that there would not be telegrams of congratulation afterwards, since these tended to upset the people's confidence in justice.[4]

Concerning the legal question, he was in agreement with the Reichs-Chancellor, Dr. Frank and Dr. Liszt that there needed to be changes in the law to demarcate the line between civil and military authority, and he was quite in agreement with the suggestions of Dr. Frank and the very detailed examination and proposals by Dr. Liszt that there should be legislative action on this. The majority of the great legal scholars was convinced that the Cabinet Order of 1820 and the service regulations of 1899 were invalid and therefore it had been illegal to use them in the trial of Colonel von Reuter as sources of authority. This uncertainty had to be removed. Dissimilarity in the law among the various contingents of the Federal States was the result, and this had to be removed. Territorial rights had to be respected as they had been originally in the beginnings of the Empire when Baden in 1872 had made military agreements with Prussia and there the interference of the military in civil matters had been allowed only upon the request of the civil authorities. This case proved that no one had thought of regulations in Prussia where the military could step in without being called upon by the civil authorities. This, he advocated, should be the principle used in the forthcoming new legislative enactments. Although he agreed with Dr. Liszt and the National Liberal Party as well that there needed to be a conclusive regulation encompassing the whole Empire and weighing the rights of the civil authority carefully, when it came to the means of enacting this legislation he disagreed with Dr. Liszt that it should be done through the Reichstag. Although there was no doubt in his mind that the Reichstag was competent to legislate in this case, he believed that no one should interfere in the rights of the individual states to determine this matter. He emphasized that all states should set up regulations which would guarantee similar regulations throughout the German army. He pointedly suggested that this had to be done soon for although only one case of the use of the Cabinet Order of 1820 had been recorded, nevertheless a quick-tempered lieutenant might do anything.[5]

Regarding the future of Alsace-Lorraine, he believed that the Alsatians should be satisfied that the Reichstag was a responsible organization looking out for their interests. As to the demands of the second chamber of Alsace-Lorraine, he stated that the first demand, the demarcation between powers of civil and military authorities, would come to pass; the second, a reform of the military court system, he believed that all of Germany wanted, and it would be achieved; the third, federal statehood for Alsace-Lorraine, would take time and would depend on the solution to the problem of excessive nationalism within Alsace-Lorraine. In the meantime, Alsace-Lorraine would have to be satisfied with the constitution she had.[6]

With regard to Prussian particularism and the militaristic spirit of Prussia as was shown at the meeting of the Preussenbund in Berlin, he emphasized that there had to be a German army which could be watched and trusted by the people and it should be responsible to the people. The outbursts of Lieutenant General Wrochem at the Preussenbund congress, according to Fehrenbach, indicated a spirit which had to be eliminated from the army. Herr Wrochem had said that a terrible danger was hovering over our army and if the rabble of all the classes were victorious-there was a mob in all classes-"the heart of our Monarch would be pierced."[7] Herr Fehrenbach saw this as an attitude of weakness, for the individuals within the army ought to be able to be criticized without this criticism's being considered as a condemnation of the whole army.

Concerning the power of command, which the Conservatives had complained was being destroyed, Herr Fehrenbach referred to the remarks of Count Yorck von Wartenburg in the Prussian Upper House as typical of an attitude used with some success on both suitable and unsuitable occasions since the end of the Reichstag meeting in 1906. the Count had considered as an intervention in the Imperial Supreme Command the resolution of the Reichstag to replace active with inactive officers, the change of the present pension plan, the use of inactive officers as commanders, and the renunciation of adjutants by princes. Concerning these and also General Wrochem's remarks that Erzberger's reforms were daring and impudent attacks on the army, Herr Fehrenbach stated that his colleague Erzberger ahd been only attempting to improve the finances and pensions of the military, and that for the most part the items listed above concerned the budget, that even the refusal to allow three new cavalry regiments was involved with the budget. When the refusal of a budget demand became intervention in the power of command, one might as well be as absurd as to say that the demands of the government, simply by setting up a budget, also constituted interference with the power of command. At this latter remark some deputies in the Reichstag said "Quite right," and general hilarity erupted in the Center. Fehrenbach concluded that if this were carried to the extreme, the end result would be pure absolutism.[8]

Of late the Reichstag had come under a good deal of criticism, according to Herr Fehrenbach, and he is quite opposed to this as detrimental to the representatives of the people who must act together for the benefit of the nation. Recently, he stated, a member of the Prussian House of Representatives had said concerning the budget finance bill that the people's representatives in the Reichstag could go to the Devil. With regard to the army finance bill Fehrenbach remarked that the Prussians had no reason to complain when the Prussian paid in direct taxes only nine Marks per head while the citizen of Baden paid fifteen. He implied that the Reichstag was interested in the protection of Germany but that the Prussians were not or they would not have opposed the finance bill. Even the military did not seem to be interested in protecting Germany, he implied, for, if they were, members like Lieutenant General Wrochem would not be flying into a towering rage and calling the Reichstag names because of the military bill passed six months earlier, and conservatives like Dr. Yorck von Wartenburg would not state that the bill must not be passed without critical debate. How could anyone say that who wanted to protect the German Empire with blood and material support? Words like those of Dr. Yorck, he continued, built an indestructible wall between northeastern Prussia and the rest of Germany. He asked if that were necessary? Such words were fitting for beer-hall speeches, but not for Berlin, where they were heard with joy by foreign countries. He condemned the Prussians for the worst particularism and was cheered by both left and center when he stated emphatically that this was not the way to serve the fatherland, nor was it patriotic to oppose the protection of the country by opposing the army bill. He concluded his speech with a plea both against particularism, whether northern or southern, and for a united Germany.[9]

Herr Bassermann, representing the National Liberals, approved the performance of the Imperial-Chancellor and supported him despite the fact that the demarcation line between the civil and military authority had not yet been drawn. He appealed to all to unite in healing the wounds as the Imperial-Chancellor had asked and not to provoke trouble. He and his party friends had complete confidence in the Imperial-Chancellor both for his support of the power of the Emperor and for his love for the army.

The Imperial-Chancellor had stated, according to Herr Basserman, that he had been watching the foreign press and that through the false propaganda of the Social Democrats it had been receiving the impression that the sabre ruled in Germany. This press also had an erroneous belief, stated Herr Bassermann, that by repressing the power of the Emperor, Germany would be handed over to Parliamentary rule. This showed the fear of the Conservatives which Dr. Frank had tried to dispel. One thing neither they nor the Social Democrats had learned was that throughout all of the upsetting events of the Zabern Affair and its aftermath, the solidarity of the army with the middle class had not been shaken. That could be seen in the army bill of the preceding year and it was hoped that this bill would strengthen the army and that there would be no gulf between officers and men. The middle class had increasingly been working for the officers as was shown by the increasing number of officers allowed to be on leave of absence from the army as a consequence of middle class temporary replacements. Military mistakes were diminishing in number and the officer was not only the leader but also the comrade of the men.[10]

With regard to Dr. Frank's criticism of him earlier, Herr Bassermann suggested that his way, which was opposed to both the radical left and right, like Cordelia's in King Lear, was the right way. Both the right and the left had reproaches from the National Liberals for supporting a strong army bill the previous year, in 1912 and in 1911. He did not, however, reproach the majority of the Reichstag because they did not have the heart nor the understanding of the need for a strong army. He rebuked his colleague, Herr Fehrenbach, for the critical statement he had made and approved more than ever the remark of Bismarck on June 14, 1882, that:

> the German military organization, which through respect and antipathy binds together our well-led battalions with our well-taught intelligence, is the foundation of the political future. We must not weaken the army.[11]

Regarding the accusation thrown at the National Liberals during the last month and a half that the vote of mistrust against the Imperial-Chancellor constituted a blow against the army, Herr Bassermann used extensive quotations to show that the National Liberals had been neutral and in the vote of mistrust had referred only to a specific incident at a specific time and that this in no way had constituted either a blow against the army or disruption of the power of command by the Emperor. He quoted Dr. von Calker in the Reichstag on the third of December and von Rochling in the Prussian House of Representatives of the thirteenth of January, 1914, to show that the vote of mistrust had been against neither the army nor the civil power. He even pointed out that Herr Rochling had shown that the Imperial-Chancellor had put off the decision in order to decide what was politically necessary and that this might even be a positive virtue. As for the accusation made by the Conservatives that the Reichstag had destroyed the command power of the Kaiser, he cited the Handbook for the Army and Navy[12] from the year 1913 which defined the command power as partially composed of the decisions of the Reichstag and that the budget power of the Reichstag, the legal competence of the Reichstag as a factor in law giving, which they highly esteemed, was considered part of that power of command; the Reichstag had the power to approve or disapprove every request for money for the army.[13]

Concerning the Strasburg trials and the legality of Cabinet Order of 1820, Herr Bassermann agreed with Herr Fehrenbach that the court decision had the force of law, but he denied that the Reichstag could pass on the legality of the Cabinet Order. He cited the various authorities both pro and con and was content to leave any changes that should be made with respect to the Order to the Emperor; unlike Herr Fehrenbach he did not stress the need for uniformity among the Federated States.[14]

Concerning Alsace-Lorraine, he was also in basic agreement with Herr Fehrenbach. He emphasized that there were two sides to the problems there and that both sides seemed to have been guilty of illegality. He condemned more emphatically than Herr Fehrenbach the nationalistic excesses in Alsace-Lorraine and declared that the past had shown these provinces to be untrustworthy and that their future had to depend on their Germanization. He accepted the decision of the court in the Reuter case that the civil authorities had been lax in the administration of their police duties. He was much more critical of the civil authorities in Zabern than Herr Fehrenbach had been. This was seen by his emphasis on the necessity for a more vigorous civil authority to be maintained in Alsace-Lorraine; one which would energetically carry out its duties in an authoritative manner.

On the other hand, Bassermann upheld as much as Herr Fehrenbach the power of the Reichstag. He brought up the speech made by Count von Schwerin at the Stettin Conservative Party Conference in which Schwerin admonished all the elements in Germany who supported a German government that would be established on the basis of constitutional monarchy. Herr Bassermann emphatically supported a constitutional monarchy-form of government for Germany. He stated that his party wished that the Reichstag be treated and esteemed as a real part of the Constitution so that the legislation of the Reichstag would have real meaning with regard to the Constitution. According to him, the Constitution appertained to the Reichstag and when von Wrochem denounced this body using such words to describe it as "gang," "mixed society" and other expressions, he could only regret that the Reichstag representatives who were at the Prussian conference (Preussentag) had not replied to this slander by recalling that throughout this year of 1913 the Reichstag had celebrated this bicentennial of 1813 by passing the army bill and the budget. He condemned the Prussian anti-Reichstag attitude that divided Germany. He also castigated the people who grew angry over the expanding role of the Reichstag, stating that its importance would increase because of the growing demands on the nation and because of the necessity of financing the new army bill in the face of so few means for doing so. Concerning means, he supported the army-finance bill's property tax by quoting both Herr von Heydebrand and Count von Westarp, both of whom had advocated such a tax in 1911 for the financing of the army. He thus condemned the Right for opposing the property tax bill in 1913, and so acting contrary to their own words of two years before.[15]

Concerning the Preussenbund, Herr Bassermann agreed with those who had condemned it for insulting and slandering the Reichstag and Imperial institutions. He insisted that the National Liberals were just as anxious as those who composed the Preussenbund that a strong Prussia and a strong Prussian army be maintained within the German Empire, but he was equally insistent that the Reichstag had to protect the nation against those insulting and slandering Imperial institutions. The people were condemning the particularistic attitude of the Preussenbund in Diets all throughout the Empire and, he emphasized, he stood with them in support of that Empire. The great development of Germany had taken place only because of the cooperation of two elements, the Regime and the Parliament. Without this cooperation he believed no such development could have taken place nor would it take place in the future. In world politics and colonial development it had been the cooperation of these two elements which had provided for the development of German strength through the power of the Navy and the Army. He hoped that the thought of the Empire would in future increasingly permeate Alsace-Lorraine.[16]

The Conservative Representative, Count von Westarp, was condemnatory, like Herr Bassermann, of the nationalistic elements growing in importance in Alsace-Lorraine. Unlike Herr Bassermann, however, he added democratic elements to the list of those condemned. It was against these elements that the army had to be supported in the provinces. He stated that the acts of a lieutenant had been unjustly exploited and that Colonel von Reuter had acted rightly in protecting him and had shown the fine Prussian tradition in doing so. He condemned the Social Democrats for trying to undermine both the army and the loyalty of the soldier to his outfit.[17]

With regard to the intervention of the military in civil affairs, Westarp stated that in the absence of an Imperial law concerning the actions of the army, the military had to follow the laws of the individual states. He did not recognize that the Reichstag had any right to discuss the drafting of any Imperial laws on this subject, since the right to legislate belonged to the individual states.

Concerning the power of command mentioned by Fehrenbach, Westarp and his party considered that power to be infringed upon when the army contingent leaders were subject to the legislation of the Empire and not to the power of command of the individual states. It was also disruptive of the power of command when the Reichstag construed its authority in such a way as to diminish the responsibility of the Imperial-Chancellor and the Minister of War. He attacked the Social Democrats, the Alsatians and the Progressive People's Party representatives for this and especially for trying to regulate the army leadership by means of Imperial law, which he regarded as the worst inroad on the power of command. He condemned both Fehrenbach and Bassermann for linking the question of the power of command with the Zabern Affair and the army budget finance bill; between these matters he saw only a loose connection, and therefore, he refused to offer the Conservative views on the budget finance bill for the army.[18]

Although Count Westarp denied that the Preussenbund and also the Preussentag were organizations of the Conservative Party, he asserted that they represented opinions not altogether to be ignored. Particularly important here was the view that the powers of the monarch of Prussia were being lessened while this Prussian King William's Imperial powers grew in importance. This objective, he stated, was especially sought by the Social Democrats and the Progressive People's Party representatives.

In his concluding remarks, Count von Westarp appealed in the name of the Conservatives for maintaining the Imperial constitution as it was. He stated that the Conservatives had every desire to support the Empire but not at the expense of encroachments on the power of the individual states. The rights of these individual states had to be preserved in a Federal type of constitutional state like that of the Empire, but the goal of the Conservatives was not only to protect the Empire and the Constitution but also to protect and preserve the exceptional position of Prussia within that Empire which was guaranteed by the Constitution.[19]

Representative Schultz of the Imperial party, another conservative, compared the present Reichstag attitude with that of the third and the fourth of December and found the former to be completely different. Since that time, he said, with the exception of the Social Democrats, the Reichstag members seemed to have become cautious. He implied that the furor had not been lessened but had been pushed in a different direction, in the direction of questioning the demarcation between the power of command (Kommandogewalt) and civil power. According to him, the country was not pleased that the Reichstag criticized its army on the third and fourth of December. The no-confidence vote given at that time had been in reality an unconstitutional attack not on the Imperial-Chancellor, who supposedly had been held responsible for the events in Zabern, but against the army.[20] It had not been cast against the individuals of the army who were a part of the actual events of Zabern but against the spirit that ruled in the army, and this latter view was what was believed by the people in the country today. He implied that the third and fourth of December had been days when the passions of all parties had been caught up in the impassioned oratory of the Social Democrats and had voted the mistrust vote under the influence of the accusations of military dictatorship and praetorianism leveled at the army because of the events in Zabern; thus under this influence they had actually voted against the spirit of the army rather than against the Chancellor. Schultz implied that they had now changed their opinion, now that the courts martial at Strasburg had revealed the unbelievable difficulties the soldiers had encountered in their relationships with the Westmark (Alsace).

Concerning the character of Colonel von Reuter, Schultz's comments were most commendatory, and to show that they reflected not only his own German view, but others, he cited the words of a French army officer writing in the conservative French journal, La France Militaire. This French officer lauded Colonel Reuter for taking upon himself the responsibility for all that his subordinates had done and asked rhetorically how many French officers would have done the same. Schultz concluded that this conduct showed not only the universally recognized fine character of Colonel von Reuter but also the fine leadership within the German army.[21]

On the subject of the Cabinet Order of 1820, he, like Count von Westarp, believed that the subject should not have been discussed in the Reichstag because this body had no authority either to change or to criticize it. However, and also in agreement with Count von Westarp, Schultz followed the views of Professor Laband, who had said in the upper chamber of the Alsace-Lorraine Diet that the Cabinet Order had been legal according to Article thirty-six of the Prussian Constitution and had applied to Alsace-Lorraine since the law of the twenty-third of January, 1872. According to Professor Laband, as cited by Herr Schultz, there had been no civil authority in Zabern at that time and that this law's stipulation that the military could intervene in case of inner unrest without the request of the civil authorities when these authorities were either unable to bring about or too slow to request such intervention had been shown to be valid by the many voices in the last weeks and months within Alsace-Lorraine inimical to Germany. Schultz therefore accused those had who voted mistrust on the fourth of December of giving the impression to the French Alsatian nationalists that the Reichstag was on their side. He condemned the two houses of the Alsace-Lorraine Diet, which had called the army rule "military dictatorship," as enemy voices and declared that they and the introduction of the constitution of Alsace-Lorraine were part of a great plan for victory of the nationalistic-French party. Here, as elsewhere in his remarks, he was interrupted by calls of "quite right" from the right. In condemning the Constitution of Alsace-Lorraine he was condemning the Imperial-Chancellor, indirectly, as the latter had introduced it, but this was in opposition to his opening remark in his speech of this day when he had said that many had said wrongly, he thought, that the Right had just as much if not more reason to vote a declaration of mistrust against the Chancellor as the other parties of the

Reichstag had had.[22]   Yet, the Right had voted a disagreement with the Chancellor and it had condemned this Constitution in the past also in the Prussian Landtag.

Despite what Herr Schultz and Count von Westarp had to say, all the other parties in the Reichstag on this twenty-third of January, 1913, were in favor of an extension of the role of the Reichstag in government, although the National Liberals emphasized that this had to be in harmony with a constitutional Monarchy-type of Empire with cooperation between Reichstag and Kaiser, with perhaps more federalism under the Kaiser and decentralization of power to the individual states.

The Radical Party position, given by Dr. Friedrich Naumann, deplored the weakness of the Reichstag and stated that the Left in general favored a parliamentary type of government not subordinated to any other branch of the government. He asked the members why the Reichstag sat at all or passed resolutions, if it merely threw them in the wastebasket. His solution was to enhance the power of the Reichstag. Its power at that time, he said, was as void as that of what was called "a house of echoes" and those who devoted themselves to it merely frustrated themselves in futile gestures. The Reichstag could do no more than accept and amend laws, criticize and control the administration at varied points and here and there bring about an improvement or repress an overzealous policeman who illegally attended a meeting. It could even regulate many things as an aid in carrying out the everyday administration of the nation, but it did not in any way play an important part in German history.[23]

With regard to Herr Schultz's suggestion that the vote of mistrust was aimed not at the Chancellor but the German army, Herr Naumann emphasized that there was more to keeping the internal order of a country than seeing that regulations were carried out. He suggested that if a lieutenant and a colonel were to act in Baden, Wurttemburg, or Bavaria, as they had in Zabern, the result would have been disastrous for them. What he suggested was that the army have more respect for civilians. If it were a people's army, why had it not more respect for the people? The people of Zabern had been called the masses, but they were, after all, the fathers, brothers, and sisters of those who made up the nation in arms; they were the people on whose enterprise and industry rested the entire system of the military. He castigated the attitude of Dr. von Jagow who had called Alsace-Lorraine almost enemy country and emphasized that the officers must not play a political role and decide whether blood will flow or not, for if they did, they would be regarded as foreign elements, not as a people's army.

Returning to his original thought, Dr. Naumann stated that the question today was whether force was to be united with intelligence and humanity in the German army, whether the people of Germany possessed mind as well as power. Colonel von Reuter, to Dr. Naumann, represented the latter and was indicative of the political soldier's order of values. He was therefore applauded from all over Germany by those who wanted to break down the democratized order of society, as being the epitome of the real soldier who stood by regulations and suffered "no nonsense" from civilians.[24]

With regard to the relationship between Prussia and the Empire, he showed that the Prussians were nervously aware that Prussia was losing power as a state to the Empire. This was shown, he implied, by the speech of Count Yorck von Wartenburg in the upper chamber and by that of Herr von Heydebrand in the lower chamber of the Prussian Diet in which they warned the Imperial Chancellor not to be too imperial, not to show too much feeling for the Empire, for Prussia was the basis of the Empire. This supposition Dr. Naumann was quite ready to admit, but the Empire had changed in that it had advanced far beyond its original condition during the preceding fifty years and had become strong, more German, and less Prussian. The Prussians asked how could Prussianism survive, he said, and the day that Bismarck foretold in 1877 had now come, when there would be an Imperial Finance Minister whose enemy was the Prussian Finance Minister. The uneasy tension of the Prussians would continue as they observed that their former certainty that Prussianism would be carried out by the Imperial Finance Minister gave way to increasing doubt of this that they considered their birthright.[25]

The final speaker of the day, the Socialist Herr Ledebour, criticized the militarism of Herr Schultz and Count von Westarp, but his major criticism was of the Crown Prince. Like Dr. Frank, Herr Ledebour denounced the part played in the recent events by the future ruler of the German Empire, the Crown Prince. He castigated the sending of telegrams to the military in Strasburg and Zabern by the Crown Prince. He was equally condemnatory of his militaristic farewell message to his Danzig regiment, and his supposed friendship with the ultra conservative Herr von Oldenburg-Januschau. Ledebour accused the Crown Prince of friendship with those who opposed parliamentary government and who agitated for a coup d'état against the Constitution. Herr Ledebour emphatically declared that the monarchy was an obsolete institution, which was incompatible with the modern state, and that the spirit of the Crown Prince exemplified this incompatibility. His actions in sending two telegrams of encouragement to Colonel von Reuter had not been denied and even the Imperial Chancellor had admitted this; these telegrams had been sent at a time when legal proceedings had been started. The Crown Prince acted as if he had the monarchial privileges, whereas as the heir to the throne, he was entitled to no more privileges under law than anyone else.[26]

Since the Imperial Chancellor was absent at that time, Herr Ledebour was answered by Herr Delbruck, the Secretary of State for the Imperial Ministry of the Interior.   He stated that the Crown Prince had a natural reason for his friendship with Herr Oldenburg-Januschau, since he had been stationed at Danzig near the latter's home.   Herr Delbruck also criticized the Social Democrat for bringing the Crown Prince into the discussion as this was not customary in the Reichstag.   As far as the subject of the Crown Prince's spirited goodbyes to his troops were concerned, Herr Delbruck said that that lay outside the present discussion, although this sentimental attachment to his unit showed the fine spirit which lived within the German army and was well exemplified in the conduct of the Crown Prince and he was glad to see it.

The reactions of the opposing sides concerning the Zabern Affair had polarized on one issue. All but the Conservatives had become more insistent that the allegiance of all Germans should first be given to the Empire and that the various federated states should be given only secondary allegiance. The Prussian Army which had hithertoo been the German Army had to become now a German Imperial Army operating under an Imperial Constitution which guaranteed that the power of command over it be exercised through the budgetary powers of the Imperial Reichstag. In the midst of the polarized sides on the issue, the Reichs-Chancellor, Bethmann-Hollweg, was supported and yet criticized by both sides. On the other hand, his statements of foreign expressions of public opinion and their influence on the reputation of Germany had had the affect of influencing the opposing sides to find commen cause in pride in a united Germany. The question yet unanswered was "how to sew up the wounds of an injured Germany so that the patient will be more healthy than before the wound was acquired?" This question was still unanswered at the outbreak of World War I, seven and a half months later.

NOTES

[1]Verhandlungen des Reichstags, 292, p. 6753.
[2]Ibid.
[3]Ibid.
[4]Ibid.
[5]Ibid., p. 6755.
[6]Ibid., p. 6757.
[7]Ibid.
[8]Ibid.
[9]Ibid., p. 6759.
[10]Ibid.
[11]Ibid.
[12]Handbuch fur Heer und Flotte.
[13]Verhandlungen des Reichstags, 292, pp. 6760-6761.
[14]Ibid.
[15]Ibid., p. 6763.
[16]Ibid., p. 6764.
[17]Ibid., p. 6765.
[18]Ibid., p. 6766.
[19]Ibid., p. 6768.
[20]Verhandlungen des Reichstags, 292, p. 6769.
[21]Ibid.
[22]Ibid., p. 6768.
[23]Ibid., p. 6773.
[24]Ibid., p. 6774.
[25]Ibid., p. 6776.
[26]Ibid., pp. 6782-6785.

CHAPTER X

HEALING THE ZABERN WOUNDS?

The parties in the Reichstag on the twenty-third of January believed that it was time to stop digging in the wound created by the Zabern Affair and allow it time to heal. Yet, their verbal intentions were belied by their practices; without exception they continued to agitate the wound. The conservatives and the democratic parties acted at the radical extremes while the Centre and National Liberals parties were fearful of both these extremes; yet they did not regret nor deny their mistrust vote of the fourth of December, and they remained more critical of the right than of the left. Indeed, the newly emphasized issue of Prussian particularism had made them even more emphatically against Prussian domination of the Empire than normally and even more vigorous in supporting a strong Reichstag under a constitution. No party in the Reichstag on the twenty-third of January was satisfied with the Imperial Constitution; all advocated changing it, although no two parties agreed on the procedure nor on what the final version of a new constitution should be.

Nevertheless, a new Imperial Constitution would have pleased everyone. Yet, some, like the Social Democrats, were so disturbed that the Conservatives did not observe the present Constitution that they wondered if any Constitution would suffice. To them, the military wanted to rule the state and, supported by the Crown Prince[1] and his Constitution-hating cronies, were determined to bring about a coup d'état[2] eliminating any constitution forever. The main theme of Dr. Frank's Interpellation concerned the maintaining of constitutional rights.[3] Dr. Frank suggested that the Social Democrats were quite willing to aid the other parties in changing the Constitution.[4] On the other hand he asked the Imperial Chancellor what he would do to assure Imperial unity in the face of the scurrilous attacks by the members of the particularist Preussenbund. He encouraged the middle class to abandon the antiquated relics of the past

193

and to stand up for the Constitution.[5] Yet, the constitution to which he referred was one he imagined for the future, for it would have allowed the Reichstag to legislate on all matters pertaining to the army, and one under which the Reichstag's legislative power would have made it a governing body with power approaching that of the Kaiser. Yet, his implications were quite clear: the past would restrict Germany to a military-police state, while the future, in order to avoid the past, had to include participation of the Reichstag in a constitutional government cooperating with the Kaiser within an Imperial setting.

The Conservatives on the twenty-third of January criticized the Constitution on the ground that the Reichstag possessed too much budgetary and financial power already and that these powers were regulating army needs so much that this unconstitutional authority had stretched to legislating on such issues as whether cavalry regiments were even necessary. Furthermore, the Reichstag had been misled into suggesting legislation on what the pension or finances of an officer should be. This criticism of the Reichstag had gone so far that when Herr Fehrenbach of the Centre Party was speaking, he was interrupted by Conservative members' comments from the floor questioning whether the Reichstag had any right at all to set up or even consider an army budget, because such consideration would interfere with the power of command of the King of Prussia, the Emperor.[6] To the parties of the Right, any Imperial legislation or suggestion for it that might interfere with the leadership of the army was unconstitutional, whether such consideration involved the budget or a reform of the military law or of the military court system. This conception, which had been supported by Imperial Party Representative Schultz, however, was one which, like that of Dr. Frank's, would have required a change in the Constitution in order for it to apply.[7]

The Centre Party position on the Constitution, as stated by Deputy Fehrenbach assumed that the Reichstag had the power to legislate reform of the military law but preferred that this be left to the province of the federated states. His justification for this view was that the army had to be a trustworthy agent of the people and that the people had to have the power to watch it and control it, for it controled or protected all states and therefore should represent the participation and regulation of all the states. Therefore, the federated states had to meet and discuss the development of a uniform set of laws for such an army. Thus he too was advocating a change in the Constitution,[8] since he objected to the dominating role of Prussia and its King, the Kaiser, in the army. He opposed the Conservative's position which would not allow the Reichstag to replace leave-taking active officers with reserve (non-aristocratic) officers as commanders, a measure which the middle classes which dominated the inactive officer-list had urged for some time.[9] He emphasized that the power of the Reichstag to do all of this resided in the power of the purse.

The National Liberals voiced their desire for a constitutional change through the agency of a well-argued speech of Herr Bassermann. This speech went to the extreme position of demanding the introduction of a completely new form of government which would include a Constitutional Monarch under which the Reichstag would act as a parliamentary body with actual legislative initiation authority and a government that would be based on this cooperation between the Emperor and the Reichstag.[10]

That this issue inspired by the Zabern Affair was of immediate importance was demonstrated by the fact that this controversy over the power of the Reichstag within the Constitution or within a new Constitution was the major issue of the day and all other issues were connected with it or were made to relate to it. All parties except those of the Right were in agreement that the powers of the Reichstag should be expanded. Deputy Bassermann had stated that the individual states of the Empire could not cope with the demands of the modern state in this modern industrial, technologically mechanized world and that there had to be central direction for the needs of the navy and the army by an Imperial representative body. In the words of Deputy Naumann representing the Democrats, the Reichstag must no longer be a "House of Echoes."[11]

None of the parties on this day opposed a strong Prussia within the Empire. However, all except the conservative parties objected to militarism, dominance of military over civil law without justification, and Prussian particularism; and all these parties wished a reform of the military law. When Deputy von Westarp of the Conservatives had stated that the vote of mistrust had not been against the Imperial Chancellor but had been against the spirit of Prussia exemplified in the actions of Colonel von Reuter, he had been very near the truth.[12] Deputies Fehrenbach, Bassermann, Naumann, and Ledebour called for a people's army and Deputy Naumann expressly refuted Count von Westarp's view of Colonel von Reuter as an honorable man by stating that the army, if it were a people's army, had to respect the fathers, sons, daughters, and mothers of its members, unlike the behavior of Westarp's army which would be ready to kill any of them if necessary. His suggestions included the exclusion of officers from politics. On the other hand, Dr. Liszt of the Progressive People's party had said, when he had presented a bill to the Reichstag to reform the army laws, that he did not oppose the spirit of Prussia, that spirit which had fought the War of Liberation a hundred years before. But, he did oppose the new spirit; that of swaggering miles gloriosus represented by Colonel von Reuter and the members of the Preussenbund.[13] The Centre Party under Fehrenbach was equally condemnatory of this spirit of militarism shown by the <u>Preussenbund</u> member, General Wrochem, who had emphasized that the Reichstag sought to substitute mob rule over the army for that aristocratic rule which had preserved it in the past and which had defeated the great enemies of Germany by its spirit.[14]

The Zabern Affair revived Prussian nationalistic particularism which maintained that Prussia and the Prussian Junker-led army had a more important place within the Empire than other states and their armies. This was primarily because it had been the Prussian army that had led in the War of Liberation and had dominated other armies in the Franco-Prussian War that had unified the German states and had thus brought about the German Empire. On the other hand, the Imperial states, especially Bavaria and Saxony, found that these particularistic claims weakened their position within the Empire and questioned the viability of the developing institutions that were supposed to serve the Empire as a whole, rather than merely one part. All the parties in the Reichstag, except those of the right, were opposed to this inference that the inherent superiority of the Prussian aristocracy within the army as well as within the Empire should assure their dominance. While many members of the Reichstag, especially those from southern Germany, felt more closely associated with their states than with the relatively new German Empire, nevertheless, they were well aware that their state's interests were served better by the unity found in the Reichstag of the Empire than by their heart-felt ties to their "grass roots."

Old values survived in these "grass roots" areas, but the new modern spirit of the Reichstag seemed imminently preferable. While there was always the question from the old whether something or some idea was good just because it was new, nevertheless, technological development in this increasingly mechanized world had brought an increasingly literate population to realize that success came to those whose health allowed them the opportunity to educate themselves, go into business, acquire capital, invest it and use the dividends to purchase property. These middle-class values were in direct contrast to those associated with Prussian heredity, aristocratic domination of an officer corps; this was a way of life many believed to rooted in an antediluvian, medieval age in which rural feudal nobility protected the peasants on their estates. These antiquated assumptions no longer appealed to the possessors of modern middle-class values. It is with these views in mind that members of Centre, National Liberal and Social Democratic Parties regarded the very important issue of whether Prussian aristocratic officers and their values were to be maintained in control of the German army to the exclusion of middle-class officers, whose technical and educational expertise made them at least equal if not better officers than the Prussian Junkers. Dr. Frank asked whether Germany should remain backward in restriction or press forward to modern freedom of opportunity in a future Germany not hidebound by privilege. He quoted statements from the Prussian aristocratic views taken from the Kreuz-Zeitung and the Deutsche Tageszeitung to the effect that even to consider any modification, not to speak of the replacement, of the Cabinet Order of 1820 and the service regulations of 1899 would automatically destroy Prussia.[15] Dr. Frank attacked the military aristocracy for monopolizing the officer corps of the army and for not allowing non-aristocrats to become officers. He said that the aristocrats of Prussia even prevented reform in the Prussian electoral system which the middle-class had been wanting for so long and which they had been promised.[16] Nevertheless, the Junkers had maintained their gentlemen-class society.[17]

According to Dr. Frank, the Junkers weren't content with their society; they wanted even more. They wanted a revolution which would destroy the Reichstag and break up the Empire and its Constitution. In referring to the class conflict between the Junkers and the middle class, he stated that the only way in which Junkers would not be able to obtain their revolution was one wherein the middle-class overlooked the defeats of the last fifty years in the Prussian Landtag and united with the other parties for justice and the Constitution.[18]

Progressive People Party representative Dr. Liszt was quite proud of the service of the aristocracy to the Fatherland and its self-sacrifice, but he emphasized that it should be a people's aristocracy serving the people in the army and should be regulated by the representatives of the people in the Reichstag.[19] He attacked this aristocracy for using the claim "that the democrats usurped the power of command" as a device or tactic in order to play off the monarchy against democracy and vice-versa. Thus, he said, the aristocracy was trying to protect its power and economic privileges by this ruse, and further emphasized that this aristocracy was really the main enemy and opposition to the monarchy, as anyone who had ever studied constitutional history should have known.[20]

Centre Party Deputy Fehrenbach was quite in agreement with the view that the aristocracy exploited the issue of the power of command as a ruse, and he pointed to its use in the case of Herr Erzberger's attempt to help the military during the previous May. According to him, if Count Yorck von Wartenburg insisted that the replacement of active officers by inactive officers and the use of reserve officers as commanders was usurpation of the power of command, then he was denying the right of the Reichstag to carry out its constitutional budgetary powers. Fehrenbach asserted that the importance of this accusation of Count Yorck von

Wartenburg was that the reserve officers mostly were members of the middle classes and that the Count was trying to preserve the monopoly of the officer-corps by the Prussian aristocracy.[21]

Herr Bassermann, of the middle class-dominated National Liberal Party, implied that the values of the Junker aristocracy were not the values needed in the army that he believed necessary for the future of Germany. He stated that he and the other National Liberals were very much in support of the army, as their approval of the army bill had shown, but that the values of that army needed to include an ideal noticeably absent from the behavior of its officers. He hoped the Junker officers would cease the harsh and even brutal treatment of soldiers. Herr Bassermann hoped that there would be no gulf between soldiers and officers that had characterized the Prussian officer-led army. He cited the officer characteristics that had been described by Deputy Fehrenbach on the fourth of December from experiences he had had in the army which had included lack of officer courtesy toward and even extended to brutality to common soldiers. Then again, on the twenty-third of January Dr. Frank had cited actions running the gamut from mere discourtesy to brutality to soldiers. Herr Bassermann added that in the previous year in May the National Liberals had asked for an investigation of army officers and under-officer brutality toward common soldiers and recruits.[22] Attendant to and equally middle class in its expression of sentiment was the hope expressed by Herr Bassermann that there would be in the future German army a true spirit of comradeship between officers and men. He also indicated that the middle class had been working for the officers as was shown by the fact that there had been an increasing number of officers on leave of absence from the army.[23] What he did not mention, but what others had, was that there had been great resistance of the Junker officers to this practice because these officers on leave had been replaced by reserve officers of middle-class origin.[24]

What was clear from all these comments of the aristocracy was that the remarks in the Landtag of Prussia on the thirteenth and fourteenth of January, 1913 and especially of that aristocratic preserve, the House of Lords, had provoked the anger of the members of the Reichstag and had led to wholesale criticism of the Prussian aristocracy. Especially bringing common condemnations from the more liberal members of the Reichstag were the comments of Count von Westarp and Herr Schultz in the Reichstag, of Count Yorck von Wartenburg in the House of Lords of the Prussian Landtag, and Lieutenant General Wrochem at the Berlin meeting of the Preussenbund that had maintained Prussian particularism. Notably, they seemed to reflect the Prussian aristocracy's views that they, the Junkers, stood to lose the basis of their class system and the basis of their control of the political system through a combination of changing attitudes, all of which seemed to have been exacerbated by the Zabern Affair and brought to a head by the insolence of the Reichstag. First, that insolence had been shown by the Reichstag's emphasis on the Empire and the Imperial power of command dominating that power of the Prussian Monarch and thereby subject to the financial control of the Reichstag which assumed that the sacrosant Cabinet Order of 1820 should be modified or destroyed; second, the army budget bill had opened a mare's nest of reforms by the Reichstag that brought intervention in the control of the officer's wages, pensions and, in general, regulation of the Prussian Monarch-controlled army by a Reichstag appealing to the Emperor to replace the Prussian Monarch and make this army an Imperial army; third, the passage of this feared army budget bill had included a tax on property which the Prussian aristocracy would have great difficulty in paying and the non-payment of which would force the sale thereof thus causing the loss of voting privileges in the Prussian Landtag; the result of this would be the success of the long-sought middle class-led reform to eliminate the three class voting system of Prussia, which the aristocracy had always dominated because of its property ownership.   Thus, the middle class would become the ruling class in Prussia and the aristocracy might be subservient to the insufferable insolence of commoners.   The liberal members of the Reichstag had good reason to find common cause against the aristocratic assumptions of these privileged Junkers.

Obviously, one of the major issues that had been influential in encouraging the Reichstag to take its stand against the aristocracy of Prussia, that of the civil rights of the provincial people of Alsace-Lorraine, was no longer the central interest of those still engaged in the controversies emerging from the Zabern Affair. Both Deputies Fehrenbach and Bassermann had been critical of the nationalism present in Alsace-Lorraine and both had maintained that the decisions of the Strasburg trials had been established as unassailable legal decisions.   In this they were in agreement with the Conservative Party representative Schultz, but they could not possibly have common cause with his assertion that this nationalism had been linked with the subversive group advocating Franco-Alsatian nationalism. To Herr Schultz, Bethmann-Hollweg's phrase "heal the wound" meant that the Centre and National Liberal Parties in the Reichstag ought to drop their support of the Alsatian claims for justice concerning the Zabern related elements involving officers Reuter, Schad, and Forstner.   An important aspect of this interpretation of "heal the wound" was the assumption shared by Herr Schultz with Dr. von Jagow, police-chief of Berlin, and Dr. von Zedlitz, Deputy in the Prussian House of Representatives, that the Imperial Reichstag supported democratic elements within and reform of the army, for the passing of the army budget bill had demonstrated that, and therefore the Reichstag was opposed to that spirit of Prussia that should protect and therefore rule Germany. Yet, all other parties except the Conservative had insisted in the preceding year that they considered the passage of this bill both the height of Imperial German nationalism and indicative that the Empire still preserved that spirit of Prussia which history as well as the Kaiser's speeches had demonstrated was the core of the War of Liberation of 1813. Indeed, the Reichstag majority had linked this army bill with the future of the German Empire and thus by implication if the Conservatives attacked it they would be attacking the future of Imperial Germany and they had not anticipated that. But, they had been surprised as the Zabern Affair had brought out the latent conservative animosities, for not only did the conservatives condemn it, they also condemned the democratic tendencies of the Reichstag for even discussing the issue and, indeed, compounding the felony by addressing the issue and bringing it into public view in connection with the embarrassment of the Zabern Affair.[25]

Conservative reaction inspired the judgments in the Reuter, Schad trials and by the reversal in the Forstner appeal trial came to its highest point of opposition to the Empire in the debate over the Interpellations on the twenty-third of January. It had come a long way from the rather meek opposition to the Mistrust Vote before the first Forstner trial on the nineteenth of December. So vitriolic had the condemnations become by the twenty-third of January, that Imperial Chancellor Bethmann-Hollweg's reference to "nipping in the bud" the recent attempts to divide the Empire might be as much a reference to the conservatives, or at least the rabidly Prussian nationalistic Preussenbund wing therein, as it was to the Social Democratic Party. This development of such opposition leading to polarization might also be attributed to the Centre and National Liberal Parties. Social Democrat Dr. Frank illustrated the point in his quotation from the Reichstag speech of Herr Scheidemann of the tenth of December, 1913, that fear of the Conservatives by the middle-class parties had in the past prevented action despite broken promises by the latter.[26] He referred obliquely to the Centre Party but more directly to the National Liberals who had made their peace with the Conservatives after the Franco-Prussian War with great expectations, but had been prevented in the Prussian Landtag from gaining their goals, among them the liberal reform that would have changed the Prussian election law and thereby have given them more representation because of the anticipated elimination of the three-class voting system in Prussia. Yet, by the twenty-third of January this National Liberal peace with the Conservatives had been broken, for Herr Bassermann had openly deplored the nationalistic, Prussian particularism despite their intimidations.[27]

Both Herr Bassermann and Herr Fehrenbach opposed the suggestions of the Preussenbund that the Kaiser dissolve the Reichstag and that the Prussian Monarch stage a coup d'état. Such intimidations of its members by threats of the dissolution of the Reichstag were not even limited to the Preussenbund but existed in the Prussian Landtag in which a Conservative asked von Bethmann-Hollweg why he had not dismissed the Reichstag when this Imperial institution had passed the army budget finance bill in June, 1913.[28] Thus, the Imperial-Chancellor could with good reason have posed the threat that the Empire would be destroyed if there were no attempt to "heal the wound" by unification; and the destruction might very well have come from the Right as from the Left, for the ultras were in the lead among the Conservatives and Bethmann-Hollweg as well as the liberals were all condemned under the common label of socialist collaborators. Herr Schultz's[29] condemnation of the Alsatian Constitution of 1911 as being a victory for the nationalistic French party was also a condemnation of the Constitution's originator and most ardent supporter, the Imperial Chancellor, for being a French nationalist. Dr. Schultz had even gone so far as to imply that the middle-classes had been caught up in the same hands, for they had been the victims of both the impassioned oratory and the press reports of the socialists, and because of this and their weakness, they had passed the vote of mistrust.[30] This same middle-class vote had passed a Prussia-damaging army budget finance bill and then insisted on the uniformity of military law within the Empire, and this plus the Kaiser's examination of military orders gave fear to the Conservatives that the dominance of Prussian officers over the civil authorities had come to an end. This fear had an even greater motivation for if the cooperation of the Reichstag in the government made it a meaningful legislative body, the end of Prussian dominance in the German Empire would result. The Prussian Conservatives had great reasons to object strenuously to the annulment of the Prussian Cabinet Order of 1820 by a new Imperial law on the army, since the new law would favor an Imperial army officer corps that might eliminate the ancient Prussian Junker domination of this aristocratic preserve. Thus, their insistence that reform of the military law by the Kaiser would be the end of the favored position of the Prussian army within the Empire and therefore the termination of the special position of Prussia within the Empire and ultimately the destruction of Prussia was adamantly maintained.[31]

Thus, the Centre and the National Liberal parties had little choice but to support the Imperial Chancellor. Furthermore, the National Liberals needed to do so because of internal party dissention. Their own constituents had labeled them Socialists and this was being published in the assertion of Dr. Pechmann's letter to the Preussenbund that he was quitting the party because of its socialistic leanings and because he supported this Prussian nationalist organization.[32] The National Liberal newspaper, Goester Kreisblatt, condemned their leader, Herr Bassermann, for his Social Democratic led condemnations in the mistrust vote.[33] Therefore, the National Liberals were not at all secure on the twenty-third of January and thus the pleas of the National Liberal organ, the Kölnische Zeitung, that the Zabern Affair should now be forgotten[34] seemed to have been embraced by Herr Bassermann despite his opposition to Prussian Nationalism.

Yet there was an attempt by the Reichstag to do more than merely remain a "hall of echoes," for the members appointed a committee to advise and suggest military reforms to the Kaiser. They attempted to bring into existence what on the twenty-third of January all of the parties except those of the Right had been advocating, that the powers of the Reichstag be augmented and that there be a government of both the Kaiser and the Reichstag based on a new constitution that anticipated a modern Imperial Germany.

No motions on the interpellations were passed on the twenty-third of January. However, on the twenty-fourth, the Centre Party initiated a motion that was passed. It asked the Federal Council to assure that the conditions upon which the military could intervene in civil police affairs should be uniform throughout the Empire and in such a manner that maintained the independence of the civil authority. The second motion approved by the Reichstag was the National Liberal motion that the Reichs-Chancellor keep that assembly informed of the result of the Imperial inquiry into the army orders. Thus, despite internal division and intimidation the National Liberals acted in support of Imperial interests rather than Prussian. This also set up the above-mentioned committee of twenty-one members which was to review the Socialist, Alsatian, and Radical motions concerning special laws about the military powers and jurisdiction and to advise the Emperor on the basis of any suggestions taken from these motions.[35]

There were not any members of the government present at the Reichstag of the twenty-fourth of January. When the Reichstag passed motions from the floor, the regime absented itself because of the unconstitutionality of this action. Such action assumed that the government had some responsibility to the Reichstag or that there was some basis for negotiation between the two over a motion entered in the Reichstag, when there was not. The Reichstag's bid for extension of its powers was, as usual, ignored by the Imperial government.

NOTES

[1]Verhandlungen des Reichstag, 292, p. 6738.
[2]Ibid., pp. 6736-6784.
[3]Ibid., p. 6739.
[4]Ibid., p. 6733.
[5]Ibid., p. 6739.
[6]Ibid., p. 6757.
[7]Ibid., p. 6769.
[8]Ibid., p. 6755.
[9]Ibid., p. 6757.
[10]Ibid., p. 6763.
[11]Ibid., p. 6740.
[12]Ibid., p. 6749.
[13]Ibid., 6745.
[14]Ibid., p. 6757.
[15]Ibid., p. 6731.
[16]Ibid., p. 6732.
[17]Ibid., p. 6733.
[18]Ibid., p. 6739.
[19]Ibid., p. 6748.
[20]Ibid., p. 6749.
[21]Ibid., p. 6757.
[22]This accusation will be revived in the Reichstag on the sixth of May, 1914.
[23]Verhandlungen des Reichstags, 292, p. 6754.
[24]Karl Demeter, Das deutsche Heer und seine Offiziere. Berlin, 1930, p. 30. Hans Herzfeld, Die deutsche Rüstungspolitik vor dem Weltkrieg, Bonn, 1923, p. 62f.
[25]Verhandlungen des Reichstags, 292, p. 6766.
[26]Ibid., p. 6739.
[27]Ibid., p. 6763.
[28]Verhandlungen des Preussischen Hauses des Abgeordneten, pp. 140ff.

[29]Verhandlungen des Reichstags, 292, p. 6749.
[30]Ibid., p. 6770.
[31]Ibid., p. 6766.
[32]See pp. 71-75, this manuscript.
[33]Deutsche Tageszeitung, January 9, 1914.
[34]Kölnische Zeitung, January 14, 1914.
[35]Verhandlungen des Reichstags, 292, p. 6789.

CHAPTER XI

GERMAN REACTION TO THE ZABERN AFFAIR

Questions that might be asked at this time when the Reichstag parties had determined to "heal the wound" were: was the Zabern Affair with its attendant issues concluded? What significance, if any, did it have in terms of changes made in the government or of positive action taken by the government? The London Times correspondent in Berlin said with reference to the Zabern Affair and Bethmann-Hollweg's ignoring of the Reichstag motions of the twenty-fourth of January, "There the matter ended as so many other 'constitutional crises' have ended."[1] The Paris Journal de Debats, said that Germany, except for the Socialists, was once more united.[2] The Allgemeine Zeitung of Munich, on the other hand, expressed the National Liberal view that agreed neither with the Times nor with the Journal de Debats, for it commented that the unity of Germany was wishful thinking and that it would be good if this were true about other things than just the Zabern Affair. "There lie before Germany," it went on, "dangerous disputes as a result of the growing opposition between militarism and the middle-class spirit," and it felt that the danger was that whether the dispute was short or long Germany would disintegrate.[3]

It is this dispute, which the Zabern Affair through the Reichstag sharpened to great magnitude, which was to continue to plague the internal peace of the German Empire. Yet, for a time, at least, there seemed to have been a period of quiescence while the Reichstag was awaiting both the decision of its newly appointed committee on the reform of the military, the decision of the Kaiser on the military orders reform, and while the Reichstag had a chance to catch up on all the past business that it had ignored or glossed over during that Zabern Affair and the issues that that affair had aroused as a result of having been driven by the Conservatives to radical action.

The committee appointed by the Reichstag to discuss the motions made by the Social Democrats, Alsatians, and Radicals for change in the military law did not last very long. At its second and final meeting on the twenty-sixth of February, it was dissolved because of controversy among the members of the parties and lack of cooperation by the government. The committee, called the Zabern Commission in the Deutsche Tageszeitung, had little chance of success from the very beginning. It was supposed to consider motions of the Reichstag for possible future legislation, but any such initiated legislation was unconstitutional, and the motions would have meant little except as thorns in the side of the Conservatives. The Conservative Deutsche Tageszeitung reminded the Committee that it had no powers under the constitution and that it was only duplicating the service that was being performed by the Emperor, who had taken under consideration changes in the military law. Any attempt to use a motion as pressure or to legislate was, the Conservatives held, a further disruption of the power of command of the Emperor.[4] The government was asked to provide information concerning the individual states' military laws so that the Zabern Commission would have a basis upon which to act, but the government was not ready, although it had emphasized that the work was already finished. The Centre Party thereupon asked for adjournment, but the Conservatives, not wanting a discussion, opposed the request. The Centre Party refused to take part in any debate after a Socialist attacked the government. The main proposals were voted on and defeated, the Radicals withdrew the remaining proposals and the commission broke apart.[5]

The fear of a discussion by the Conservatives represented only one instance of a growing general fear of democracy and of Parliamentary government, which had been a result of the twenty-third and twenty-fourth of January debate on the Zabern Affair. Although the fear had existed before the affair, the spread and deepening of it resulted generally from the affair as a whole. An example of this fear came on twenty-first of February, the same day as the Deutsche Tageszeitung's reminder to the Zabern commission of the unconstitutionality of its work, when there appeared in the Allgemeine Zeitung of Munich the declaration of policy of the League of Landowners (Bund der Landwirte). This league meeting in Berlin, included Dr. Roesicke, Dr. Diederich Hahn, Dr. Oertel, and Herr von Oldenburg-Januschau. They, along with other members, declared that they intended to work for the monarch, for the Empire, and for the whole people against the unholy development of democracy. In all areas of legislation within the Empire, they said, the growing wishes and interests of democracy concerning the military, taxation, society, and politics were being followed. They stated that the events in Zabern and the entire handling of the Zabern Affair, the desire to set aside the boundaries of the Kaiser's power of command and that of the federation of princes in order to strengthen parliamentarism, the overriding by the Empire of the taxation policies of the individual states, were all marks of infringement by the developing democracy in Imperial Germany.[6]

Herr Oldenburg-Januschau in his Memoirs went much further than the "League" in his condemnation of the Reichstag. He attributed the destruction of the German Empire to the Reichstag that Bismarck had created and so the responsibility for this destruction must be laid at the feet of this first Germany Reichs-Chancellor. The foundation of the governing system as developed by Bismarck, according to these Memoirs, seemed to have been the administration of the government by two opposing forces, the civil power with its center in the liberally elected government of the Reichstag and the military power with its center being the Kaiser. The bond between the two constituted the liberal authority. Oldenburg-Januschau insisted that the power of this Bismarckian device, the Reichstag, had been great as early as the end of von Bulow's administration but that the policies of Bethmann-Hollweg enabled this power to expand greatly. The Imperial minister's indecisiveness and incompetence were responsible for this expansion. Bethmann-Hollweg had begun the game of the two centers of power, the Reichstag and the Kaiser, each jockeying for position, opposing each other at every turn: the game would end only when the German Empire would be destroyed. According to Oldenburg-Januschau the Left and the Centre party under Erzberger had a major part in this destructive process, since they had taken advantage of Bethmann-Hollweg's indecisiveness and lack of ability and thereby had augmented in their own interests the unconstitutional Reichstag dominance of the Empire. He emphasized that some people would attribute the source of the destructive forces to the misuse of the Imperial authority, but that this basis too was the result of the Bismarckian system. The foundation of the weakness of the whole system of Imperial authority was that the power of the War Minister was limited by his dependence upon the budget, which was created by the decrees of 1861 giving control over the War Minister to popular authority. The Centre Party under Erzberger had begun to agree with the Left and this agreement had brought democratic control and thus the destruction of the German Empire.[7]

The Zabern Affair had acted as a catalyst on this growing power of the liberal-democratic elements that Oldenburg-Januschau maintained had destroyed the German Empire even before World War I. Ministerial responsibility and parliamentary government had been demanded by the leaders of that majority in the Mistrust Vote and continued to be demanded on the twelfth of January when National Liberal Party leader, Herr Bassermann had demanded that the Reichstag have an equal voice in the government.[8] No less insistent had been the voice of Radical Party leader Naumann when he maintained on the twenty-third of January that the Reichstag was a parliament and as such should govern a parliamentary state. This was more than merely another Social Democrat speaking as was shown by the Freisinn-Konservative Allgemeine Zeitung of Munich statement that Herr Naumann was no mere demagogue, that he actually meant what he said.[9] Other examples of this demand came from such party leaders as Fehrenbach, Liszt, Frank, and Ledebour.[10] The insistence on strengthening the power of the Reichstag did not end on the twenty-third of January as was shown by the declaration of the league of "League of Landowners" of the twenty-first of February, nor did it end on the twenty-sixth of February when the Zabern commission dissolved, as was shown by Herr Naumann's demand for a Parliamentary state on the fourteenth of March as reported by the Freisinn-Konservative Allgemeine Zeitung of that day.

The statement that Herr Naumann really meant what he said and was not merely another Social Democrat opposed to everything that did not promote socialism was recognition that serious consideration was being shown for parliamentary principles, whether favorable or not. Distinctly unfavorable consideration was delivered on the part of the Conservatives who feared revolutionary change in the relationship of the state to the Imperial government. Count von Schwerin-Lowitz delivered a speech at the Pomeranian Conservative Party Conference on the twenty-fifth of January in which he said that the middle-class members and the supporters of the social democracy were united in a three-part program which included extending the constitutional rights of the Reichstag until it became a full-fledged parliamentary government, restricting the power of command of the Emperor and democratizing the Prussian electoral rights, or, if they are not able to do this, mediatizing Prussia and the other federated states through depriving them of financial independence. He linked the National Liberals and the Centre Party members with a middle-class desire for an English-constitutional monarchy and with the newly reformed Social Democrats who had given up their economic egalitarianism and now wanted a republican-state form of government. He stated that both forces collaborating for their common goals constituted a grave danger for the future of the German Empire, for there existed now a weak regime dominating the government. Furthermore, he insisted that these forces with their separate goals were basically wrong for Germany because there had been no historical development nor experience in German history to support either.[11]

The controversy over parliamentary initiation of legislation in the Reichstag that the Zabern Affair had encouraged took new forms in February beginning with the introduction of proposals by the Polish Centre and Social Democratic Parties for a change in the laws on association. All three wanted the abolition of the law forbidding young people to join associations or attend meetings. In addition, the Centre sought restrictions on police supervision over public meetings and an end to imprisonment for breaking curfew. The Social Democrats went even further by demanding that the regulations concerning mandatory reports and observation of political meetings be abolished, and that the police authority over a situation rightfully controlled by Imperial laws on association be excluded and restrictions on political associations and the right of nonpolitical associations to political affairs be eliminated. All three proposals were unconstitutional in view of the fact that the Reichstag lacked the right to bring about changes in a law; but Dr. Lewald, the Conservative Imperial Ministerial Director, stated that the change must be executed individually by the Landtags of the states.[12] He and the Conservatives Veit and Mertin reminded the Reichstag that it could not legislate reform. The next day, the fifth of February, the National Liberal, Herr Junck, declared that his party was opposed to the proposals on the law of association, and Dr. Muller-Meiningen of the Progressive People's Party agreed with him. There ensued a heated debate between the latter and the Centre Party advocate of the proposal, Dr. Groeber, but the meeting closed with the subject dropped from the succeeding day's agenda.[13] Both Representatives Junck and Muller-Meiningen agreed that it was within the scope of the Reichstag to consider such a proposal, but they regarded the law on association in existence as liberal and the problem behind the proposals to be merely one of the inconveniences of administering the law through the proper police authorities. In other words the complaints were caused merely by the "red tape" involved in the existing law. The Deutsche Tageszeitung, a conservative daily, could not decide who was more wrong, Dr. Muller-Meiningen or Representative Groeber of the Centre Party.[14]

Further attempts to legislate occurred when the Prussian reform bill for the military penal code came before the Reichstag on the twenty-first of February. Again it was a member of the Centre Party, Dr. Spahn, who proposed that the reform bill introduced to the Prussian War Minister von Falkenhayn be referred for consideration to the Zabern Commission. The National Liberal Representative Dr. von Calker opposed the reform altogether because it dealt with peripheral problems and was not the fundamental military penal code reform needed. Dr. Muller-Meiningen wanted to accept the reform because he believed it to be a brilliant justification of the "Mistrust" views expressed in the Reichstag in the preceding year. He also pointed out that it would be better to have this reform than to wait many years for a complete reform of the entire military law. This would be a Prussian inspired law and not one coming as a result of the consideration of the Emperor, which was still going on. Nevertheless, Dr. Muller-Meiningen, speaking for the Progressive People's Party, considered the Zabern commission unsuitable and was quite willing to accept the bill as an installment on the eventual fundamental reform of the entire military penal code.[15]

Count von Westarp also opposed sending the military penal code bill to the Zabern commission but his reason for such opposition was that he viewed that commission as one set-up by the Social Democrats for Social Democratic purposes, which were identical with those stated by Rosa Luxemburg in the previous year, when she claimed that the army wanted to bring Germany into a war to the death against the French and that the Social Democrats must oppose this and the army as well. He continued with the typical tirade of the Conservatives against the Social Democrats as anarchists opposed to all army law. He was answered by Fehrenbach of the Centre party, who reminded him that the Zabern Commission had been set up by the combined vote of the majority of all parties and that apart from use of the name "Zabern," which might embarrass the Conservatives, he could see no reason why the Zabern Commission should not examine the Reform Bill.[16] The Social Democrats, represented by Herr Noske, agreed with the National Liberals that the reform bill should not be sent to the Zabern commission; they maintained that it should be voided altogether. The result of the debate was that a special commission of twenty-one members was created to consider the War Minister's military penal code reform bill.

It was clear that the Zabern commission was tainted because it had been set up originally to consider proposals from the floor of the Reichstag and to propose changes in the military law to the Emperor in the form of legislation. Neither the Centre, National Liberal, nor Social Democratic Parties questioned the constitutional right of the Zabern commission to exist on the twenty-first of February, and it was equally obvious, considering the character of the Zabern commission as it had been set up, that these parties expected it to attempt to draft its own military penal code reform bill. The Centre party, almost a month after the Zabern Commission had been set up, still expected that the Zabern commission would be an agent in changing the Constitution in order to give the Reichstag legislative power and to influence the Kaiser and with these views the National Liberals and the Social Democrats concurred. The wish, however was a futile one for as we have seen, the commission broke up on the twenty-sixth of February.[18]

Reform of the military law, about which the majority of the members of all parties of the Reichstag had sought to legislate, was accomplished on the eighth of April, 1914, by the Emperor. He approved new regulations concerning cooperation of the military with civil authorities and the use of arms by the military in the suppression of internal disturbances. The regulations which had been drawn up by the Prussian Minister of War would apply to Prussia, to all the states which had no special military privileges, and to Alsace-Lorraine, and, by the agreement of the Bavarian, Saxon, and Wurttemberg governments, to the troops from those states which were stationed in Alsace-Lorraine.

The regulations suppressed the parts of the Cabinet Order of 1820, which had allowed Colonel von Reuter and the officers of Zabern to take over civil authority. They provided that the military could intervene only when there was a clear necessity due to the nonfunctioning of the state authorities, that is, when they were not in a position to call upon the military. Furthermore, no arms would be used by the military until all other means had failed. The regulations were a distinct concession to public opinion led by the Reichstag, and thus a distinct concession to this body. The use of old Cabinet Orders, and thus Prussian Cabinet Orders to justify military rule had thus been brought to an end.[19]

The Reichstag had succeeded in limiting the freedom of the military of Prussia. Yet, despite the fact that the 99th infantry regiment came back to Zabern without both Colonel von Reuter and Lieutenant von Forstner and was welcomed peacefully and even with some show of pleasure, the Reichstag was not satisfied. The Emperor had not gone far enough in the eyes of many, and both on the sixth and twentieth of May, 1914, the Reichstag questioned the government about the adequacy of the military law and showed a continued desire, as at the time of the Interpellations in the Zabern Affair, to legislate on the issue.

As far as the Cabinet Order of 1820 was concerned, the Reichstag, with the exception of the Social Democrats, was satisfied with the Kaiser's new regulations. On the sixth of May, the Prussian Minister of War was able to placate the members by referring to the nature of the new regulations and by assurances of his own that the new regulations would be carried out. Essentially the main reason he gave for the necessity of the new regulations was that the general nature of the Cabinet Order assumed that the civil government would not then be in operation if the military were forced to take over but did not specifically state it. He emphasized that the new regulations were not to conflict with the special regulations of the federal states but were to apply to all contingents within the provinces. The main difference among the state regulations that he knew about at that time was that in Saxony all troops were to be under the jurisdiction of the state. As far as Bavaria and Wurttemburg were concerned, he had not been instructed about special regulations there. The New regulations specifically stated that it was the duty of the civil authority to put down unrest independently unless it asked the military for aid. If this authority of the civil government no longer existed, then the military would take over. Whether the military should interfere had to be the decision of the officers as to whether the civil government was in operation, and he would not answer any questions by the Reichstag members on this point. The army officers, he thought, knew that they carried a weighty responsibility and would respect it. More than any other reason this assurance made this part of the new regulations acceptable to the Reichstag. On the other hand, as was said, these regulations could be considered only one step forward rather than a permanent solution to the military problem.[20]

The reform of the Cabinet Order was not the only issue arising out of the Zabern Affair that was brought up this sixth of May. The second most discussed issue of the day concerned whether the National Defense League (Wehrverein) would turn into another Preussenbund. The specific question asked concerned what the Prussian War Minister intended to do about the threat of the Wehrverein to become another Preussenbund as it celebrated the victory of that organization in discussing political problems that had been associated with the Zabern Affair. Critics accused General von Deimling, in command at Strasburg where the Wehrverein conference had been celebrated, of being in collusion with the Wehrverein and suspected that he would allow officers to talk on any subject regardless of how offensive this might be to the local population. Dr. Muller-Meiningen protested against the Wehrverein speech of General Kracht because of its insults to Bavaria, which the former represented in the Reichstag. Furthermore, as a member of the Progressive People's Party, he condemned the militarism that both the Preussenbund and the Wehrverein reflected.[21]

War Minister von Falkenhayn disclaimed any link existing between the Wehrverein and the army; they both have the same goal he said, which was the protection of the Fatherland. He maintained emphatically that many ex-army officers belonged to the Wehrverein and that the bonds between them were too strong to break. However, he insisted that officers in the Wehrverein should not speak on political issues and that General von Deimling and his fifty subordinate officers would have to leave the assembly of the Wehrverein if any political subjects were discussed.[22] The Reichstag rumblings of discontent indicated that hardly anyone but members of the Right were pleased by this statement.

Another important issue that had developed during the Zabern Affair was that of ministerial responsibility and it continued to be an issue in the repercussions of that Affair here in the spring of 1914. On the sixth of May, the Reichstag majority believed that the Prussian Minister of War, who was also the Imperial Minister of War, ought to be responsible to the Reichstag because of the budgetary powers controlled by the Reichstag. Von Falkenhayn, however, was emphatic in his denial that the Reichstag had any part to play concerning the military might of Prussia, which was the dominant power in the Imperial army. He cited that by provisions of the Imperial Constitution, which included those of the Prussian constitution, the King of Prussia-Emperor of Germany regulated the army through conventions with the other federated states. He insisted that he, as War Minister, was solely responsible for his actions to the King of Prussia; there was no ministerial responsibility to any legislating organization. Therefore, according to General von Falkenhayn, it was an unconstitutional expansion of the Reichstag's power for either the Left or Herr Muller-Meiningen to keep the War Minister on short summons in the budget business after he had expressed the desires of the King. To do so would be to deprive Prussia of its own institutions. He stated that the army had only one base, and this base was the king of Prussia. The only defense against ambitious party leaders working for a party dominated constitution that would destroy the Prussian army was this base. "The monarchy is the only safe refuge left for the Prussian army; it must not be shaken."[24]

This statement of the War Minister brought to everyone's attention one of the major issues that had developed as a result of the Zabern Affair, the issue of whether Prussian particularism would dominate the Empire or whether the growing demands of the National Liberal, Centre, and Social Democratic parties that Imperial power be dominate over states' rights would prevail.

The increasing attempts of the Reichstag to determine through its budgetary powers what the Prussian army would be in the future, and what the position of that Prussian contingent would be within the Imperial army, evoked the assertion of the Prussian army's independent position and source of strength independent of the Reichstag by the War Minister, but in his acknowledging the growing strength of the parties and their leaders under the Constitution and in using the phrase "safe refuge" with reference to the King of Prussia, the War Minister showed the weakening position of the Prussian Army within the Empire.

That this weakening position was known by the Prussian army's enemies was evidenced by the increasing criticism of the army in the Reichstag discussions on the fifth and sixth of May, 1914. The Social

Democrats as well as the Centre Party leader, Herr Erzberger, quoted General von Einem's militaristic views when these Reichstag representatives condemned the systematic ill treatment of subordinates by officers.[25]   Herr Erzberger asked for economy in the construction of housing for soldiers and officers and then requested that special rooms be built for the under-officers.[26] He and Muller-Meiningen of the Progressive People's Party and Von Bieberstein on the sixth of May suggested a better rank for the officer of sanitation.[27]   Muller-Meiningen and the Left demanded social equality among all officers, which would include making the fore-mentioned middle-class sanitation officers equal to Junker aristocrats.[28] National Liberal leader Bassermann suggested that an office of information or press reports be set up for the War Ministry; in agreement with Bieberstein, he asked for the expanding of cavalry divisions in peace time.[29] Yet, von Bieberstein anticipated that the cavalry would become more mechanized as he criticized the remounting of the army,[30] and thereupon the Social Democrats claimed that the army was old-fashioned, that the army that had won the Franco-Prussian War could not win a modern war.[31]   They demanded in the spirit of Gneisenau, Scharnhorst and Boyen a people's army instead of a monarchical army.[32] Representative Muller-Meiningen claimed that all the graduates from the military academy were joining guard regiments instead of line regiments and also, he suggested, that the War Ministry take over the military cabinet.[33]   The Polish Representative supported by the Social Democrats asked that Polish recruits be allowed to speak Polish in the army hospital when their parents came to visit because their parents did not understand the German they were forced to speak in a government institution.[34]

Every one of these demands and claims except that for an increase in cavalry officers was denied by the War Minister. The press report bureau which General von Falkenhayn wanted, was denied him on the twentieth of May by the Reichstag, seemingly in retaliation for the denial of everything that the Reichstag had wanted by the War Minister. Thus, the power of the Reichstag was being tested since the Zabern Affair in ways that had never been used before. The Reichstag was taking more interest in controlling and reforming the army than ever before. Herr Muller-Meiningen even went so far as to suggest that the Prussian Army through the War Ministry was usurping the Reichstag's parliamentary authority.[35] There was good reason for the War Minister to complain that the Prussian Army was being attacked from all sides; it was!

Despite the fact that the demands and claims of fifth and sixth of May were largely ignored, the Reichstag was not finished with its demands on the army and its plans for change in the army. The spirit of Zabern was displayed once again when in the week beginning Monday, the eighteenth of May, and ending on the day of adjournment of the Reichstag, the twentieth of May, the budget commission came forth with a long list of proposals for reforms in the army. The reforms were exactly what the Zabern Commission would have recommended if it had continued its action beyond the twenty-sixth of January. Among the changes demanded in this Reichstag army bill of 1914 was the application of the army penal code to mustered reserves and not before or after. The abolition of close confinement by the army had been demanded when the Prussian Military Penal Code Reform was first presented to the Reichstag on the twenty-first of February by Dr. Frank of the Social Democratic Party,[36] and it was now proposed by the multi-party members of the budget commission.[37] Of course, the administration rejected these proposals as unconstitutional and unacceptable; it stated that there could not be a change in the military penal law until the penal law as a whole was reformed.[38] That ended the legislative attempt to reform the Prussian military, but the financial considerations attendant to the army budget went on. On the second reading of the budget, every party in the Reichstag except the Centre voted to raise the salary for certain lower civil officials and to change the regulation concerning the position of higher postal officials. The Imperial authorities declared that this Social Democratic proposal was unconstitutional and therefore unacceptable, and it introduced a counter-proposal in which certain under officials in the postoffice and telegraph services would receive salary raises beginning the first of January, 1916. The compromise was opposed by the Centre Party which was now joined by the Social Democrats and together they defeated the compromise proposal of the government by a vote of 152 to 149. It was unusual for the Centre Party not to support the original proposal. Because of this opposition the liberal journals declared that the Centre Party was not voting objectively but was taking a negative attitude for political reasons.[39] The Munich Allgemeine Zeitung, a Freisinnige Konservative journal, declared that the Centre Party was only concerned with allowing the Imperial administration to enhance its position of power, and the Imperial administration ought to react to this attitude of complete opposition by dissolving the Reichstag.[40] The result of the debate on the last day of the Reichstag's meeting was that the budget passed without a raise in salaries of lower officials, which every party except the Social Democrats and the Centre had wanted, and without the press report bureau for the War Ministry, which the Imperial regime, and especially the War Ministry, had wanted and urged passage.[41]

The attempts by the Reichstag to initiate legislation had been frustrated by the Imperial government. The effects of such frustration were manifested in several ways at the close of the session. One representative shouted <u>Vive la France</u>. Instead of rising and marching out of the chamber when the three hurrahs for the Emperor were to be given the Social Democrats remained seated in silent contempt.

The remarks of Oldenburg-Januschau concerning the coalition of the Social Democrats and the Centre Party in opposition to the Imperial administration seem to be borne out by the actions of these two Parties in this period from the fourth through the twentieth of May. Whether, as Oldenburg-Januschau claimed, this coalition started the opposition that was to overthrow the Imperial regime at the end of World War I would be difficult to prove, as stated, and even more difficult without including certain members of the National Liberal Party that had taken an active part in the Zabern Affair.[42]

H.V. Zwehl, Erich von Falkenhayn's biographer and friend, as well as fellow general in the Prussian army, stated that the Zabern Affair that ended on the sixth of May permanently damaged the reputation of the army through the exploitation of the affair by the newspapers. "During World War I," he wrote, "this damage to its reputation aided the enemy's effort to undermine the army by revealing what propaganda lines to exploit and where this propaganda would be effective." He even went so far as to castigate the Emperor for not dissolving the Reichstag in May 1914.[43]

Whatever the effects of the Zabern Affair were to have in 1918, there was no doubt in 1914 that a new aggressive spirit had appeared in the Reichstag and that the Prussian army was attacked from all sides, as von Falkenhayn had said, and that it had become the prime target of criticism in the proceeding year. If this spirit had been maintained in the Fall sitting of the Reichstag, and if no war had occurred, what might have happened to the fundamental structure of the Imperial German government? Perhaps that spirit was applied four years later?

NOTES

[1]The Times (London), January 26, 1914.
[2]Journal de Debats, as stated in the Allgemeine Zeitung of Munich, January 31, 1914.
[3]Allgemeine Zeitung of Munich, January 31, 1914.
[4]Deutsche Tageszeitung, February 21, 1914.
[5]Ibid., February 27, 1914.
[6]Allgemeine Zeitung of Munich, February 21, 1914.
[7]Oldenburg-Januschau, Erinerungen, (Berlin: Verlegt bei Koeler und Amelung, 1936), pp. 106-107.
[8]Deutsche Tagezeitung, January 12, 1914. See Verhandlungen des Reichstags, 1913, p. 6162, 6170 for suggestions and questions concerning Imperial constitutional change by Fehrenbach, Peirotes et al.
[9]Allgemeine Zeitung of Munich, March 14, 1914.
[10]See pp. 177-178, this monograph.
[11]Deutsche Tageszeitung, January 25, 1914.
[12]Verhandlungen des Reichstag, 292, 7002.
[13]Ibid., p. 7016.
[14]Deutsche Tageszeitung, February 6, 1914.
[15]Verhandlungen des Reichstags, 292, 7547-7548.
[16]Ibid., pp. 7550-7551.
[17]Verhandlungen des Reichstags, 292, p 7552.
[18]See p. 208, this monograph.
[19]Nord Deutsche Allgemeine Zeitung, April 8, 1914. See also The Times, April 9, 1914.
[20]Verhandlungen des Reichstags, 294, pp. 8520-8522.
[21]Ibid., pp. 8494, 8521, 9523.
[22]Ibid., p. 8520.
[23]Ibid., p. 8521.
[24]Ibid., p. 8472.
[25]Ibid.
[26]Ibid., p. 8473.
[27]Ibid., pp. 8474, 8490-8494.

[28]Ibid., pp. 8494, 8520-8521.

[29]Ibid., pp. 8475, 8492.

[30]Ibid., p. 8491.

[31]Ibid., p. 8520-8521.

[32]Ibid.

[33]Ibid., pp. 8493-8498.

[34]Ibid., pp. 8505-8506.

[35]Verhandlungen des Reichstags, pp. 8493-8498.

[36]Ibid., pp. 7545-7546.

[37]Ibid., pp. 9055-9058, 9076.

[38]Ibid., pp. 9105, 9107.

[39]Munich Allgemeine Zeitung, May 23, 1914.

[40]Ibid.

[41]Ibid.

[42]See p. 77,180, this monograph.

[43]H.V. Zwehl, Erich von Falkenhayn General der Infanterie, Eine biographische Studie (Berlin: Verlegt bei E.S. Mittler und Sohn, 1926), p. 50.

CHAPTER XII

ISSUES AND ENCORES

The aristocracy of Prussia prior to the First World War, but especially after the Daily Telegraph Affair of 1908, in many ways resembled the French aristocracy of the period usually called the Ancien Regime. Like the French aristocrats, the Prussian Junkers were fighting a determined battle for survival of their idealism, honor, and position in an increasingly materialistic, practical society in which new invention, new technological advance, new medical discoveries, new armaments bringing new tactics and strategy and new educational opportunities bringing new opportunities for success in new areas hitherto non-existent made the word "new" a synonym for progress toward a better life and, by contrast, "old" came to have lesser value as a word describing a good life. In this time of great change in science, industry, government and warfare, when the economically prestigious were demanding a political prestige as well, these Junker nobles were protecting themselves against the intrusion into their privileged world of such economic, social, political, intellectual and religious groups as might in any way threaten their dominating power position. They tried to maintain the aristocratic rules regarding social mobility which emphasized that only through marriage or, for example, through special ability and achievement, such as that of the historian von Ranke, could members of the middle class hope to reach the august position of the aristocracy in society and the officer corps in the army. Like the French aristocracy of the Ancient Regime, but even more deeply entrenched, the Junker had created a conservative caste system perpetuating the honorific privileges pertaining to his position as a member of a natural aristocracy based on land ownership and service in the bureaucracy and the army of Prussia.

Deputy Hauss, of the Centre Party, indicated in his Reichstag speech of the fourth of December, 1913, that the army had changed in that in

223

1913 there was even more emphasis on aristocratic privileges being maintained in the army than there had been twenty years before. He emphasized that in 1913 there was more desire for class prestige among the officers than earlier, and that no longer was ability the criterion for advancement in the army as much as was social position. The class of authority sought to maintain the army free from the new liberal elements who were demanding a place in society and to protect the army against the middle-class spirit. The Centre, Radical, and National Liberal parties in the Reichstag exemplified the middle class spirit in their attempts to regulate the army officer corps through the use of their budgetary powers as justification. The Junker aristocratic protectors of their officer monopoly called these attempts unconstitutional.[1]

Like the pre-1789 French aristocracy, the Junker sought to maintain his function as a cavalry officer or as a civil servant in the upper echelons of the bureaucracy and in pursuit of these goals swore allegiance to that other pillar of Prussia, the King, and sought to exclude those of the lower social orders from these positions. The interconnection of state function and social prestige, both matters of practical and theoretical considerations, was the basis for the Junkers often outspoken declaration that they were the backbone of the state, the protector of its present and future and the natural rulers of the masses of people of both Prussia and Germany. Therefore, the policy of this caste in politics was to perpetuate the foundations of their authority: the Prussian army-cavalry, the Prussian bureaucracy, protection of its property from taxes, and the protection of the authority of the Prussian King over the German Empire through his power as Commander-of-Chief of the army. Any innovations in politics such as an increase in the authority of any assembly, a Landtag, or the Reichstag, and any increase in the independence of a federated state or province in opposition to the King of Prussia's authority would weaken their hold. Any reform in the rule or administration of the army, such as the adoption of non-Prussian rules of weapon usage, limitations on the actions of the army with or without civil authority, or the rise in prestige of newly important technical officers, for example those in the sanitation corps or artillery, who were not members of the aristocracy would be anathema to them. Perhaps, even more to be dreaded by the Junker would be the competition of a federal army with the Prussian army through both independent officers or laws governing the peace or wartime use of that army. The army must even be maintained in a superior position above the navy and not take second place. Concerning the most fundamental basis of Junker political and economic power, in landowning, it must be protected at all costs from having this basis weakened or reduced by taxes or inheritance duties.

Yet, all that the Junker feared seemed destined to come about in the future in the German Empire, and apprehension of this future led many of the Prussians to mistrust the Empire and to emphasize Prussianism. By the sixth of May, the War Minister had to remind those who feared the Empire that the Emperor was also the King of Prussia and as such the sole prop for the umbrella under which the Prussian army must shelter itself.[2] The army budget of 1913 had given three more cavalry divisions to the Prussian Army, a gift for which the army-officer-aristocracy was grateful, but this sop of three cavalry regiments given to the Junkers was not sufficient to give lasting satisfaction. To the Prussian aristocrat it seemed that even the Emperor had turned against them, for Bethmann-Hollweg as his representative had accepted the Erzberger-Bassermann army finance bill, which threatened through property, capital gains, and inheritance taxes the very basis of the Junkers existence and aroused for a time complete opposition on the part of the Junker to any financial support of the Empire. Nearly a year later it seemed that the Emperor still opposed the King of Prussia, for, as a result of the Zabern Affair, he had compromised the Junker domination of the army through making laws allowing to Saxony independent control of its army.[3] Even worse, the Emperor had changed what had become considered by 1914 the almost sacred Cabinet Order of 1820, replacing it by an Imperial edict allowing the civil authorities to remain completely independent, unless they asked for army interference or unless they no longer existed. In other words, the Emperor had made the Prussian army a servant of the people of any province and had given up what the army thought it had won by the trials of Colonel von Reuter, Lieutenant Schad and Lieutenant von Forstner. To the Junkers the trial verdicts had become meaningless army successes, for the King, submitting to public opinion and the Reichstag as its representative, had won a victory over aristocratic privilege and that age-old pillar of Prussia, its army.

Clearly evident was the basic division in German administrative circles between the military and middle class administration which, as Theodore Heuss pointed out on the twenty-first of January, 1914, mistrusted and even hated each other. The victory of the Reichstag was a victory of the middle-class administration over the Prussian military. But, the Prussian military had the last word and the ultimate victory, for this military replaced the civil administration and the government in the First World War. Heuss wrote that the Zabern Affair was only a symptom of the hatred between the two rival classes. According to him the Colonel did not go to the District Director because the latter was under his class, and the latter did not go to the Colonel because the civil authorities could not intrude into the barracks.[4] The way of life of the Junker could not be changed merely to permit the reign of peace in Alsace-Lorraine.

War Minister von Falkenhayn was ready to give up this way of life on the sixth of May, 1914, if maintaining it meant that because of backwardness of the army, a charge made by Herr Schulz, a future war would be lost; but he hastily added that the army that had won in 1870-1871 could win in 1914, since the way of life of the Junker with its emphasis on bravery and patriotism had not changed.[5]   As long as the system remained intact, he went on, those who had voted the no-confidence of the Reichs-Chancellor and who had attempted to change and control the army by Reichstag legislation would not repeat the attempt in the present and would be unsuccessful in the future.[6]

The attack by the Reichstag and by much of Germany upon the Junkers and upon Prussian particularism during the Zabern Affair at times centered on the Prussian electoral law, the very foundation of Junker control and of the value system of Prussia, without which the Junker and Prussia could not dominate the Empire.   According to the Conservatives, a change in this electoral law might increase the influence of the middle class and the army might be ruined by the substitution of middle-class materialistic officers for idealistic, dedicated professional soldiers, the Junkers.[7]   The repeated attempts to change this had been unsuccessful, and both Bethmann-Hollweg, the Prussian Prime Minister in December, 1913, and his replacement in June, 1914, President von Lubbell, had the same excuse for the refusal by the Emperor to bring about the long sought reform: "The time was not ripe yet."   Both obscured the fact that the army officer class could not afford to lose its electoral power,[8] and the Emperor, in turn, could not afford to lose his army.

Opposing the values of the Junker aristocracy, stood the spirit of the middle classes, which the Zabern Affair had stirred as never before. The Radical, Centre, and National Liberal parties were ready to change the Imperial Constitution by insisting on ministerial responsibility of the Reichs-Chancellor to the Reichstag and by legislating new army laws in the Reichstag. It was true that the National Liberals' anger subsided, and the party broke away to some extent from the coalition in February because of internal party dissension and because of its wish to counter claims that the Social Democrats were leading the National Liberals to Socialism.   The National Liberals even went so far in Munich as to condemn any link between their party and the Social Democrats. By so doing they hurt their own chances in the next election to the Reichstag; they won many seats only because the Social Democrats withdrew their own candidates in order to let them win. The Zabern Affair might have meant for them an even greater percentage of the vote than the 34.8 percent they had received in the election of 1912. Yet, despite this defection, the Radicals and the Centre continued to show this middle-class spirit until the end of the last Reichstag meeting before the war, the twentieth of May, 1914.

The Zabern Affair clearly revealed both the opposition to Prussian militarism from December, 1913, to the end of May, 1914, and the weakness of the Reichstag as a representative body in a nonparliamentary state. On the other hand, it was also apparent that the Reichstag intended to convert this weakness into strength through introducing the principle of ministerial responsibility, and that it continued attempts to change the Constitution by attempting to legislate as a parliamentary body.

The antagonism between Prussia and the Empire that became exacerbated through the Zabern Affair was not the only example of division. The affair aroused animosity between north and south Germany, resulting in the alienation of Saxony and the resumption by the King of Saxony of the command of his troops, and in Bavaria an alienation even greater than that of Saxony. The alienation of Bavaria came from insults directed at this state by the Preussenbund, from the greater amount of sympathy found within Bavaria for Alsace-Lorraine, an area south-German in spirit, and from the sympathy found in Bavaria for fellow Catholics in Zabern, also victims of Prussian prejudice.

Part of the importance of the Crown Prince's role in the Zabern Affair and of the subsidiary issues developing out of it, was that the princely support of Colonel von Reuter, Lieutenant von Forstner, and General von Deimling led to the encouragement of the conservative reaction and the Preussenbund's establishment and thus to the greater alienation of Bavaria and South Germany than ever before. It caused the alliance of the Old National Liberals[9] with the Social Democrats in Bavaria against Prussianism, and thus rejuvenated the waning political fortunes of the Social Democrats there.

The Preussenbund and General Kracht made Prussianism unpopular especially in Bavaria, and General Wrochem aroused even more anger. The Crown Prince's encouragement of the Conservatives thus became a prime element in the loosening of Imperial unity in the middle of January, 1914. His contribution to the conservative reaction in conjunction with that of Berlin police president von Jagow's were the most important factors in the success of this reaction. The attitude of the future Emperor greatly encouraged the Right at a crucial moment of conservative weakness in the face of public opinion.

One of the important results of the Zabern Affair was a growing animosity between German and French newspapers. There had been some increase of feeling over the new German army bill, which had aroused the press of the two countries and the ill treatment of downed German airmen at Nancy and Luneville had caused conservative journals to condemn France. By summer, 1913, the furor had died down, but the efforts of both governments to preserve peace received a setback through the Zabern Affair.[10] The animosity showed clearly at the time of the Strasburg trials of Colonel von Reuter, Lieutenant Schad, and Lieutenant Forstner. There had been some French comment on the Zabern incident before these trials, but the comment had been to the effect that Germany was divided into two parts; namely, the army supported by the Crown Prince, and the civil administration supported by the Emperor. The French press questioned whether sword or law was to prevail within the Empire. Prior to the article of the sixth of January in Le Temps just cited, the French press had reported factually the events and subsidiary developments concerning the Zabern Affair and without comment.[11] This objectivity was attested to by The Times Paris correspondent on the tenth of January and by the German Ambassador to France, Baron von Schoen, who even went so far as to attribute it to the influence of the French government.[12] The Times correspondent explained that the French press regarded the conflict over the Zabern Affair as a strictly internal German affair involving a division of interests between the civil and military authorities. Baron von Schoen thought that because the two governments were at that time negotiating a trade treaty France did not want any antagonisms aroused and thus put pressure on the major newspapers to refrain from condemnation. Whatever the reason, the attitude abruptly changed as a result of the Strasburg trials of the fifth of January and the plea of the sixth of January by Colonel von Reuter. Yet, even on the sixth of January when Le Temps condemned von Reuter's testimony as Pan Germanism, the writer stated that the issue was still in doubt as to whether Pan Germanism or William II's drive for peace would prevail in Germany.[13] This doubt was to be dispelled by the outcome of the Strasburg trials.

The comment of Le Temps on the eleventh of January was quite different in tone than that of the sixth. On the eleventh that journal stated that France had to deal with a Germany which was crystallized in divine right and military right and far more closely resembled the monarchy of Louis XIV than any contemporary regime. The writer further stated that in international relations and competition in armaments the Germany with which France had to deal was not concerned with the liberal and humanitarian dreams which in France and England had won the paths to power. "From the political and practical point of view, the Germany to which French Socialists appeal in order to reassure us simply does not exist."[14] This same journal, as a result of the Reichstag debates of the twenty-third and twenty-fourth of January, was even more pessimistic.

The author of an article on the thirtieth of January said that it was not important whether the Cabinet Order of 1820 applied or not. What was important was whether a majority of the people in Alsace-Lorraine could find material or moral security. If the Reichstag demanded new Orders for Alsace-Lorraine and they were given them, the only result would be that they would be under just as much control and sabre rule as before, but that the Reichstag would no longer be concerned about them.[15]

The Munich Allgemeine Zeitung replied to this article by accusing the French of wishing for that which had occurred in Alsace-Lorraine, an area known for dissatisfaction under all circumstances. The author stated that only the blind could not see that the demonstrations against the military in Zabern were brought about by French propaganda in the provinces. This conservative point of view from the Freisinnigge Konservative author went so far as to stress that no end would come to such propaganda until the day revanche brought the French attack on Germany. The Reichstag majority mistrust vote furthered the French armament efforts; France was lucky.[16]

On the fourth of April, Ludwig Thoma published in März an article which he wrote called "Pfaffen," in which he condemned in vitriolic terms the stupidity shown in an article in the French journal Liberté. He repeated the charge made above by the Munich Allgemeine Zeitung that French chauvinism in Alsace-Lorraine had caused the recent activities regarding the Prussian Army, and he asked if the writer had forgotten Abbé Wetterlé. He touched on what he considered the cause of this great chauvinism, the Catholic clerical plan for religious dominance which had emanated from Lourdes and elsewhere. He stated that" Germany must not forget that the real enemy is Papism".[17]

The issues involved in German-French animosity ran the gamut from Alsatian-French chauvinism, French propaganda, to "revanche" and "Papism." The spirit of revenge for the taking of Alsace-Lorraine in the Franco-Prussian War had died down in France. Now the Zabern Affair became the occasion of the latent animosity's flaring up.

Further results of the Zabern Affair lay in the field of finance concerning the over-all economy of Germany in 1913-1914. The Munich Allgemeine Zeitung in an article dealing with the growth of the economy in Germany in 1913 and the first month of 1914, brought out that there was a slight growth over all in the economy the previous year but that the political unrest within the country in   the latter part of the previous year had prevented greater growth in the economy. The writer stated that if there was brought about political peace within Germany in the next year the economy should improve. Specifically, because of the inner unrest and disruptions in Alsace-Lorraine, Germany was hurt by withdrawal of

foreign investments.   Whether there would be a return of such
investments, the author did not say, but he declared that Germany did not
need foreign investments for its development.   The author did not say
where the investments were lacking or from what source.   The demand for
textiles and steel was down and consequently so were prices in these two
industries.   Foreign purchases perhaps were also curtailed by the Zabern
Affair.

Nineteen-thirteen.   The year of great promise for Germany, the year
of the great celebration for the centenary of the War of Liberation.
Nineteen thirteen might subsequently have been considered a great year
for Germany if there had not been a world war.   It was perhaps the most
important year up to that time in the development of Germany's slow
movement toward a democratic Government.   The new willingness of the
Reichstag to condemn the actions of the Imperial Chancellor was
comparable to the "Declaration of the Rights of Man" or the sitting-
together of the Estates General in 1789 insofar as it, like those, renewed
the courage and solidarity of people who had heretofore doubted their own
judgement and had lacked confidence in the decisions of others.   The first
vote in history of "No confidence in the government" took place in
January, 1913, and concerned the distribution of Polish lands.   An equal,
if not greater anti-government act was constituted by passage in June of
that year of the Erzberger-Bassermann army finance bill.   From that time
on, the army was the subject of leading articles of the newspapers.   First,
the newspapers revealed corruption in the Krupp Affair and then the
brutality and militaristic aspects of the Zabern Affair.   These events
caused loss of faith in the army by many, and the loss of support for
Bethmann-Hollweg and thereby the government, resulting in less power for
the Conservatives.   Bethmann-Hollweg and the government were isolated
by the Zabern Affair, but even more isolated was that Reichs-Chancellor,
himself who had lost support from the Kaiser and had to deny his support
for the civil authorities and support the view of the military that they had
done no wrong in Zabern.   The "division" voted against him in the
Prussian Landtag damaged his prestige and led to his loss of power there
as well as his influence over the Prussian army which waned so that he
lost the influence over army then and also in World War I.   The Mistrust
Vote of the fourth of December showed that the government lacked the
support of all parties except the Right and the support there was not very
strong.   Indeed, the ultra conservative-Prussian Landtag added another
statement of its disapproval in January.   The newspapers had a "field-
day" so to speak.

The Zabern Affair marked the fruition of the efforts of the new
unstable coalition of the Centre, National Liberals, Social Democratic, and

Radical Parties against the army and the government that had arisen during the events of the preceding year. They had censured Bethmann-Hollweg, the Kaiser, the government, the army, and the Conservatives. The events in Zabern, the trials and Reichstag debates culminated in the promise of the Emperor to re-examine the Cabinet Order of 1820 and, eventually, the promulgation by him of regulations limiting the interference of army officers in peacetime activities. Next, the coalition submitted legislation to the Emperor and appointed a Zabern Commission to help him draw up new army laws. Their criticism of the Prussian army led to Preussenbund and Wehrverein inspired Prussian nationalism that led to Bavarian and Saxon secessionist movements and the independence of the Saxon army and the Imperial army. They "opened the can of worms" of Prussian Conservative Junker aristocratic opposition to the Empire and by so doing also gave prestige to their support for a middle class officer corps, middle class civil administration, and to a parliamentary system of government. They condemned the verdicts in the trials of Reuter, Schad, and Forstner. Their influence on Saxony created an unprecedented event. There was no provision in the Constitution of 1871 for the separation of the Saxon army from the Imperial army. No legislation since that time had given independent status to any federated state army. It was unconstitutional and showed the tremendous divisive effect of the Zabern Affair.

In truth, an anti-government coalition had finally, after forty-three years, surfaced in Germany. The actions of this coalition had shown the power that the Reichstag could have with a strong majority in criticizing policy. That the coalition began to lose its solidarity with the negative impact of foreign and especially French criticism was undeniable. That divisions within the National Liberals brought inaction, there was also no doubt. On the twentieth of May, 1914, the Social Democrats for the first time in history refused either to leave the Reichstag or to stand when the customary cheers for the Kaiser were given. The Centre Party had taken a position of intransigent opposition to the government and, foreshadowing its 1917 action, almost seemed in agreement with the Social Democrats. Their vote on the salary issue on that day proved to be a majority against the proposal sponsored by the War Minister and the government. This agreement of views perhaps is indicative of what the government might have had to expect when the Reichstag was to meet again in the Fall of 1914. If only the Socialists had been opposed, the Kaiser, the Reichs-Chancellor, the War Minister, and the General Staff would not have had to face a great adversary; but the coalition which had been twice effective in 1913 might have been more effective due to weakening army opposition in 1914-1915. In view of the menacing international situation and the arms race, this opposition to the government would have been a potential threat to the Emperor and might have been a potential revolutionary force. Thus the year 1913-1914 was a year of promise for the German Empire, but it was not for Prussia and the Conservatives.

The Zabern Affair was one of a catalytic nature which exploded a potentially dangerous situation. The dissatisfaction over the power of the Reichstag within the German Empire, the dissatisfaction over the relations between Prussia and the Imperial government and between Prussia and the individual states of the Empire were remnants of the nineteenth century. The Zabern Affair antagonized the long term sufferers from Prussian domination who accused Prussia of despotism. The outcome of the affair was to reduce that domination by changing part of the Prussian military code to an Imperial military code and promises made by the Kaiser to examine the whole code in order to develop a truly Imperial army.

The role of the Zabern Affair in causing antagonisms to the Prussian army officer-aristocracy could only have been effective as the culmination in the sequence of condemnations: the Army Budget Finance Bill, the Krupp Affair and then Zabern. Yet, the constitutional disruptions of the Winter and Spring of 1914 would never have occurred without the opposition to Prussian militarism that the Zabern Affair aroused. The strength of the institutions was evident in the Conservative reaction. Yet, this same reaction underlined what the Zabern Affair had already demonstrated to Germany and to the world, that these same institutions were anachronisms in the modern world. It was ironic that these institutions perhaps used Bismarck's example of gaining support and solidarity through war as it seemed that the intervention of war would have been the only alternative to evolutionary extinction and in this case it was World War One.

See W.F. Bruck, Social & Econ Hist of Ger 1888-1938 NY 1938

Gerschenkron, Bread & Democracy in Germany Russell & Russell Univ of CA

Halperin, S. Wm. Germany tried Democracy NY 1918-33 Norton + Co.

Barraclough, Geoff. Origins of Modern Ger. NY, Capricorn

Rosenberg, Art. Imp Ger

NOTES

[1]Verhandlungen des Reichstags, Vol. 291, p. 6253.
[2]Ibid., 294, p. 8515.
[3]Ibid., p. 8514.
[4]Theodor Heuss, "Die Zaberner Schussel," Marz, 8, jg. January 21, 1914, IBd, p. 133.
[5]Verhandlungen des Reichstag, p. 8510.
[6]Ibid.
[7]Ibid., 292, 6732-6734.
[8]See Allgemeine Zeitung of Munich, June 1, 1914 for von Lubbell's decision and for Bethmann-Hollweg's see p. 193, this monograph.
[9]Deutsche Tageszeitung, January 12, 1914.
[10]Freiherr Wilhelm Edward von Schoen, The Memoirs of an Ambassador, A Contribution to the Political History of Modern Times, trans. Constance Vesey (London: George Allen and Unwin Ltd.), 1922.
[11]See pp. 147, the monograph.
[12]German Diplomatic Documents, 4, 307. November 26 letter from von Schoen to Bethmann-Hollweg.
[13]See p. 177, the monograph.
[14]Le Temps, January 11, 1914.
[15]Ibid., January 30, 1914.
[16]Allgemeine Zeitung, January 31, 1914.
[17]Ibid., March 28, 1914.

BIBLIOGRAPHY

Documentary Sources

Delbruck, Hans (ed.). Preussische Jahrbucher. 115 Januar-Marz, 1914.

Dodd, Walter Fairleigh (ed.). Modern Constitutions: A Collection of the Fundamental Laws of Twenty-two of the Most Important Countries of the World with Historical and Bibliographical Notes. Vol. I. Chicago: University of Chicago Press. London: T. Fisher Unwin, 1909.

Dugdale, E. T. S. (ed.). Documents Relating to Origins of World War I. New York: Harper and Bros., 1931. Vols. IV and XXXIX.

Schulthess, S. Europaischen Geschichtskalendar. LIV, LV.

Stenographische Berichte uber die Verhandlungen des Preussischen Hauses der Abgeordneten. 22 Legislatur-periode, 2 Session 1914-1915. IBd.

Stenographische Berichte des Verhandlungen des Reichstag, Bd. 288-296. 1913-1914.

Stenographische Berichte uber die Verhandlungen des Preussischen Herrenhause in der Session 1914-1915.

Literature by Contemporaries

Bulow, Bernhard Prince von. Memoirs 1900-1919. Translated by Geoffrey Dunlop. 4 vols. London: Charles Whittingham and Griggs, Lts. Chiswick Press, 1920.

Chapman-Huston, Desmond, Major (ed.). Daisy Princess of Pless by Herself. New York: EIP Dutton and Co., Inc., 1929.

Hohenzollern, Wilhelm. Memoirs of the Crown Prince of Germany. New York: Charles Scribner's Sons, 1922.

Delbruck, Hans. Government and the Will of the People.
Translated by Roy S. MacElves. Oxford University Press,
1923.

Gerard, James W. Face to Face with Kaiserism. New York: George
H. Doran Co., 1918.

Gerard, James W. My Four Years in Germany. New York: George H.
Doran Co., 1917.

Hauptmann, Gerhard Johann Robert. Festspiel Am Deutsche
Reiman, Samtliche Werke. Herausgeben von Hans-Egon Hass, Band
II Dramen, Propylaen Verlag. Frankfurt: Verlag Ullsteire Gmb. H.
Berlin, 1965.

Höflich, Sergeant. Affäre Zabern: Mitgeteilt von einen der
beiden Missetator. Berlin, Verlag fur Kulturpolitik, 1951.

Hohenlohe-Schillingsfurst. Fürst Chlodwig-zu. Denkwurdigkeiten
der Reichskanglerzeit. A. von Muller, ed. Stuttgart: Deutsche
Verlagsanstalt, 1931.

Liebknecht, Karl. Militarism. New York: B. W. Huebsch, 1917.

Luxemburg, Rosa. Ausgewahnts Reden und Schriften. Berlin:
Dietz Verlag, 1951.

Naumann, Friedrich. Werke: Schiften zur Tagespolitik. Funfter
Band, Köln und Oplaten: Westdeutscher Verlag, 1964.

Oldenburg-Januschau. Erinnerungen. Leipzig, Verlegt bei
Koehler und Amelang, 1936.

Scheidemann, Philipp. Memoiren eines Sozialdemokraten. Dresden:
Reissner Verlag, 1928.

Schoenberner, Franz. Confessions of a European Intellectual.
New York: The MacMillan Co., 1946.

Sommerfeld, Adolf (von). Der Fall Zabern: Die Kronprinzen
Depesche und die öffentliche Meinung. Berlin: Kommissionsverlag
Verlag Continent GMBA, 1914.

Ursula, Countess von Eppinghoven, dame du Palais to Her Majesty
the Empress Queen. Private Lives of William II and His Consort:
Secret History of the Court of Berlin. Vol. I. New York: World
Publishing Co., 1909.

Wetterlé, Abbé, Behind the Scenes in the Reichstag. Translated
from the French by George Frederic Lees. New York: George H.
Doran Co., 1918.

Wolff, Theodor. The Eve of 1914. (Der Krieg des Pontius Pilatus)
Translated by E. W. Dickes. New York: Alfred A. Knopf,
1936.

Newspapers (Partial list)

Allgemeine Zeitung of Munich. July, 1913-July, 1914.
Allgemeine Rundschau. January and February, 1914.
Bayrische Staatszeitung. March, 1913-May, 1914.
Berliner Tageblatt. December 1913. January and February, 1914.
Deutsche Tageszeitung. November, 1913-May, 1914.
Frankfurter Zeitung. October, 1913-February, 1914.
Kölnische Zeitung. November, 1913-January, 1914.
Kreuz-Zeitung. October, 1913-February, 1914.
Le Temps. November, 1913-February, 1914.
National Zeitung. December, 1913.
Nord Deutsche Allgemeine Zeitung. 1911-1914.
Die Post. December, 1913.
Strasburg Post. January, 1914.
The Times (London). 1913-1914.
Vorwärts. December and January, 1913-1914.
Vossische Zeitung. January, 1913. December, 1913. January, 1914.

Periodicals

Archiv fuer Militaer Recht. January, 1913.
Barker, J. Ellis. "Autocratic and Democratic Germany. The Lesson of Zabern," The Nineteenth Century.
Die Friedens Wärte. 1914.
Harden, Maximillan. Die Zukunft. December, 1913-March, 1914.
Heer und Politik. January, 1914.
Heuss, T. "Die Zaberner Schussel," März, Eine Wochenschrift 7 Jhrg. 4Bd. Gegrundet von Albert Langen und Ludwig Thoma. Geltet von Dr. Theodor Heuss. Verlag GMBH Munich. October, 1913, bis December, 1914., Munchen, Verlag GMBH.
Jorden, David Starr. "Alsace-Lorraine: A Study in Conquest," Atlantic Monthly, 113, 5. 1914.
Kunstwärt. Februar heft, 1914. Jhrg. 27, Heft 9. Vol. XXVII, 2 Januar bis Marz, 1914.
Landshut, Sigfried. "The Development of Democracy in Germany in the Nineteenth and Twentieth Century," German Social Science Digest. Clausen Verlag. Hamburg, November, 1955.
Maehl, William. "The Triumph of Nationalism in the German Socialist Party on the Eve of the First World War," The Journal of Modern History, XXIV, 1952, 15-41.
Militär Wochenblatt. January, 1914.

Rauscher, V. "Die Zaberner Schlacht," März, January 24, 1914.
_____. "Von Zabern bis Zaberze," März, February 14, 1914.
Simplicissimus. November, 1913-February, 1914. Jhrg 18-19.
München.
Die Tat
Thoma, Ludwig. "Pfaffen," März, March 14, 1914.
Wehler, Hans Ulrich. "Fall Zabern," Der Fall Zabern: Ruckblick
    auf eine Verfassungskrise des Wilhelminischen Kaiserreichs.
Wagner, F. "Fall Zabern," Volker Friede: Zeitschrift der deutschen
    Friedensgesellschaft, 15 Jhrg, January, 1914.
Wold, Alfred. "Von Patriotismus in Elsass-Lothringen,"
    Sud Deutsche Monatshefte. November, 1913-January,1914.

                Interpretive Books (Partial List)

Barraclough, Geoffrey. The Origins of Modern Germany. New York:
    Capricorn Books, 1946.
Bruck, W. F. Social and Economic History of Germany from
    William II to Hitler, 1888-1938: A Comparative Study. New York:
    Russell and Russell, Inc., 1938.
Craig, Gordon A. The Politics of the Prussian Army. New
    York: Oxford University Press, 1955.
Dawson, William Harlbutt. The Evolution of Modern Germany.
    London: T. Fisher & Unwin, 1919.
_____. The German Empire, 1867-1914 and the Unity Movement.
    2 vols. New York: The MacMillan Co., 1919.
_____. What is Wrong with Germany. London: George Allen
    and Unwin, 1915.
Edwards, Marvin L. Stresemann and the Greater Germany, 1914-
    1918. New York: Bookman Associates, 1963.
Epstein, Klaus. Mathias Erzberger and the Dilemma of German
    Social Democracy. Princeton: Princeton University Press, 1959.
Eyck, Erich. Das personliche Regiment Wilhelm's II: Geschichte
    des Deutschen Kaiserreiches von 1890-1914. Erlenbach-Zurich:
    Rentsch, 1948.
Gershenkron, Alexander. Bread and Democracy in Germany. Berkeley
    and Los Angeles: University of California Press, 1943.
Goerlitz, Walter. A History of the German General Staff.
    New York: Proeger, 1960.
Goldschmidt, Hans. Das Reichs und Preussen im Kampf an die
    Fuhrung: Von Bismarck bis 1918. Berlin: Carl Heymanns Verlag,
    1931.

Haller, Johann. Philipp Eulenburg, The Kaiser's Friend. 2 vols.
    Translated by E. C. Mayne. New York: A. Knopf. 1930.
Halperin, S. William. Germany Tried Democracy: A Political
    History of the Reich from 1918 to 1933. New York: W. W.
    Norton & Co., Inc. 1946.
Hazen. Alsace-Lorraine Under German Rule. New York: Henry
    Holt & Co., 1917.
Heidegger, Hermann. Die deutsche Sozialdemokratie und der
    nationale Staat 1870-1920. Gottingen, Musterschmidt Verlag, 1956.
Jonas, Klaus W. The Life of Crown Prince William. Translated
    by Charles W. Bangert. Pittsburg: University of Pittsburg Press,
    1961.
Krieger, Leonard. The German Idea of Freedom: History of a
    Political Tradition. Boston: Beacon Press, 1957.
Landauer, Carl. European Socialism. 2 vols. Berkeley and
    Los Angeles: University of California Press, 1959.
Roth, Gunther. The Social Democrats in Imperial Germany: A
    Study in Working Class Isolation and national Integration.
    Totowa, New Jersey: The Bedminister Press, 1963.
Rosenberg, Arthur. Imperial Germany: The Birth of the Republic.
    Translated by Ian F. D. Morrow. Boston: Beacon Press, 1964.
Rovere, Julien. L'Affaire de Saverne, November, 1913-Janvier,
    1914. Paris Editions Bossard, 43 Rue Madame 43, 1919.
Russell, Bertrand. German Social Democracy. New York:
    George Allen & Unwin, 1915. Longmans Green, 1896.
Schoenbaum, David. Zabern 1913: Consensus Politics in Imperial
    Germany. New York: George Allen & Unwin, 1982.
Schenk, Irwin. Der Fall Zabern. Druck von W. Kohlhammer.
    Stuttgart: 1927.
Schorske, Carl E. German Social Democracy, 1905-1917: The
    Development of the Great Schism. New York: John Wiley &
    Sons, Inc., 1955.
Stenkewitz, Kurt. Immer Feste Druff: Zabernaffäre 1913.
    Berlin: Rutten und Loening, 1962.
Tuchman, Barbara W. The Proud Tower: A Portrait of the World
    Before the War, 1890-1914. New York: The MacMillan Co., 1966.
Vagts, Alfred. A History of Militarism: Civilian and Military.
    Revised edition. New York: Meridian Books, Inc., 1959.
Zmärzlich, Hans Gunter. Bethmann-Hollweg Als Reichskanzler.
    Beitrage zur Geschichte des Parlamentarismus und der politischen
    Parteien. Band II, Dusseldorf: Droste Verlag, 1965.
Zwehl, H. (von). Erich von Falkenhayn, General der Infanterie

Eine biographische Studie.   Berlin: Verlagt bei E. S.
Mittler & Sohn, 1926.

INDEX

Ablass, Dr., 66, 86.

Albrecht, 66,71, 86.

Allgemeine Zeitung, Munich 119, 120 "still longer effects", 217 Freisinnige-Konservativ journal vs Centre, 229 French Propaganda caused Zabern Affair.

Alsace-Lorraine, 2,3 10, 29 history, 30, 31 Constitution of 1911, 48 Zabern Affair, 56 and Prussia, 59 civil and military law in,60-2 civil rights 63ff.

Alsatians, 66 political party.

Amstrichter, 80 judge in a civil court.

An Mein Volk, 6, 9.

Army, 3 power of, 4 Bill of 1912, 31 Bill of 1913, 32 Bill of 1914, 9, 12, 16, 18 Bethmann-Hollweg's defense of, 20, 21, 75-76 People's army of 1806 compared to that of 1913, 83 Haass' people's army.

Arnold, Mathew, 119 "Sea of faith".

Balkan Conflict, 10.

Barker, J. Ellis, 2 Sicily.

Barth, Colonel, 59.

Bassermann, 96 vs Scheidemann, 143 pro modern, democratic, bourgeois state, 144, 181 vs Prussian Particularism, 182 pro constitutional monarchy, 183 power of Reichstag upheld, 183 middle-class replacements for Prussian Officers, 198.

Battle of Nations, 4.

Bavaria, 5, 94 Civil Rights, Catholicism, 167 Preussenbund insults to Bavarian army.

Bayrische Staatszeitung, 15 Bavarian government organ.

Beemelmans, Judge, 127 Public Prosecutor at Colonel von Reuter's Trial.

Behr-Behrenhoff, Graf, 137 began Prussian Herrenhaus debate on Zabern January 10.

Berlin, 6, 8 University.

Berliner Börsencourier, 143 changed from pro to anti military after Reuter verdict.

Haeusler, Major General, Bavarian Centre Party member, 18 opposes "Prussian Army".

Hardenburg, von., 6.

Hauss, Centre Party deputy to Reichstag from Alsace-Lorraine, 60-3, 223-4 aristocratic privilege in Prussian army more in demand today than twenty years ago.

Harden, Maximilian , 9, Die Zukunft.

Hatzfeld, Prince von, 140 moved closure of debate in Prussian Herrenhaus (upper house), 1/10/1914, vs Bethmann-Hollweg.

Haussmann, Progressive Peoples Reichstag deputy, 103 agrees with Center party Erzberger on German civil rights protection vs militarism, 120 Zabern Affair-aroused democratic force declining, 1/10/1914, Naumann.

Hauptmann, Gerhard, 11 Festspiel

Heeringen, von, General and Prussian War Minister before Krupp Trial revelations, 4, 20

Heuss, Theodore, 225 middle-class and military administrators mistrusted each other. Hatred between rival classes.

Heydebrand, 167 Prussia wants to put-down revolution bloodily.

Himmeldonnerwetter policy, 101 military repression of civil unrest.

Hoch, Social Democrat Reichstag deputy, 102 summarized debates of previous days and sets forth the issues, 103 meaning of the vote of mistrust-coalition no longer passive in politics, 106.

Höflich, Sergeant, 32-34 protagonist in Zabern Affair.

Hohenlohe-Schillingsfurst, former Reichs-Chancellor, 62.

Imperial Party, 185 Conservative Schultz represented it in Reichstag. Interpellations, 1, 71 Roser, Albrecht, Delsor, Ablass, 163 1/14/1914 Radicals, Social Democratic and Alsatian Deputies presented these.

Iron Cross, Order of, 6.

Jagow, Dr. Juris von, Police President of Berlin, 98 fear of new Social Democratic power, 109 letter to Kreuz Zeitung "Zabern almost in enemy country", 110 all but Conservatives condemned his chauvinism, but feted by them, General Staff, Crown Prince, 119 close friend of Emperor, 130, 167, 227.

Journal de Debats, Parisian journal, 207 Germany once more united.

Jaures, Jean, French Socialist, 56.

Junker, Prussian cavalry officer, 223-4 emphasizing continuance of old aristocratic caste system.

Kaempf, President of the Reichstag, 163 opposed Yorck von Wartenburg's accusations.

Kahn, Bank official, 125 resisting Lt. Schad's arrest in Zabern.

Kalesch, Judge, 127 leaked